Beyond mind over matter, enter the universe of
soul over matter with Dr. Zhi Gang Sha

Praise for Dr. Sha and his #1
New York Times bestselling
OUL POWER SERIES

"Jusı : thoughts can influence water, our souls can bring healing
and ː to our selves, our loved ones, and our world today. Dr. Sha
is a tant teacher and a wonderful healer with a valuable message
abc ɔower of the soul to influence and transform all life."

—Dr. Masaru Emoto, *New York Times* bestselling
author of *The Secret of Water*

"ɪ ɪakes available secret techniques and insights that were only
av ı the past to a select few. He shares in simple terms the in-
sig ːools that took him more than thirty years of hard work and
dis o attain. He gives you access to information and techniques
tha otherwise be unattainable."

—Dr. John Gray, #1 *New York Times* bestselling author of
Men Are from Mars, Women Are from Venus

"Dʲ ɪne-tested results have proven to thousands of students and
reaɪ healing energies and messages exist within specific sounds,
mɔ and affirmative perceptions. Weaving in his own personal
exː Dr. Sha's theories and practices of working directly with
thɪ energy and spirit are practical, holistic, and profound. His
reɪ hat Soul Power is most important for every aspect of life is
vit ng the challenges of twenty-first-century living."

-Dr. Michael Bernard Beckwith, founder and spiritual director of
ɪ International Spiritual Center and author of *Spiritual Liberation*

This title is also available from Simon & Schuster Aud⁀
and as an eboc⌐

Other Books in the Soul Power Series

DIVINE SOUL MIND BODY HEALING AND TRANSMISSION SYSTEM

The Divine Way to Heal You, Humanity, Mother Earth, and All Universes

Dr. Zhi Gang Sha

ATRIA PAPERBACK
New York   London   Toronto   Sydney

Heaven's Library
Toronto

ATRIA PAPERBACK

Heaven's Library
Toronto, ON

A Division of Simon & Schuster, Inc.
1230 Avenue of the Americas
New York, NY 10020

The information contained in this book is intended to be educational and not for
diagnosis, prescription, or treatment of any health disorder whatsoever. This information
should not replace consultation with a competent healthcare professional. The content
of the book is intended to be used as an adjunct to a rational and responsible healthcare
program prescribed by a healthcare practitioner. The author and publisher are in no way
liable for any misuse of the material.

First Atria Paperback edition October 2010

ATRIA PAPERBACK and colophon are trademarks of Simon & Schuster, Inc.

Heaven's Library and Soul Power Series are trademarks of Heaven's Library Publication Corp.

For information about special discounts for bulk purchases,
please contact Simon & Schuster Special Sales at 1-866-506-1949
or business@simonandschuster.com.

The Simon & Schuster Speakers Bureau can bring authors to your live event.
For more information or to book an event, contact the Simon & Schuster Speakers Bureau
at 1-866-248-3049 or visit our website at www.simonspeakers.com.

Designed by Meghan Day Healey

Manufactured in the United States of America

10   9   8   7   6   5   4   3   2   1

The Library of Congress has cataloged the hardcover edition as follows:

Sha, Zhi Gang.
    Divine soul mind body, healing, and transmission system : the divine way to heal you,
humanity, mother earth, and all universes / Zhi Gang Sha.—1st Atria Books hardcover ed.
        p.   cm.—(Soul power series)
    Includes bibliographical references and index.
1. Spiritual life.   2. Spiritual healing.   I. Title.
BL624.S47539   2009
204'.4—dc22   2009033303

ISBN 978-1-4391-7766-2
ISBN 978-1-4391-8251-2 (pbk)
ISBN 978-1-4391-8087-7 (ebook)

Contents

Soul Power Series

*T*HE PURPOSE OF life is to serve. I have committed my life to this purpose. Service is my life mission.

My total life mission is to transform the consciousness of humanity and all souls in all universes, and enlighten them, in order to create love, peace, and harmony for humanity, Mother Earth, and all universes. This mission includes three empowerments.

My first empowerment is to teach *universal service* to empower people to be unconditional universal servants. The message of universal service is:

I serve humanity and all universes unconditionally.
You serve humanity and all universes unconditionally.
Together we serve humanity and all souls in all universes unconditionally.

My second empowerment is to teach *healing* to empower people to heal themselves and heal others. The message of healing is:

I have the power to heal myself.
You have the power to heal yourself.
Together we have the power to heal the world.

My third empowerment is to teach *the power of soul,* which includes soul secrets, wisdom, knowledge, and practices, and to transmit Divine Soul Power to empower people to transform every aspect of their lives and enlighten their souls, hearts, minds, and bodies.

The message of Soul Power is:

> *I have the Soul Power to transform my consciousness*
>   *and every aspect of my life and enlighten my soul,*
>   *heart, mind, and body.*
> *You have the Soul Power to transform your conscious-*
>   *ness and every aspect of your life and enlighten your*
>   *soul, heart, mind, and body.*
> *Together we have the Soul Power to transform con-*
>   *sciousness and every aspect of all life and enlighten*
>   *humanity and all souls.*

To teach the power of soul is my most important empowerment. It is the key for my total life mission. The power of soul is the key for transforming physical life and spiritual life. It is the key for transforming and enlightening humanity and every soul in all universes.

The beginning of the twenty-first century is the transition period into a new era for humanity, Mother Earth, and all universes. This era is named the Soul Light Era. The Soul Light Era began on August 8, 2003. It will last fifteen thousand years. Natural disasters—including tsunamis, hurricanes, cyclones, earthquakes, floods, tornados, hail, blizzards, fires, drought, extreme temperatures, famine, and disease—political, religious, and ethnic wars, terrorism, proliferation of nuclear weapons, economic challenges, pollution, vanishing plant and animal species, and other such upheavals are part of this transition. In addition, millions of people are suffering from depression, anxiety, fear, anger, and worry. They suffer from pain, chronic conditions, and life-threatening illnesses. Humanity needs help. The consciousness of humanity needs to be transformed. The suffering of humanity needs to be removed.

The books of the Soul Power Series are brought to you by Heaven's Library and Atria Books. They reveal soul secrets and teach soul wisdom, soul knowledge, and soul practices for your daily life. The power of soul can heal, prevent illness, rejuvenate, prolong life, and transform consciousness and every aspect of life, including relationships and finances. The power of soul is vital to serving humanity and Mother Earth during this transition period. The power of soul will awaken and transform the consciousness of humanity and all souls.

In the twentieth century and for centuries before, *mind over matter* played a vital role in healing, rejuvenation, and life transformation. In the Soul Light Era, *soul over matter*—Soul Power—will play *the* vital role to heal, rejuvenate, and transform all life.

There are countless souls on Mother Earth—souls of human beings, souls of animals, souls of other living things, and souls of inanimate things. *Everyone and everything has a soul.*

Every soul has its own frequency and power. Jesus had miraculous healing power. We have heard many heart-touching stories of lives saved by Guan Yin's[1] compassion. Mother Mary's

---

1. Guan Yin is known as the Bodhisattva of Compassion and, in the West, as the Goddess of Mercy.

love has created many heart-moving stories. All of these great souls were given Divine Soul Power to serve humanity. In all of the world's great religions and spiritual traditions, including Buddhism, Daoism, Christianity, Judaism, Hinduism, Islam, and more, there are similar accounts of great spiritual healing and blessing power.

I honor every religion and every spiritual tradition. However, I am not teaching religion. I am teaching Soul Power, which includes soul secrets, soul wisdom, soul knowledge, and soul practices. Your soul has the power to heal, rejuvenate, and transform life. An animal's soul has the power to heal, rejuvenate, and transform life. The souls of the sun, the moon, an ocean, a tree, and a mountain have the power to heal, rejuvenate, and transform life. The souls of healing angels, ascended masters, holy saints, Daoist saints, Hindu saints, buddhas, and other high-level spiritual beings have great Soul Power to heal, rejuvenate, and transform life.

Every soul has its own standing. Spiritual standing, or soul standing, has countless layers. Soul Power also has layers. Not every soul can perform miracles like Jesus, Guan Yin, and Mother Mary. Soul Power depends on the soul's spiritual standing in Heaven. The higher a soul stands in Heaven, the more Soul Power that soul is given by the Divine. Jesus, Guan Yin, and Mother Mary all have a very high spiritual standing.

Who determines a soul's spiritual standing? Who gives the appropriate Soul Power to a soul? Who decides the direction for humanity, Mother Earth, and all universes? The top leader of the spiritual world is the decision maker. This top leader is the Divine. The Divine is the creator and manifester of all universes.

In the Soul Light Era, all souls will join as one and align their consciousness with divine consciousness. At this historic time, the Divine has decided to transmit divine soul treasures to humanity and all souls to help humanity and all souls go through Mother Earth's transition.

Let me share two personal stories with you to explain how I reached this understanding.

First, in April 2003, I held a Power Healing workshop for about one hundred people at Land of Medicine Buddha, a retreat center in Soquel, California. As I was teaching, the Divine appeared. I told the students, "The Divine is here. Could you give me a moment?" I knelt and bowed down to the floor to honor the Divine. (At age six, I was taught to bow down to my tai chi masters. At age ten, I bowed down to my qi gong masters. At age twelve, I bowed down to my kung fu masters. Being Chinese, I learned this courtesy throughout my childhood.) I explained to the students, "Please understand that this is the way I honor the Divine, my spiritual fathers, and my spiritual mothers. Now I will have a conversation with the Divine."

I began by saying silently, "Dear Divine, I am very honored you are here."

The Divine, who was in front of me above my head, replied, "Zhi Gang, I come today to pass a spiritual law to you."

I said, "I am honored to receive this spiritual law."

The Divine continued, "This spiritual law is named the Universal Law of Universal Service. It is one of the highest spiritual laws in the universe. It applies to the spiritual world and the physical world."

The Divine pointed to the Divine. "I am a universal servant." The Divine pointed to me. "You are a universal servant." The Divine swept a hand in front of the Divine. "Everyone and everything is a universal servant. A universal servant offers universal service. Universal service includes universal love, forgiveness, peace, healing, blessing, harmony, and enlightenment. *If one offers a little service, one receives a little blessing from the universe and from me. If one offers more service, one receives more blessing. If one offers unconditional service, one receives unlimited blessing.*"

The Divine paused for a moment before continuing. "There is another kind of service, which is unpleasant service. Unpleasant service includes killing, harming, taking advantage of others, cheating, stealing, complaining, and more. If one offers a little unpleasant service, one learns little lessons from the universe and from me. If one offers more unpleasant service, one learns more lessons. If one offers huge unpleasant service, one learns huge lessons."

I asked, "What kinds of lessons could one learn?"

The Divine replied, "The lessons include sickness, accidents, injuries, financial challenges, broken relationships, emotional imbalances, mental confusion, and any kind of disorder in one's life." The Divine emphasized, "This is how the universe operates. This is one of my most important spiritual laws for all souls in the universe to follow."

After the Divine delivered this universal law, I immediately made a silent vow to the Divine:

Dear Divine,

I am extremely honored to receive your Law of Universal Service. I make a vow to you, to all humanity, and to all souls in all universes that I will be an unconditional universal servant. I will give my total GOLD [gratitude, obedience, loyalty, devotion] *to you and to serving you. I am honored to be your servant and a servant of all humanity and all souls.*

Hearing this, the Divine smiled and left.

My second story happened three months later, in July 2003, while I was holding a Soul Study workshop near Toronto. The Divine came again. I again explained to my students that the Divine had appeared, and asked them to wait a moment while I bowed down 108 times and listened to the Divine's message. On this occasion, the Divine told me, "Zhi Gang, I come today to choose you as my direct servant, vehicle, and channel."

I was deeply moved and said to the Divine, "I am honored. What does it mean to be your direct servant, vehicle, and channel?"

The Divine replied, "When you offer healing and blessing to others, call me. I will come instantly to offer my healing and blessing to them."

I was deeply touched and replied, "Thank you so much for choosing me as your direct servant."

The Divine continued, "I can offer my healing and blessing by transmitting my permanent healing and blessing treasures."

I asked, "How do you do this?"

The Divine answered, "Select a person and I will give you a demonstration."

I asked for a volunteer with serious health challenges. A man named Walter raised his hand. He stood up and explained that he had liver cancer, with a two-by-three-centimeter malignant tumor that had just been diagnosed from a biopsy.

Then I asked the Divine, "Please bless Walter. Please show me how you transmit your permanent treasures." Immediately, I saw the Divine send a beam of light from the Divine's heart to Walter's liver. The beam shot into his liver, where it turned into a golden light ball that instantly started spinning. Walter's entire liver shone with beautiful golden light.

The Divine asked me, "Do you understand what software is?"

I was surprised by this question but replied, "I do not understand much about computers. I just know that software is a computer program. I have heard about accounting software, office software, and graphic design software."

"Yes," the Divine said. "Software is a program. Because you asked me to, I transmitted, or downloaded, my Soul Software for Liver to Walter. It is one of my permanent healing and blessing treasures. You asked me. I did the job. This is what it means for you to be my chosen direct servant and channel."

I was astonished. Excited, inspired, and humbled, I said to the Divine, "I am so honored to be your direct servant. How blessed I am to be chosen." Almost speechless, I asked the Divine, "Why did you choose me?"

"I chose you," said the Divine, "because you have served humanity for more than one thousand lifetimes. You have been very committed to serving my mission through all of your lifetimes. I am choosing you in this life to be my direct servant. You will transmit countless permanent healing and blessing treasures from me to humanity and all souls. This is the honor I give to you now."

I was moved to tears. I immediately bowed down 108 times again and made a silent vow:

Dear Divine,

I cannot bow down to you enough for the honor you have given to me. No words can express my greatest gratitude. How blessed I am to be your direct servant to download your permanent healing and blessing treasures to humanity and all souls! Humanity and all souls will receive your huge blessings through my service as your direct servant. I give my total life to you and to humanity. I will accomplish your tasks. I will be a pure servant to humanity and all souls.

I bowed again. Then I asked the Divine, "How should Walter use his Soul Software?"

"Walter must spend time to practice with my Soul Software," said the Divine. "Tell him that simply to receive my Soul Software does not mean he will recover. He must practice with this treasure every day to restore his health, step by step."

I asked, "How should he practice?"

The Divine gave me this guidance: "Tell Walter to chant repeatedly: *Divine Liver Soul Software heals me. Divine Liver Soul Software heals me. Divine Liver Soul Software heals me. Divine Liver Soul Software heals me.*"

I asked, "For how long should Walter chant?"

The Divine answered, "At least two hours a day. The longer he practices, the better. If Walter does this, he could recover in three to six months."

I shared this information with Walter, who was excited and

deeply moved. Walter said, "I will practice two hours or more each day."

Finally I asked the Divine, "How does the Soul Software work?"

The Divine replied, "My Soul Software is a golden healing ball that rotates and clears energy and spiritual blockages in Walter's liver."

I again bowed to the Divine 108 times. Then I stood up and offered three Soul Softwares to every participant in the workshop as divine gifts. Upon seeing this, the Divine smiled and left.

Walter immediately began to practice as directed for at least two hours every day. Two and a half months later, a CT scan and MRI showed that his liver cancer had completely disappeared. At the end of 2006 I met Walter again at a signing in Toronto for my book *Soul Mind Body Medicine*. In May 2008 Walter attended one of my events at the Unity Church of Truth in Toronto. On both occasions Walter told me that there was still no sign of cancer in his liver. For nearly five years his Divine Soul Download healed his liver cancer. He was very grateful to the Divine.

This major event of being chosen as a direct divine servant happened in July 2003. As I mentioned, a new era for Mother Earth and all universes, the Soul Light Era, began on August 8, 2003. The timing may look like a coincidence but I believe there could be an underlying spiritual reason. Since July 2003 I have offered divine transmissions to humanity almost every day. I have offered more than ten divine transmissions to all souls in all universes.

I share this story with you to introduce the power of divine transmissions or Divine Soul Downloads. Now let me share the commitment that I made in *Soul Wisdom*, the first book of my Soul Power Series, and that I have renewed in every one of my books since:

From now on, I will offer Divine Soul Downloads in every book of the Soul Power Series.

Divine Soul Downloads are permanent divine healing and blessing treasures for transforming your life. There is an ancient saying: *If you want to know whether a pear is sweet, taste it.* If you want to know the power of Divine Soul Downloads, experience it.

Divine Soul Downloads carry divine frequency with divine love, forgiveness, compassion, and light. Divine frequency transforms the frequency of all life. Divine love melts all blockages, including soul, mind, and body blockages, and transforms all life. Divine forgiveness brings inner peace and inner joy. Divine compassion boosts energy, stamina, vitality, and immunity. Divine light heals, prevents sickness, rejuvenates, and prolongs life.

A Divine Soul Download is a new soul created from the heart of the Divine. The Divine Soul Download transmitted to Walter was a Soul Software. Since then, I have transmitted several other types of Divine Soul Downloads, including Divine Soul Herbs, Divine Soul Acupuncture, Divine Soul Instruments, and Divine Soul Transplants.

A Divine Soul Transplant is a new divine soul of an organ, a part of the body, a bodily system, cells, DNA, RNA, the smallest matter in cells, or the spaces between cells. When it is transmitted, it replaces the recipient's original soul of the organ, part of the body, system, cells, DNA, RNA, smallest matter in cells, or spaces between cells. A new divine soul can also replace the soul of a home or a business. A new divine soul can be transmitted to a pet, a mountain, a city, or a country to replace their original souls. A new divine soul can even replace the soul of Mother Earth.

Everyone and everything has a soul. The Divine can download any soul you can conceive of. These Divine Soul Downloads are permanent divine healing, blessing, and life-transformation treasures. They can transform the lives of anyone and anything. Because the Divine created these divine soul treasures, they carry Divine Soul Power, which is the greatest Soul Power among all souls. All souls in the highest layers of Heaven will support and assist Divine Soul Downloads. Divine Soul Downloads are the crown jewel of Soul Power.

Divine Soul Downloads are divine presence. The more Divine Soul Downloads you receive, the faster your soul, heart, mind, and body will be transformed. The more Divine Soul Downloads your home or business receives and the more Divine Soul Downloads a city or country receives, the faster their souls, hearts, minds, and bodies will be transformed.

In the Soul Light Era, the evolution of humanity will be created by Divine Soul Power. Soul Power will transform humanity. Soul Power will transform animals. Soul Power will transform nature and the environment. Soul Power will assume the leading role in every field of human endeavor. Humanity will deeply understand that *the soul is the boss.*

Soul Power, including soul secrets, soul wisdom, soul knowledge, and soul practices, will transform every aspect of human life. Soul Power will transform every aspect of organizations and societies. Soul Power will transform cities, countries, Mother Earth, all planets, stars, galaxies, and all universes. Divine Soul

Power, including Divine Soul Downloads, will lead this transformation.

I am honored to have been chosen as a divine servant to offer Divine Soul Downloads to humanity, to relationships, to homes, to businesses, to pets, to cities, to countries, and more. In the last few years I have already transmitted countless divine souls to humanity and to all universes. I repeat to you now: *I will offer Divine Soul Downloads within each and every book of the Soul Power Series.* Clear instructions on how to receive these Divine Soul Downloads will be provided in the next section, "How to Receive the Divine Soul Downloads Offered in the Books of the Soul Power Series," as well as on the appropriate pages of each book.

I am a servant of humanity. I am a servant of the universe. I am a servant of the Divine. I am extremely honored to be a servant of all souls. I commit my total life and being as an unconditional universal servant.

I will continue to offer Divine Soul Downloads for my entire life. I will offer more and more Divine Soul Downloads to every soul. I will offer Divine Soul Downloads for every aspect of life for every soul.

I am honored to be a servant of Divine Soul Downloads.

Human beings, organizations, cities, and countries will receive more and more Divine Soul Downloads, which can transform every aspect of their lives and enlighten their souls, hearts, minds, and bodies. The Soul Light Era will shine Soul Power. The books in the Soul Power Series will spread Divine Soul Downloads, together with Soul Power—soul secrets, soul wisdom, soul knowledge, and soul practices—to serve humanity, Mother Earth, and all universes. The Soul Power Series is a pure servant for humanity and all souls. The Soul Power Series is honored to be a total GOLD² servant of the Divine, humanity, and all souls.

The final goal of the Soul Light Era is to join every soul as one in love, peace, and harmony. This means that the consciousness of every soul will be totally aligned with divine consciousness. There will be difficulties and challenges on the path to this final goal. Together we will overcome them. We call all souls of humanity and all souls in all universes to offer unconditional universal service, including universal love, forgiveness, peace, healing, blessing, harmony, and enlightenment. The more we offer unconditional universal service, the faster we will achieve this goal.

The Divine gives his heart to us. The Divine gives his love to us. The Divine gives Divine Soul Downloads to us. Our hearts meld with the Divine's heart. Our souls meld with the Divine's soul. Our consciousnesses align with the Divine's consciousness. We will join hearts and souls together to create love, peace, and harmony for humanity, Mother Earth, and all universes.

> *I love my heart and soul*
> *I love all humanity*
> *Join hearts and souls together*
> *Love, peace and harmony*
> *Love, peace and harmony*

Love all humanity. Love all souls. Thank all humanity. Thank all souls.

Thank you. Thank you. Thank you.

Zhi Gang Sha

---

2. Total GOLD means total gratitude, total obedience, total loyalty, and total devotion to the Divine.

How to Receive the Divine Soul Downloads Offered in the Books of the Soul Power Series

*T*HE BOOKS OF the Soul Power Series are unique. For the first time in history, the Divine is downloading the Divine's soul treasures to readers as they read these books. Every book in the Soul Power Series will include Divine Soul Downloads that have been preprogrammed. When you read the appropriate paragraphs and pause for a minute, divine gifts will be transmitted to your soul.

In April 2005 the Divine told me to "leave Divine Soul Downloads to history." I thought, "A human being's life is limited. Even if I live a long, long life, I will go back to Heaven one day. How can I leave Divine Soul Downloads to history?"

In the beginning of 2008, as I was editing the paperback edition of *Soul Wisdom,* the Divine suddenly told me: "Zhi Gang, offer my downloads within this book." The Divine said, "I will preprogram my downloads in the book. Any reader can receive them as he or she reads the special pages." At the moment the Divine gave me this direction, I understood how I could leave Divine Soul Downloads to history.

Preprogrammed Divine Soul Downloads are permanently stored within this book and every book in the Soul Power Series. If people read this book thousands of years from now, they will still receive the Divine Soul Downloads. As long as this book exists and is read, readers will receive the Divine Soul Downloads.

Allow me to explain further. The Divine has placed a permanent blessing within certain paragraphs in these books. These blessings allow you to receive Divine Soul Downloads as permanent gifts to your soul. Because these divine treasures reside with your soul, you can access them twenty-four hours a day—as often as you like, wherever you are—for healing, blessing, and life transformation.

It is very easy to receive the Divine Soul Downloads in these books. After you read the special paragraphs where they are preprogrammed, close your eyes. Receive the special download. It is also easy to apply these divine treasures. After you receive a Divine Soul Download, I will immediately show you how to apply it for healing, blessing, and life transformation.

You have free will. If you are not ready to receive a Divine Soul Download, simply say *I am not ready to receive this gift.* You can then continue to read the special download paragraphs, but you will not receive the gifts they contain. The Divine does not offer Divine Soul Downloads to those who are not ready or not willing to receive the Divine's treasures. However, the moment you are ready, you can simply go back to the relevant paragraphs and tell the Divine *I am ready.* You will then receive the stored special download when you reread the paragraphs.

The Divine has agreed to offer specific Divine Soul Downloads in these books to all readers who are willing to receive them. The Divine has unlimited treasures. However, you can receive only the ones designated in these pages. Please do not ask for different or additional gifts. It will not work.

After receiving and practicing with the Divine Soul Downloads in these books, you could experience remarkable healing results in your physical, emotional, mental, and spiritual bodies. You could receive incredible blessings for your love relationships and other relationships. You could receive financial blessings and all kinds of other blessings.

Divine Soul Downloads are unlimited. There can be a Divine Soul Download for anything that exists in the physical world. The reason for this is very simple. *Everything has a soul.* A house has a soul. The Divine can download a soul to your house that can transform its energy. The Divine can download a soul to your business that can transform your business. If you are wearing a ring, that ring has a soul. If the Divine downloads a new divine soul to your ring, you can ask the divine soul in your ring to offer divine healing and blessing.

I am honored to have been chosen as a servant of humanity and the Divine to offer Divine Soul Downloads. For the rest of my life, I will continue to offer Divine Soul Downloads. I will offer more and more of them. I will offer Divine Soul Downloads for every aspect of every life.

I am honored to be a servant of Divine Soul Downloads.

What to Expect After You Receive Divine Soul Downloads

Divine Soul Downloads are new souls created from the heart of the Divine. When these souls are transmitted, you may feel a strong vibration. For example, you could feel warm or excited. Your body could shake a little. If you are not sensitive, you may not feel anything. Advanced spiritual beings with an open Third Eye can actually see a huge golden, rainbow, or purple light soul enter your body.

These divine souls are your yin companions[3] for life. They will stay with your soul forever. Even after your physical life ends, these divine treasures will continue to accompany your soul into your next life and all of your future lives. In these books, I will teach you how to invoke these divine souls anytime, anywhere to give you divine healing or blessing in this life. You also can invoke these souls to leave your body to offer divine healing or blessing to others. These divine souls have extraordinary abilities to heal, bless, and transform. If you develop advanced spiritual abilities in your next life, you will discover that you have these divine souls with you. Then you will be able to invoke these divine souls in the same way in your future lifetimes to heal, bless, and transform every aspect of your life.

It is a great honor to have a divine soul downloaded to your own soul. The divine soul is a pure soul without bad karma. The divine soul carries divine healing and blessing abilities. The download does not have any side effects. You are given love and light with divine frequency. You are given divine abilities to serve yourself and others. Therefore, humanity is extremely honored

---

3. A yang companion is a physical being, such as a family member, friend, or pet. A yin companion is a soul companion without a physical form, such as your spiritual fathers and mothers in Heaven.

that the Divine is offering his downloads. I am extremely honored to be a servant of the Divine, of you, of all humanity, and of all souls to offer Divine Soul Downloads. I cannot thank the Divine enough. I cannot thank you, all humanity, and all souls enough for the opportunity to serve.

Thank you. Thank you. Thank you.

Foreword to the Soul Power Series

I HAVE ADMIRED DR. Zhi Gang Sha's work for some years now. In fact, I clearly remember the first time I heard him describe his soul healing system, Soul Mind Body Medicine. I knew immediately that I wanted to support this gifted healer and his mission, so I introduced him to my spiritual community at Agape. Ever since, it has been my joy to witness how those who apply his teachings and techniques experience increased energy, joy, harmony, and peace in their lives.

Dr. Sha's techniques awaken the healing power already present in all of us, empowering us to put our overall well-being in our own hands. His explanation of energy and message, and how they link consciousness, mind, body, and spirit, forms a dynamic information network in language that is easy to understand and, more important, to apply.

Dr. Sha's time-tested results have proven to thousands of students and readers that healing energies and messages exist within specific sounds, movements, and affirmative perceptions. Weaving in his own personal experiences, Dr. Sha's theories and practices of working directly with the life-force energy and spirit are practical, holistic, and profound. His recognition that Soul Power is most important for every aspect of life is vital to meeting the challenges of twenty-first-century living.

The worldwide representative of his renowned teacher, Dr. Zhi Chen Guo, one of the greatest qi gong masters and healers in the world, Dr. Sha is himself a master of ancient disciplines such as tai chi, qi gong, kung fu, the *I Ching,* and feng shui. He has blended the soul of his culture's natural healing methods with his training as a Western physician, and generously offers his wisdom to us through the books in his Soul Power Series. His contribution to those in the healing professions is undeniable, and the way in which he empowers his readers to understand themselves, their feelings, and the connection between their bodies, minds, and spirits is his gift to the world.

Through his Soul Power Series, Dr. Sha guides the reader into a consciousness of healing not only of body, mind, and spirit, but also of the heart. I consider his healing path to be a universal spiritual practice, a journey into genuine transformation. His professional integrity and compassionate heart are at the root of his being a servant of humankind, and my heartfelt wish for his readers is that they accept his invitation to awaken the power of the soul and realize the natural beauty of their existence.

Dr. Michael Bernard Beckwith
Founder, Agape International Spiritual Center

How to Read This Book

*I*N EVERY BOOK of my Soul Power Series, I reveal soul secrets and teach soul wisdom, soul knowledge, and soul practices. Secret and sacred wisdom and knowledge are important. *Practice is even more important.* Since ancient times, serious Buddhist, Daoist, qi gong, and kung fu practitioners have spent hours and hours a day in practice. Their dedication empowers them to develop and transform their frequency, their consciousness, and their purification further and further. In the modern world, successful professionals in every field similarly spend hours a day for months and years in practice. Their commitment empowers them to develop and transform their power and abilities further and further.

Every book in my Soul Power Series offers new approaches to healing, rejuvenation, and life transformation. Along with the teachings of sacred wisdom and knowledge, I also offer Divine Soul Downloads as a servant, vehicle, and channel of the Divine. I am honored to serve you through these books. However, *the most important service offered in these books is the practices.* In this book I lead you in many practices. If you spend four or five minutes to do each practice, I fully understand that it will take you some time to finish all of them. Do a few practices today. Tomorrow do another few practices. Do a few more the day after tomorrow. The practices are vital. If you do not do them, how can you experience their power and benefits? If you do not experience their power and benefits, how can you fully understand and absorb the teaching?

My message to you is that as you read this book, make sure you do not miss the practices. I deliberately guide you in this book to do spiritual practices using the power of soul for healing, prevention of sickness, rejuvenation, prolonging life, and transforming every aspect of life, including relationships and finances. Reading this book is like being at a workshop with me. When you go to a workshop and the teacher leads you in a meditation or practice, you do not run off to do something else, do you?

Do not rush through this book. Do every practice I ask you to do. You will receive ten, fifty, a hundred times the benefit that you would receive if you simply read through the book quickly. Especially, to receive Divine Soul Downloads does not mean you automatically receive their benefits. You must invoke them and practice to experience and receive divine healing and blessing. Remember also that going through this book just once is not enough. My advanced students go through my books many times. Every time they read and do the practices, they reach more and more "Aha!" moments. They receive more and more remarkable healing, purification, and life-transformation results.

These are important messages for you to remember as you read this book. I wish each of you will receive great healing, rejuvenation, purification, and life transformation by doing the practices in this book. Receive the benefits of *soul over matter,* which is the power of soul.

Practice. Practice. Practice.

Experience. Experience. Experience.

Benefit. Benefit. Benefit.

Hao! Hao! Hao!

Thank you. Thank you. Thank you.

List of Divine Soul Downloads

Chapter Three

Chapter Four

Chapter Five

Introduction

PEOPLE WORLDWIDE TALK about body, mind, and spirit. Spirit is soul. I prefer the order soul, mind, and body. Why? Because I have realized deeply through my life's study that *soul is the boss*. Some of you may not agree. You may think your mind is the boss, because you think you decide to do something using your mind. For example, this is how you may think you decide to open a business, find a partner, go to a concert, or join a workshop. You believe your mind decides what you want to do.

Let me share my understanding. At the moment you think about what you want to do, your soul is involved with your thinking. Generally speaking, your soul agrees with what your mind thinks you want to do. But sometimes your soul does not agree with your mind's thinking. What will be the result if your soul agrees with your mind's thinking? Things could be smooth and pleasant. If your soul does not agree with your mind's thinking, but your mind still insists on doing what it thinks, things could be blocked or difficult.

There may be many blockages in your life. What I want to

share is that *your soul can block your life.* Pay great attention to this vital issue that I have shared with humanity in my previous books. I have deeply realized this fact. Therefore, I believe **soul is the boss.** I use the order soul, mind, and body.

In 2006, I published one of my major books on soul healing: *Soul Mind Body Medicine: A Complete Soul Healing System for Optimum Health and Vitality.*[4] In this book, I revealed the one-sentence secret:

Heal the soul first; then healing of the mind and body will follow.

In the last few years, this teaching has benefited hundreds of thousands of people worldwide. There are thousands of heart-touching and moving stories from the teachings and practices of *Soul Mind Body Medicine.* One day, when I was teaching a Soul Mind Body Medicine workshop, a lady I had never met came to tell me, "Thank you, Master Sha. I cannot thank you enough. I healed my cancer by applying the soul healing program for cancer recovery in this book. I am very grateful." This made me very happy. I replied, "I'm very glad to hear this. Congratulations! Continue to do more soul self-healing."

Soul Mind Body Medicine teaches the Four Power Techniques. These four practical techniques for self-healing are:

Soul Power. Using the power of soul to heal. This is *soul over matter.*

Body Power. Using specific hand and body positions to heal.

---

4. 2006, Novato, California: New World Library.

Mind Power. Using creative visualization, intention, and the potential power of the brain to heal. This is *mind over matter.*

Sound Power. Using sacred healing mantras or vibratory healing sounds to heal.

Each of the Four Power Techniques is simple, powerful, and effective, but *Soul Power is the most powerful technique.* Soul Power is the fundamental teaching of my entire Soul Power Series. Let me explain some of the key teachings about Soul Power now.

One key teaching is that Soul Power can be summarized in one sentence: Say *hello.* This is the formula for soul self-healing. I call it Say Hello Healing. It has five steps:

Say *hello*. *Dear soul, mind, and body of my* _____ [name a system, organ, or part of the body that needs healing],

Give love. *I love you.*

Make an affirmation. *You have the power to heal yourself.*

Give a command. *Do a good job!*

Express gratitude. *Thank you.*

We will use the Say Hello formula in every practice in this book.

There are two basic ways to apply Say Hello Healing:

• Say *hello* to inner souls.

• Say *hello* to outer souls.

Say *Hello* to Inner Souls

You can say *hello* to your inner souls, which are the souls of your own body, systems, organs, cells, DNA, and RNA, to self-heal.

For example, if you have a knee problem, here is how to do Say Hello Healing. Simply say:

> *Dear soul, mind, and body of my knees,*
> *I love you.*
> *You have the power to heal yourselves.*
> *Do a good job!*
> *Thank you.*

Repeat this formula over and over, silently or aloud, for three to five minutes. For chronic knee conditions, the more times you practice and the longer you practice each time, the better. There are no time limits.

Let me share a heart-touching story with you. About three years ago, a lady in the San Francisco Bay Area was working in her garden. She spent several minutes squatting. When she tried to stand up, there was pain everywhere. It was excruciating in her knees. She thought, "Oh, my God, I can't walk. It feels like I've pulled every muscle, ligament, and tendon there." She could only cry because she could barely move. She stood up gingerly and hobbled over to a chair. A devout Catholic, she said, "Oh, my dear Jesus, what do I do?" Suddenly, she remembered that her son always said, "You have the power to heal yourself," and had taught her the Say Hello Healing formula. She practiced like this:

> *Dear my beloved and beautiful knees,*
> *I love you, honor you, and thank you.*
> *You have the power to heal yourselves.*
> *Do a good job.*

I appreciate it.
Thank you. Thank you. Thank you.

As soon as she said this formula once, she could feel she was receiving healing. She was amazed. Within two minutes, her pain disappeared! She stood up and walked normally. She was in awe. She couldn't believe her excruciating pain could disappear so quickly. All she could say and think was, "Wow! Wow! Thank you, Jesus. Thank you, God, for teaching this to Dr. Sha." She was so deeply moved and grateful that she shared her story with hundreds of people in one of my teleconferences.

Does Say Hello Healing really work? People using the Say Hello Healing formula have shared thousands of heart-touching stories like the one you just read. I wish you will give it a try now. Choose one part of your body. Now add some Body Power: Put one palm on that area. For example, whether you have back pain or a stiff neck or a sore elbow—whatever part of the body needs healing—put one palm over the problem area. Then say *hello* like this:

> *Dear soul, mind, and body of my* _____ [back, neck, elbow, or whichever part of your body you chose to focus on],
> *I love you, honor you, and appreciate you.*
> *You have the power to heal yourself.*
> *Do a good job!*
> *Thank you.*

Repeat this formula for at least three minutes. Tap your palm on the problem area as you repeat the Say Hello Healing formula. After these three minutes, you may notice significant improvement. You may feel a little better. You may feel nothing at all. Even if you feel no improvement, it does not mean Say Hello Healing does not work. Serious or chronic conditions often take longer to improve. Be patient. Practice more. You may notice results after another practice or two.

Say *Hello* to Outer Souls of Saints

You can say *hello* to outer souls, which are souls that do not reside inside your body, such as the souls of holy saints, buddhas, healing angels, ascended masters, gurus, lamas, and all kinds of spiritual fathers and mothers in all layers of Heaven. You can apply the Say Hello Healing formula to invoke Jesus, Mary, Guan Yin, Shi Jia Mo Ni Fuo, A Mi Tuo Fuo,[5] and other high-level beings to help you. For example, you can say *hello* like this:

> *Dear beloved Jesus,*
> *I love you, honor you, and appreciate you.*
> *Please heal me.* [Make your personal request for
>   healing.]
> *I am very grateful.*
> *Thank you.*

Then repeat over and over again:

---

5. Guan Yin is known as the Bodhisattva of Compassion and, in the West, as the Goddess of Mercy. Shi Jia Mo Ni Fuo, the Chinese name of the founder of Buddhism, is also known as Shakyamuni and Siddhartha Gautama. His name in Chinese is pronounced *shee jya maw nee fwaw.* A Mi Tuo Fuo (Amitabha in Sanskrit) is the buddha who leads the Pure Land in Heaven.

Jesus, heal me. Thank you.
Jesus, heal me. Thank you.
Jesus, heal me. Thank you.
Jesus, heal me. Thank you.

Practice like this for at least three minutes, the longer, the better. In these few minutes, you could feel Jesus' healing. You could be very surprised by the results. The Bible has so many miracle stories. The teaching here is to tell you and every reader that Jesus' soul is available twenty-four hours a day. Jesus is a divine son and an unconditional divine servant for humanity and all souls.

You can invoke Mother Mary to offer you healing in the same way:

Dear beloved Mother Mary,
I love you, honor you, and appreciate you.
Please heal me. [Make your personal request for
    healing.]
I am very grateful.
Thank you.

Then repeat over and over again:

Mother Mary, heal me. Thank you.
Mother Mary, heal me. Thank you.
Mother Mary, heal me. Thank you.
Mother Mary, heal me. Thank you.

Practice like this for at least three minutes, the longer, the better. In these three minutes, you could feel Mother Mary's great love. You could receive remarkable healing results. Mother Mary is also available twenty-four hours a day. She is an unconditional divine servant for humanity and all souls.

You can invoke Guan Yin, the Goddess of Compassion. Her new name in the Soul Light Era is Ling Hui Sheng Shi—pronounced *ling hway shung shr*—which means *Soul Intelligence Saint Servant:*

> *Dear beloved Ling Hui Sheng Shi,*
> *I love you, honor you, and appreciate you.*
> *Please heal me.* [Make a specific request for healing.]
> *I am very grateful.*
> *Thank you.*

Then repeat over and over again:

> *Ling Hui Sheng Shi, heal me. Thank you.*
> *Ling Hui Sheng Shi, heal me. Thank you.*
> *Ling Hui Sheng Shi, heal me. Thank you.*
> *Ling Hui Sheng Shi, heal me. Thank you.*

Practice like this for at least three minutes, the longer, the better. After three minutes, you could feel Ling Hui Sheng Shi's heart-touching compassion and receive great healing results. Ling Hui Sheng Shi is available to each of us all the time. She is a divine daughter and another unconditional divine servant for humanity and all souls.

Say *Hello* to Outer Souls of Nature

You can apply Say Hello Healing to invoke the souls of nature. For example, say *hello* to the soul of the sun:

> *Dear soul of the sun,*
> *I love you, honor you, and appreciate you.*
> *You have the power to heal me.*
> *Please heal me.* [Make your personal request for healing.]
> *Thank you.*

Then repeat this Say Hello formula for at least three minutes, the longer, the better.

The soul of the sun can give you great blessing for your yang energy. The soul of the sun has great healing power. When you invoke the sun in this way, the soul of the sun will respond instantly to give you a healing and a blessing. The longer you practice, the more benefits you will receive from the sun. Even if it is raining or midnight when you practice, you will still receive the blessing of the sun, because you are calling the *soul* of the sun to heal and bless you.

The soul of the sun is available every day and any time. When the sun is shining during the day, you may understand easily that you can ask for a healing from the soul of the sun. How about during the night, when the sun is not shining? You can still repeat, "Soul of the sun heals me. Thank you." You will still receive healing instantly from the soul of the sun, because the soul of the sun is available twenty-four hours a day, every day.

Soul healing is very simple. You can invoke any soul in nature to heal you and to heal others. For example:

Dear soul of the sun, I love you.
My mother has cold feet.
Could you give my mother a healing now?
Thank you very much.

Then repeat, silently or aloud:

Soul of the sun heals my mother's feet.
Soul of the sun warms my mother's feet.
I am very grateful.
Thank you.

If your spiritual channels are open, you could hear the soul of the sun telling you, "I am grateful to heal your mother's feet. I am honored to be a servant to heal your mother's feet."

The true nature of any soul is to serve. Souls love to heal. They are eager and excited to offer healing and service. This is why soul healing works.

You also can invoke the soul of the moon to give you a healing. This is how to do it:

Dear soul of the moon,
I love you, honor you, and appreciate you.
You have the power to heal me.
Please heal me. [Make your personal request for
    healing.]
Thank you.

Then chant repeatedly for at least three minutes, the longer, the better:

Soul of the moon heals me. Thank you.
Soul of the moon heals me. Thank you.
Soul of the moon heals me. Thank you.
Soul of the moon heals me. Thank you.

The soul of the moon can give you great blessing for your yin energy. The soul of the moon has great healing power. When you invoke the soul of the moon in this way, it will respond instantly to give you a healing and a blessing. The longer you practice, the more benefits you will receive from the moon. Even if it is the middle of the day and you cannot see the moon, you can still invoke the soul of the moon to give you healing and blessing. You could receive great healing and blessing from the soul of the moon.

As a specific example, menopause is a major issue for millions of women. According to traditional Chinese medicine and yin/yang philosophy, difficulties associated with menopause are due to lack of yin. This is the way to do soul healing for menopause:

Dear soul of the moon,
I love you.
Please heal my menopause problems.
Do a good job.
Thank you.

Then chant repeatedly, silently or aloud:

Soul of the moon heals my menopause.
Soul of the moon heals my menopause.
Soul of the moon heals my menopause.
Soul of the moon heals my menopause.

Soul of the moon nourishes the yin of my body.
Soul of the moon nourishes the yin of my body.
Soul of the moon nourishes the yin of my body.
Soul of the moon nourishes the yin of my body.

In fact, menopause problems are due to insufficiency of kidney yin, so you can practice by chanting:

Soul of the moon nourishes my kidney yin to heal my
    menopause.
Soul of the moon nourishes my kidney yin to heal my
    menopause.
Soul of the moon nourishes my kidney yin to heal my
    menopause.
Soul of the moon nourishes my kidney yin to heal my
    menopause.

Thank you. Thank you. Thank you.

Soul healing using the Say Hello formula may sound too simple to believe. Let me share with you a renowned ancient Chinese statement:

If you want to know if a pear is sweet, taste it.

Applying this statement to soul healing:

If you want to know whether a healing technique works, experience it.

Soul healing is to invoke the soul to heal. Everyone on Mother Earth has a soul. Everything in all universes has a soul.

An herb has a soul. You can invoke the souls of herbs to heal. You do not need to have the physical herb to do soul healing. This is *soul over matter*.

One herb that nourishes kidney yin, and so benefits menopause, is Sheng Huai Shan (pronounced *shung hwye shahn*), also known as dioscorea or Chinese wild yam. Say *hello* to the soul of Sheng Huai Shan:

> *Dear soul of Sheng Huai Shan,*
> *I love you, honor you, and appreciate you.*
> *Please heal my menopause issues.*
> *I am very grateful.*
> *Thank you.*

Then chant repeatedly for at least three minutes:

> *The soul of Sheng Huai Shan heals my menopause.*
> *The soul of Sheng Huai Shan heals my menopause.*
> *The soul of Sheng Huai Shan heals my menopause.*
> *The soul of Sheng Huai Shan heals my menopause.*

Now let me introduce an acupuncture point that can help various menstrual issues, including menopause issues, as well as male issues such as erectile dysfunction and premature ejaculation: Shen Shu (Urinary Bladder 23). This acupuncture point is on the back, at the level of the L2 vertebra, and 1.5 *cun*[6] to the right of the Du meridian, which runs down the center of the back.

But for soul healing, you do not need to know where the

---

6. The *cun* (pronounced "tsuen") is a unit of measurement used in traditional Chinese medicine. One *cun* is defined as the width of the top joint of the thumb at its widest part. Although this varies from person to person, it is roughly equivalent to one inch.

Shen Shu acupuncture point is. Acupuncture points have a soul. Invoke the soul of this, or any, acupuncture point and receive healing. As always, first say *hello:*

> *Dear soul of my Shen Shu acupuncture point,*
> *I love you, honor you, and appreciate you.*
> *Please heal my menstrual issues* [you may name them].
> *I am very grateful.*
> *Thank you.*

Then chant repeatedly for at least three minutes:

> *The soul of my Shen Shu point heals my menstrual*
> * issues. Thank you.*
> *The soul of my Shen Shu point heals my menstrual*
> * issues. Thank you.*
> *The soul of my Shen Shu point heals my menstrual*
> * issues. Thank you.*
> *The soul of my Shen Shu point heals my menstrual*
> * issues. Thank you.*

As a final example of Say Hello Healing by invoking the outer souls of nature, invoke Heaven and Mother Earth to bless you at the same time. Do it like this now:

> *Dear soul of Heaven and soul of Mother Earth,*
> *I love you, honor you, and appreciate you.*
> *You have the power to heal me.* [Make your personal
> * request for healing.]*
> *Please heal me.*
> *Thank you.*

Then repeat this Say Hello formula for at least three minutes, the longer, the better.

Heaven's energy represents and carries great yang energy. Mother Earth's energy represents and carries great yin energy. When you invoke the soul of Heaven and the soul of Mother Earth together, you will receive healing and blessing from yang and yin energies at the same time. I never promise anything, but you could receive remarkable healing. Your healing result could be beyond your comprehension.

You can use the wisdom and the Say Hello formula in *Soul Mind Body Medicine* and in this section to invoke any soul of nature for self-healing. For example, you can invoke the soul of a mountain, a river, an ocean, a forest, or a flower. There is no limitation.

Say *Hello* to the Divine

The Divine is in soul form. The Divine is an outer soul. The Divine is our father and our mother. The Divine is the creator of the universe. The Divine is the source of the universe. The Divine is the top soul of the universe. To invoke the Divine is the top Soul Power secret for self-healing. Here is how to do it:

Dear Divine,
I love you, honor you, and appreciate you.
I am so grateful that you can heal me.
I cannot thank you enough.
Please heal me. [Make your personal request for healing.]
I am extremely grateful.

Then chant repeatedly:

Dear Divine, heal me. Thank you.
Dear Divine, heal me. Thank you.
Dear Divine, heal me. Thank you.
Dear Divine, heal me. Thank you.

The Divine is available twenty-four hours a day. The Divine is an unconditional universal servant. Invoke the Divine. Then you can receive soul healing blessings beyond words. There is no time limit for invoking the Divine and practicing as above.

The best way to receive healing from the Divine is to be in a meditative state and focus on the area where you want healing. Put one palm on this area and use it to do simple Soul Tapping there at the same time. Soul Tapping is soul-guided tapping. Seven chapters of *Soul Wisdom,*[7] the first book of my Soul Power Series, are devoted to the soul secrets, wisdom, knowledge, and practices of Soul Tapping. It is a practical and powerful soul healing technique and treasure. We will use Soul Tapping in many of the practices in this book.

Let me share a one-sentence secret for hands healing (Body Power), which includes Soul Tapping:

Where you put your hands is where you receive healing.

Let me share a one-sentence secret for mind healing (Mind Power), which includes creative visualization:

---

7. *Soul Wisdom: Practical Soul Treasures to Transform Your Life* (2008, New York/Toronto: Atria Books/Heaven's Library).

Where you focus your mind is where you receive healing.

The following simple soul self-healing practice by invoking the Divine, together with the Body Power and Mind Power of using your hands and mind, will greatly accelerate your healing. This practice uses all of the Four Power Techniques of Soul Mind Body Medicine:

Soul Power. Use the Say Hello formula to invoke the Divine:

> *Dear Divine,*
> *I love you, honor you, and appreciate you.*
> *Please heal me.* [Make a specific request.]
> *Thank you.*

Body Power. With one palm, do Soul Tapping on the area where you wish to receive healing.

Sound Power. Repeat the Say Hello formula or, more simply, repeat:

> *Dear Divine, heal me. Thank you.*
> *Dear Divine, heal me. Thank you.*
> *Dear Divine, heal me. Thank you.*
> *Dear Divine, heal me. Thank you.*

Mind Power. Focus your mind on the area to receive healing. Visualize golden light there.

You can apply these Four Power Techniques in every Soul Mind Body self-healing practice. This healing system is so simple and practical. After I published *Soul Mind Body Medicine* in 2006, thousands of heart-touching stories worldwide have proven that this system works.

This Soul Mind Body self-healing system can be summarized in one sentence:

You can heal yourself anywhere, anytime, without walking one step to find The Divine and other soul healing resources.

This is the power and the benefit of Say Hello Healing. This technique may be too simple for some of you to believe. But remember this one-sentence secret:

The most powerful technique is the simplest technique.

One-sentence secrets are treasures for people who are searching for healing secrets. People could study hundreds of books and join workshops for years, even decades. Yet, they may not be able to summarize the key wisdom and secrets in one sentence. I'm honored to share one-sentence secrets with you and humanity.

"Say *hello*" *is* a one-sentence secret for soul healing. The more you practice Say Hello Healing, the more blessings and "Aha!" moments you could receive.

It is very important to realize that soul healing can take time. In some cases, three minutes of soul healing practice can produce remarkable results. In other cases, you may not feel any improvement at all after three minutes of practice. This does not mean that soul healing does not work.

Sickness is due to blockages in soul, mind, and body. You could have major bad karma, which is a soul blockage. You could have strong blockages in your consciousness, which are mind blockages. You could have severe energy or matter blockages, which are body blockages. I will explain all of these blockages in depth in this book.

To remove these blockages does take time. Be patient. Be consistent. *Trust* soul healing. Think about this. Many people take medicine for an unhealthy condition, sometimes for twenty or thirty years, or even for their whole life. It could take years to see any improvement. Sometimes there is never any improvement; people take medicine just to stabilize and maintain their condition. So, please do not complain if you do not feel any improvement after only three to five minutes of practice. Saying "soul healing does not work" is not fair. Be patient and do your job. Try to do more practice. Give soul healing a fair trial.

I started to teach soul healing in 1994. People from all over the world have shared thousands of heart-touching, moving, and miracle stories that have shown the power of soul healing. These stories include transformation of pancreatic cancer, liver cancer, lymphatic cancer, lung cancer, and many other cancers, as well as recovery from arthritis, kidney failure, slipped disks, depression, sadness, anger, other emotional imbalances, and mental disorders such as schizophrenia. Visit my website, www.drsha.com, to read these stories, which demonstrate that soul healing is simple, practical, and powerful.

I always say there is no time limit to practicing soul healing. The more you practice and the longer you practice, the better. I strongly believe soul healing can offer great service to humanity. I wish you will receive great soul healing results as quickly as possible.

I am extremely grateful to all of my spiritual fathers and mothers, and to all of my great teachers—national treasures in China—of ancient Chinese arts and philosophies, including tai chi, qi gong, the *I Ching*, feng shui, kung fu, Daoism, Buddhism, and Confucianism. I am very grateful to all of my teachers in elementary school, high school, and college. I am deeply grateful to my teachers of modern Western medicine and traditional Chinese medicine. Since I was chosen as a divine servant, vehicle, and channel in 2003, the Divine teaches me directly every day. I cannot honor and be grateful to the Divine enough.

I am extremely honored to integrate the secrets, wisdom, knowledge, and practices of five thousand years of ancient Chinese arts with the essence of energy and spiritual healing, as well as with the essence of conventional modern medicine and traditional Chinese medicine. All of my life's study led me to create Soul Mind Body Medicine several years ago. I believe that it could save you a lot of time spent reading hundreds of books and pursuing all kinds of studies. I honor every book and every teaching. I also honor my hundreds and thousands of lifetimes of experiences, and especially all of the teachings I have received from my spiritual fathers and mothers and directly from the Divine.

Since July 2003, the Divine has taught and guided me daily. Within these few years, the Divine guided me to flow the following five major books and to create the Soul Power Series:

- *Soul Mind Body Medicine: A Complete Soul Healing System for Optimum Health and Vitality*
- *Soul Wisdom: Practical Soul Treasures to Transform Your Life*
- *Soul Communication: Opening Your Spiritual Channels for Success and Fulfillment*

- *The Power of Soul: The Way to Heal, Rejuvenate, Transform, and Enlighten All Life*
- *Divine Soul Songs: Sacred Practical Treasures to Heal, Rejuvenate, and Transform You, Humanity, Mother Earth, and All Universes*

Now, in 2009, the Divine has guided me further to create the Divine Soul Mind Body Healing and Transmission System. This book, *Divine Soul Mind Body Healing and Transmission System: The Divine Way to Heal You, Humanity, Mother Earth, and All Universes,* is to share with you and every reader that *a break-through divine healing system is available now.* The soul secrets, wisdom, knowledge, and practices in this book are a divine soul healing system.

The Divine teaches me these soul secrets, wisdom, knowledge, and practices through direct conversations with me or through a divine lecture. The Divine is with me as I am writing this book now. When the Divine speaks, I simply flow out the wisdom. An advanced student of mine transcribes the flow. This is also the way I wrote all of the previous books listed above. This is the way I will write all of my future books. I have created more than one hundred Divine Writers. They write books in the same way. They open their spiritual channels to "flow" wisdom from the Divine. All Divine Writers and I are honored to be vessels and servants. We are honored to receive divine teaching, and to share divine secrets, wisdom, knowledge, and practices with you and every reader.

This book will explain to you and humanity:

- what the Divine Soul Mind Body Healing and Transmission System is

- how the Divine Soul Mind Body Healing and Transmission System works
- the power and significance of this system
- how to receive the divine treasures within this book
- how to receive additional divine treasures
- how to apply them to heal you, your loved ones, pets, relationships, finances, organizations, humanity, cities, countries, Mother Earth, and all universes

The Divine Soul Mind Body Healing and Transmission System can be summarized in one sentence:

Remove soul, mind, and body blockages and receive Divine Soul, Mind, and Body Transplants to heal you, your loved ones, pets, relationships, finances, organizations, humanity, cities, countries, Mother Earth, and all universes.

I appreciate divine teaching, which is simple, practical, powerful, and effective. I wish you will enjoy the teachings of this book. Apply the secrets, wisdom, knowledge, and practices to heal all aspects of life.

I love my heart and soul
I love all humanity
Join hearts and souls together
Love, peace and harmony
Love, peace and harmony

God gives his heart to me
God gives his love to me

My heart melds with his heart
My love melds with his love

Hao! Hao! Hao![8]
Thank you. Thank you. Thank you.[9]

---

8. "Hao" (pronounced *how*) means *good, perfect* in Chinese.
9. The first "thank you" is to the Divine. The second "thank you" is to your own spiritual fathers and mothers. The third "thank you" is to your own soul.

DIVINE SOUL MIND BODY HEALING AND TRANSMISSION SYSTEM

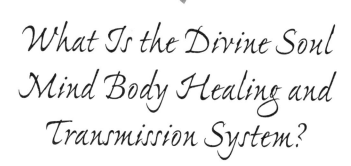

What Is the Divine Soul Mind Body Healing and Transmission System?

*I*N THE INTRODUCTION, I reviewed and emphasized some key teachings of Soul Mind Body Medicine. These teachings and practical techniques have served hundreds of thousands of people's healing journeys. They will continue to serve humanity more. In this book, I will move from Soul Mind Body Medicine to the Divine Soul Mind Body Healing and Transmission System.

Concepts and Wisdom of Soul, Mind, and Body for Everyone and Everything

In ancient times, there was a renowned spiritual statement:

Wan wu jie you ling

"Wan" means *ten thousand*. In Chinese, "ten thousand" represents *all* or *every*. "Wu" means *thing*. "Jie" means *all*. "You" means *has*. "Ling" means *soul*.

Therefore, *Wan wu jie you ling* means *everything has a soul*.

Living things have a soul. For example, human beings, animals, insects, bacteria, viruses, trees, and flowers have souls. *Wan wu jie you ling* emphasizes that *inanimate things also have souls*. For example, a mountain, a river, a table, a chair, a house, a street, the name of a business, a star, a space, a relationship, and this book, all have souls.

When you highly develop your spiritual channels,[1] including your Third Eye to see spiritual images and your direct soul communication abilities to have conversations with other souls, you will be able to see a soul clearly in every being and object. You will be able to communicate with any soul. For example, when you stand in front of a mountain, simply say, "Dear soul of the mountain, please come." Instantly, the soul of the mountain will appear in front of you. You can have a conversation with the soul of the mountain, just as you have conversations with your loved ones and friends.

Everyone and everything in the universe is made of matter. It is very easy to understand that tangible physical things are made of matter. The important secret and teaching I want to share is that even energy, light, and souls are made of matter. Energy is made of tiny matter. Light and souls are made of even tinier matter.

All matter is in motion. Matter resonates and vibrates con-

---

1. *Soul Communication: Opening Your Spiritual Channels for Success and Fulfillment* (2008, New York/Toronto: Atria Books/Heaven's Library), the second book in my Soul Power Series, offers comprehensive teachings and practical techniques for developing the four major spiritual communication channels.

stantly. When matter resonates and vibrates, it radiates energy out. Energy is life force. In ancient times, energy was named *chi* or *qi*. Five thousand years of traditional Chinese medicine theory and practice have been based on the concept of *chi*.

Qi gong was created about four thousand three hundred years ago by Peng Zu (pronounced *pung zoo*), the teacher of Lao Zi.[2] Peng Zu created *Zhi qi zhi dao*. "Zhi" means *manage* or *balance*. "Qi" means *vital energy* or *life force*. The second "zhi" is a possessive particle; it functions like an apostrophe. "Dao" is *the Way*. *Zhi qi zhi dao* means *the Way to balance qi*.

Peng Zu created this profound teaching with an entire system of practice, including singing songs and chanting mantras, meditations, visualizations, and movement. Peng Zu's system teaches practices in various positions—lying down, sitting, standing, and walking, practices for the various systems and organs of the body, practices for specific times of day, and more. It is a powerful healing, rejuvenation, transformation, and enlightenment system. With it, Peng Zu lived to the age of eight hundred eighty. He is revered in China as the Long Life Star.

Today, qi gong has spread from China and is widely popular in the world. Millions of people study qi gong to balance their energy for healing, as well as to boost their energy, stamina, vitality, and immunity. Qi gong is a great practice for rejuvenation and prolonging life.

To return to matter and energy: In a living thing, matter resides inside the cells. Cells resonate and vibrate constantly. Cells contract and expand constantly. When cells contract, matter inside the cells transforms to energy and radiates out of the cells. When cells expand, energy outside the cells transforms to matter

---

2. Lao Zi is the author of the *Dao De Jing*, the fundamental text of Daoism.

and returns to the cells. When this transformation between matter and energy is in relative balance, health and vitality result.

The important wisdom and secret to know is that *all matter carries a soul* and *all energy also carries a soul.* Let me explain further by presenting the key theory that links matter, energy, and soul.

Message Energy Matter Theory—The Key Spiritual Guidance and Principle for the Divine Soul Mind Body Healing and Transmission System

The term *soul* (*ling* in Chinese) has been used more in China and other Asian countries. *Spirit* has been used more in Western countries. *Message* is used more in the scientific field. Soul, spirit, and message are the same thing but with different names.

Everything is made of matter. Matter includes atoms, protons, neutrons, electrons, quarks, leptons, and more. Matter radiates energy. Matter and energy never disappear. They transform from one to the other.

Matter and energy are the carriers of message. Message is soul or spirit. *Soul is the boss.* Soul directs the transformation between matter and energy. This explains the one-sentence secret of soul healing, which is:

Heal the soul first; then healing of the mind and body will follow.

Soul has many layers. For example, a human being has a soul of the body (a "body soul"), which is our spirit or essence. Each human being also has a soul for each system, a soul for each organ, a soul for each cell, a soul for each cell unit, a soul for each cell DNA and RNA, a soul for each smallest particle of matter inside the cells, and a soul for each space between the cells. In fact, a human being has billions, trillions of souls, and more.

For example, scientific study has shown that the brain has billions of cells. This tells us that a brain itself has billions of souls. Each cell has many cell units, DNA, RNA, and smallest matter. Each of these also has a soul. So there will be many billions and trillions more souls of cell units, DNA, RNA, and smallest matter. Every organ has billions and billions of souls. The whole body has too many souls to count. People understand from anatomy that a human being has many systems, organs, and cells. Many people are not aware that every system, organ, and cell has a soul. I'm honored to reveal an important soul secret and wisdom that:

A human being has a complete soul system.

How is this complete soul system organized? I will now formally release some important soul secrets:

- The body soul is the boss of the system souls, organ souls, cell souls, cell unit souls, DNA and RNA souls, smallest matter souls, and space souls. (I revealed this soul secret in *The Power of Soul*.)
- The soul of the cardiovascular system is the boss of all other system souls.
- The soul of the heart is the boss of all other organ souls.
- The souls of the heart cells, heart cell units, heart DNA and RNA, smallest matter in the heart, and spaces in the heart are the bosses of all other cell

souls, cell unit souls, DNA and RNA souls, smallest matter souls, and space souls, respectively.

This is important wisdom. It tells us that the body soul, the soul of the cardiovascular system, the soul of the heart, and the souls of the cells, cell units, DNA and RNA, smallest matter, and spaces in the heart are the vital souls to heal the body, systems, organs, cells, cell units, DNA and RNA, smallest matter, and spaces.

Invoke these leader souls. Healing could be very fast. Let me give you one key practice to heal your whole body, including all systems, all organs, all cells, all cell units, all DNA and RNA, all smallest matter, and all spaces in the body at the same time:

Practice for Whole Body Healing

First say *hello*. This is **Soul Power.**

> *Dear my body soul, soul of my cardiovascular system, soul of my heart, and souls of the cells, cell units, DNA and RNA, smallest matter, and spaces in my heart,*
> *I love you, honor you, and appreciate you.*
> *You have the power to heal my body, all systems, all organs, all cells, all cell units, all DNA and RNA, all smallest matter, and all spaces in my body.*
> *Do a good job.*
> *Thank you.*

Then, chant repeatedly, silently or aloud. This is **Sound Power.**

> *Heal my whole body, my systems, organs, cells, cell*
>   *units, DNA and RNA, smallest matter, and spaces.*
> *Thank you.*
> *Heal my whole body, my systems, organs, cells, cell*
>   *units, DNA and RNA, smallest matter, and spaces.*
> *Thank you.*
> *Heal my whole body, my systems, organs, cells, cell*
>   *units, DNA and RNA, smallest matter, and spaces.*
> *Thank you.*
> *Heal my whole body, my systems, organs, cells, cell*
>   *units, DNA and RNA, smallest matter, and spaces.*
> *Thank you.*

Chant for at least three minutes, the longer, the better.

> *Hao! Hao! Hao!*
> *Thank you. Thank you. Thank you.*

Mind blockages can also be important for one's healing. They are critical to one's spiritual journey. Mind means consciousness. To heal the mind is to transform the consciousness. I have a mind and consciousness. You have a mind and consciousness. Everyone and everything has a mind and consciousness. Our systems, organs, cells, cell units, DNA and RNA, smallest matter in the cells, and spaces between the cells all have a mind and consciousness. There are many kinds of mind blockages. Major mind blockages include negative mind-sets, attitudes, and beliefs, as well as ego and attachment. Mind blockages in our systems, organs, cells, and parts of the body need to be removed for complete healing of the systems, organs, cells, and parts of the body. Mind blockages in ourselves need to be removed to progress on the spiritual journey.

Practice for Healing the Mind

Love can heal the mind. Forgiveness can heal the mind. Compassion can heal the mind. Light can heal the mind. Let us practice by invoking the souls of these four qualities:

> *Dear souls of love, forgiveness, compassion, and light,*
> *I love you, honor you, and appreciate you.*
> *You have the power to heal my mind.*
> *Please transform my consciousness and remove my negative mind-sets, attitudes, and beliefs, as well as ego and attachment.*
> *Thank you.*

Then, chant repeatedly:

> *Souls of love, forgiveness, compassion, and light,*
> *Transform my consciousness and remove my negative mind-sets, attitudes, and beliefs, as well as ego and attachment. Thank you.*
> *Souls of love, forgiveness, compassion, and light,*
> *Transform my consciousness and remove my negative mind-sets, attitudes, and beliefs, as well as ego and attachment. Thank you.*
> *Souls of love, forgiveness, compassion, and light,*
> *Transform my consciousness and remove my negative mind-sets, attitudes, and beliefs, as well as ego and attachment. Thank you.*

Souls of love, forgiveness, compassion, and light,
Transform my consciousness and remove my negative
mind-sets, attitudes, and beliefs, as well as ego and
attachment. Thank you.

Chant for at least three minutes, the longer, the better.

A body has systems. A system has organs. An organ has cells. A cell has cell units, DNA and RNA, smallest matter, and spaces. They are all made of matter. Matter resonates and vibrates to radiate energy. Energy is *chi*.

For five thousand years, traditional Chinese medicine has emphasized *chi*. *The Yellow Emperor's Internal Classic*, the authoritative textbook of traditional Chinese medicine, stated:

If chi flows, one is healthy. If chi is blocked, one is sick.

Many healing modalities worldwide focus on *chi* healing, such as acupuncture, qi gong, Reiki, prana healing, magnet therapy, and hundreds more kinds of energy-based healing. *Chi* healing is very important. *Chi* healing has benefited millions of people's health throughout history.

Let me release one secret wisdom and practice of *chi* healing. Practice like this:

Practice for Chi Healing

Choose one part of your body where you have problems, which could include pain, stiffness, heaviness, fullness, inflammation, a cyst, a tumor, cancer, or other issues. Put one palm on that area.

Then, chant repeatedly:

Chi flows.
Chi flows.
Chi flows.
Chi flows.

Practice for at least three minutes, the longer, the better. In these three minutes of chanting this two-word sentence, you could receive remarkable healing that you can hardly believe. You could receive significant improvement. You could feel a little better. You could feel no improvement at all. If you feel no improvement, it does not mean that it does not work. Practice more. You could feel results soon.

Why is this wisdom and practice a vital secret? To chant *chi flows* is to give a Soul Order to the affected systems, organs, cells, cell units, DNA and RNA, smallest matter in the cells, and spaces between the cells. This order stimulates cellular vibration. *Chi,* which is energy, flows instantly. As long as *chi* flows, you could feel better instantly.

If *chi* flows, matter blockages will dissipate also. How? Remember, matter is inside the cells. *Chi* is outside the cells. When *chi* flows, the matter inside the cells will transform to *chi* outside the cells. This will remove matter blockages naturally.

In this book, I am introducing the Divine Soul Mind Body Healing and Transmission System. We understand that everyone and everything has a soul. Divine Soul Mind Body Transplants mean that the Divine will change the soul, mind, and body of our unhealthy systems, organs, cells, cell units, DNA, RNA, smallest matter, and spaces for divine healing. If our systems, organs, cells, cell units, DNA, RNA, smallest matter, and spaces are already healthy, Divine Soul Mind Body Transplants can offer us new divine souls, minds, and bodies for divine rejuvenation and longevity.

A Divine Soul Transplant is a light being created by the Divine. This light being is a new divine soul to replace an original soul of your systems, organs, cells, cell units, DNA, RNA, smallest matter, or spaces, in order to heal and transform the soul.

A Divine Mind Transplant is another light being created by the Divine. This light being carries divine consciousness to replace an original consciousness of your systems, organs, cells, cell units, DNA, RNA, smallest matter, or spaces, in order to heal and transform the mind and remove negative mind-sets, attitudes, and beliefs, as well as ego and attachment.

A Divine Body Transplant is also a light being created by the Divine. This light being carries divine energy and divine tiny matter to replace original energy and tiny matter of your systems, organs, cells, cell units, DNA, RNA, smallest matter, or spaces, in order to heal and transform the energy and tiny matter.

To receive Divine Soul Mind Body Transplants for a system, organ, cells, cell units, DNA, RNA, smallest matter, and spaces does not mean that the system, organ, or cells are healed and recovered from their unhealthy condition. Divine Soul Mind Body Transplants carry divine frequency and vibration, with divine love, forgiveness, compassion, and light. They *could* heal the soul, mind, and body of a person's system, organ, or cells very quickly and also rejuvenate the soul, mind, and body of the system, organ, or cells. In this book, I will lead you in practices to apply Divine Soul Mind Body Transplants for healing, rejuvenation, and life transformation.

I am very grateful to be a servant of humanity and the Divine. I am extremely honored that I can be a vessel and channel to offer Divine Soul Mind Body Transplants. I started to offer Divine Soul Transplants in July 2003. Thousands of heart-touching and moving stories have proven the power of Divine Soul Transplants.

This book will share with every reader the whole picture of Divine Soul Mind Body Transplants. The Divine Soul Mind Body Healing and Transmission System will bless every reader, humanity, Mother Earth, and all universes.

The Divine Soul Mind Body Healing and Transmission System is a breakthrough divine healing system for you, your loved ones, pets, relationships, finances, organizations, humanity, cities, countries, Mother Earth, and all universes.

The Divine offers the Divine Soul Mind Body Healing and Transmission System.

We receive healing.

We receive rejuvenation.

We receive transformation.

We receive enlightenment.

We are honored and blessed.

Thank you. Thank you. Thank you.

Soul Mind Body Medicine—A Complete Soul Mind Body Self-healing System

In 2006, I published *Soul Mind Body Medicine: A Complete Soul Healing System for Optimum Health and Vitality.* That book introduced a self-healing system that everyone can apply to empower themselves to heal, prevent sickness, rejuvenate, and prolong life.

I have already shared the Four Power Techniques of Soul Mind Body Medicine to self-heal and heal others. I would like to give one new teaching and practice to explain the Four Power Techniques further.

Traditional Chinese medicine has a key teaching: the theory of Five Elements, which are Wood, Fire, Earth, Metal, and Water. This theory and philosophy uses these five natural elements to represent and interpret the major internal organs, sense organs, and tissues of the body, as well as emotions and any aspect of life and the universe. I have shared this wisdom in the fourth book of my Soul Power Series, *Divine Soul Songs*. In this book, I will give you a practical technique for applying the Four Power Techniques together with the Five Elements to heal yourself and balance your emotions. Here is a simple chart showing how the Five Elements characterize the body and the directions:

Table 1. Five Elements of the Body and Directions

Element	Yin Organ	Yang Organ	Body Tissue	Finger	Sense	Emotion	Direction
Wood	Liver	Gallbladder	Tendons	Index	Sight Eyes	Anger	East
Fire	Heart	Small Intestine	Blood Vessels	Middle	Taste Tongue	Depression Anxiety Excitability	South
Earth	Spleen	Stomach	Muscles	Thumb	Speech Mouth	Worry	Central Middle
Metal	Lung	Large Intestine	Skin	Ring	Smell Nose	Sadness Grief	West
Water	Kidney	Urinary Bladder	Bones	Baby	Hearing Ears	Fear	North

HEAL THE WOOD ELEMENT

The index finger represents the soul, mind, and body of the Wood element, which includes the liver, gallbladder, tendons, eyes, anger in the emotional body, and the eastern direction. To heal pain, inflammation, cysts, tumors, or cancer in any of these, and to balance the emotion of anger, this is the way to apply the Four Power Techniques:

Soul Power. Say *hello:*

> *Dear soul, mind, and body of my liver, gallbladder,*
>   *tendons, and eyes,*
> *I love you.*
> *You have the power to heal yourselves.*
> *You have the power to heal anger in my emotional*
>   *body.*
> *Do a good job.*
> *Thank you.*

Body Power. Squeeze your left index finger with your right hand as tightly as possible for thirty seconds, then release (totally let go) for thirty seconds. Then squeeze again for thirty seconds; release again for thirty seconds. Squeeze a third time for thirty seconds; release a third time. (Your total practice time is three minutes.)

Sound Power. Repeat *jiao* (pronounced "jow"—rhymes with "cow") aloud when squeezing, silently when released.

Mind Power. Focus on the area where you wish to receive healing and visualize bright golden light radiating and vibrating there.

Practice three to five times a day. For serious, chronic, and life-threatening conditions, practice more often and practice longer each time. There are no time limits.

HEAL THE FIRE ELEMENT

The middle finger represents the soul, mind, and body of the Fire element, which includes the heart, small intestine, blood vessels, tongue, over-excitement and over-joy in the emotional body, and the southern direction. To heal pain, inflammation, cysts, tumors, or cancer in any of these, and to balance the emotion of over-excitement or over-joy, this is the way to apply the Four Power Techniques:

Soul Power. Say *hello:*

> *Dear soul, mind, and body of my heart, small intestine, blood vessels, and tongue,*
> *I love you.*
> *You have the power to heal yourselves.*
> *You have the power to heal over-excitement and over-joy in my emotional body.*
> *Do a good job.*
> *Thank you.*

Body Power. Squeeze your left middle finger with your right hand as tightly as possible for thirty seconds, then release (totally let go) for thirty seconds. Then squeeze again for thirty seconds; release again for thirty seconds. Squeeze a third time for thirty seconds; release a third time. (Your total practice time is three minutes.)

Sound Power. Repeat *zhi* (pronounced "jee") aloud when squeezing, silently when released.

Mind Power. Focus on the area where you wish to receive healing and visualize bright golden light radiating and vibrating there.

Practice three to five times a day. For serious, chronic, and life-threatening conditions, practice more often and practice longer each time. There are no time limits.

HEAL THE EARTH ELEMENT

The thumb represents the soul, mind, and body of the Earth element, which includes the spleen, stomach, muscles, mouth and gums, worry in the emotional body, and the central or middle direction. To heal pain, inflammation, cysts, tumors, or cancer in any of these, and to balance the emotion of worry, this is the way to apply the Four Power Techniques:

Soul Power. Say *hello:*

> *Dear soul, mind, and body of my spleen, stomach,*
>   *muscles, and mouth and gums,*
> *I love you.*
> *You have the power to heal yourselves.*
> *You have the power to heal worry in my emotional*
>   *body.*
> *Do a good job.*
> *Thank you.*

Body Power. Squeeze your left thumb with your right hand as tightly as possible for thirty seconds, then release (totally let go) for thirty seconds. Then squeeze again for thirty seconds; release again for thirty seconds. Squeeze a third time for thirty seconds; release a third time. (Your total practice time is three minutes.)

Sound Power. Repeat *gong* (pronounced "gōhng") aloud when squeezing, silently when released.

Mind Power. Focus on the area where you wish to receive healing and visualize bright golden light radiating and vibrating there.

Practice three to five times a day. For serious, chronic, and life-threatening conditions, practice more often and practice longer each time. There are no time limits.

HEAL THE METAL ELEMENT

The ring finger represents the soul, mind, and body of the Metal element, which includes the lungs, large intestine, skin, nose, sadness and grief in the emotional body, and the western direction. To heal pain, inflammation, cysts, tumors, or cancer in any of these, and to balance the emotion of sadness or grief, this is the way to apply the Four Power Techniques:

Soul Power. Say *hello:*

> *Dear soul, mind, and body of my lungs, large intestine, skin, and nose,*
> *I love you.*
> *You have the power to heal yourselves.*
> *You have the power to heal sadness and grief in my emotional body.*
> *Do a good job.*
> *Thank you.*

Body Power. Squeeze your left ring finger with your right hand as tightly as possible for thirty seconds, then release (totally let go) for thirty seconds. Then squeeze again for thirty seconds; release again for thirty seconds. Squeeze a third time for thirty seconds; release a third time. (Your total practice time is three minutes.)

Sound Power. Repeat *shang* (pronounced "shahng") aloud when squeezing, silently when released.

Mind Power. Focus on the area where you wish to receive healing and visualize bright golden light radiating and vibrating there.

Practice three to five times a day. For serious, chronic, and life-threatening conditions, practice more often and practice longer each time. There are no time limits.

HEAL THE WATER ELEMENT

The baby finger represents the soul, mind, and body of the Water element, which includes the kidneys, urinary bladder, bones, ears, fear in the emotional body, and the northern direction. To heal pain, inflammation, cysts, tumors, or cancer in any of these, and to balance the emotion of fear, this is the way to apply the Four Power Techniques:

Soul Power. Say *hello:*

> *Dear soul, mind, and body of my kidneys, urinary*
> *   bladder, bones, and ears,*
> *I love you.*
> *You have the power to heal yourselves.*
> *You have the power to heal fear in my emotional body.*

Do a good job.
Thank you.

Body Power. Squeeze your left baby finger with your right hand as tightly as possible for thirty seconds, then release (totally let go) for thirty seconds. Then squeeze again for thirty seconds; release again for thirty seconds. Squeeze a third time for thirty seconds; release a third time. (Your total practice time is three minutes.)

Sound Power. Repeat *yu* (pronounced "yü") aloud when squeezing, silently when released.

Mind Power. Focus on the area where you wish to receive healing and visualize bright golden light radiating and vibrating there.

Practice three to five times a day. For serious, chronic, and life-threatening conditions, practice more often and practice longer each time. There are no time limits.

These new Five Elements practices utilize the Four Power Techniques taught in *Soul Mind Body Medicine.* The essence of Soul Mind Body Medicine is to apply the Four Power Techniques to self-heal and heal others. You could experience remarkable results. There are so many heart-touching stories worldwide from applying these Four Power Techniques. These teachings will continue to benefit humanity's health, prevention of sickness, rejuvenation, and longevity.

Divine Soul Mind Body Healing and Transmission System

So far, you have understood the basic concepts of soul, mind, and body. You have realized and experienced the importance and power of self-healing and healing others using the Four Power Techniques of Soul Mind Body Medicine. Soul Mind Body Medicine uses the power of your own soul, the power of all of your inner souls, and the power of outer souls to heal, prevent sickness, rejuvenate, prolong life, and transform every aspect of life, including relationships and finances. I am honored to have been guided and taught by the Divine, and by all of my teachers in the soul form and the physical form, to create this complete soul healing system for humanity. I wish it will continue to serve you and all humanity well.

Now, in 2009, the Divine has guided and taught me to release the Divine Soul Mind Body Healing and Transmission System to humanity. The Divine Soul Mind Body Healing and Transmission System is a *divine* way to heal, prevent sickness, rejuvenate, prolong life, and transform every aspect of life, including relationships and finances. It is a complete *divine* soul healing system for humanity. I wish it will serve you and all humanity well also.

Everyone and everything has a soul, mind, and body. A human being has a soul, mind, and body. A system, an organ, a cell, a cell unit, a DNA, an RNA, a smallest matter, and a space between cells—each and every one has a soul, mind, and body. A relationship also has a soul, mind, and body. A business has a soul, mind, and body.

The Divine Soul Mind Body Healing and Transmission System is powerful and effective because it offers divine soul healing for the soul, mind, and body. This divine soul healing system can be summarized in three steps:

- **Remove** soul, mind, and body blockages
- **Receive** Divine Soul Mind Body Transplants

- Invoke and **practice** with Divine Soul Mind Body Transplants

The Divine has the Soul Power to remove the soul, mind, and body blockages of everyone and everything. The Divine has the Soul Power to offer Divine Soul Transplants, Divine Mind Transplants, and Divine Body Transplants for everyone and everything. But to receive Divine Soul Mind Body Transplants does not mean you recover from sickness right away or that a relationship or business is transformed right away. It means you have received permanent divine treasures. These treasures carry divine frequency and vibration, with divine love, forgiveness, compassion, and light. Divine love, forgiveness, compassion, and light can heal, rejuvenate, and transform all life.

After receiving these divine soul, mind, and body treasures, you must invoke and practice with them to heal, rejuvenate, and transform your life. In this book, I will teach you how. You will see that the divine way is extremely simple.

One of the most renowned statements in Daoist teaching is:

Da dao zhi jian

"Da" means *big*. "Dao" means *The Way*. "Zhi" means *extremely*. "Jian" means *simple*.

The Big Way is extremely simple.

The Divine Soul Mind Body Healing and Transmission System is the divine way for healing, rejuvenation, and life transformation. Since I was chosen as a divine servant, vehicle, and channel in 2003, there have been thousands of heart-touching and moving stories of divine soul healing by receiving divine treasures and practicing with them. Here is one story that is extremely heart-touching:

My name is Lothar. I live in Kempten, Bavaria, Germany. In June 2008, I suddenly had severe pain in my left lower abdomen. I could not eat or sleep. I went to see my doctor, who ordered an ultrasound, MRI, and CT scan. Right afterward, he also performed a biopsy. I was diagnosed with a seventeen-centimeter cancerous tumor in and on my pancreas. That was quite a shock.

The doctor told me that I needed surgery to remove the tumor right away. He also said I needed painkillers to reduce the pain.

I told my doctor, "I have a spiritual father who taught me soul self-healing. I believe I can heal myself. I do not want to have an operation. I do not want to take painkillers."

The doctor replied, "You are a little crazy!" This doctor was a friend of my family. He had known me since childhood. He loves me and cares for me. He was very upset with me. He is an oncologist. He did not want me to take any chances with my health. He told me about a report on ten thousand pancreatic cancer cases. Not one of those patients survived. Every one of them died because of his or her cancer. That was how serious my condition was. My doctor told me that I could die before Christmas.

I decided to do soul self-healing on the spot because I believe in Master Sha's teaching. I have seen many miracle results from his divine healing blessings and the self-healing techniques he teaches. I have seen that they have really worked for many others.

The next day, one of my friends called the Institute of Soul Healing and Enlightenment to report my condition to Master Sha. I was very moved when Master Sha called me back the same day. Over the phone, he gave me a divine karma cleansing to remove my spiritual blockages. He further offered a Divine Soul Transplant for my pancreas. He told me, "Please practice at least two hours per day. Chant repeatedly:

Divine soul treasures heal me.
Thank you, Divine.
Divine soul treasures heal me.
Thank you, Divine.
Divine soul treasures heal me.
Thank you, Divine.
Divine soul treasures heal me.
Thank you, Divine.*"*

Master Sha also told me to sing Divine Soul Songs, such as the Divine Soul Song of Yin Yang and the Divine Soul Song of Five Elements, as well as my own Soul Song.

I followed Master Sha's advice. I chanted a lot—six to eight hours per day. In just a few days, my pain started to diminish. In a few weeks, it was reduced by at least 25 percent. Although the pain was still constant, I was at least able to eat and sleep again. I understood and appreciated that this was already a huge blessing. I continued to chant, chant, chant with great faith and confidence.

At the end of August, Master Sha began to offer Divine Soul Energy Matter Transplants to humanity. From July 2003 to August 2008, Master Sha had offered only Divine Soul Transplants as a divine vehicle and channel. After more than five years, the Divine guided him to begin to offer Energy Transplants and Matter Transplants, which means the Divine will change the energy and the tiny matter of a system, an organ, or a part of the body.

Hundreds of people worldwide responded by receiving these newest divine treasures remotely in one of Master Sha's Sunday Divine Blessings teleconferences. I was one of them. I received Divine Soul Energy Matter Transplants for Pancreas.

After receiving those transmissions, my pain was reduced instantly by another 50 percent. That was quite a dramatic relief from my constant pain. I was so happy and grateful. It encouraged me to practice more. I did. My practice increased to eight hours or more per day. The pain continued to diminish. My energy was much better. I slept well. I ate well. By the end of August, the pain had been reduced by about 75 percent.

In September, I went to see my oncologist again for a new MRI and CT scan. My cancerous tumor had shrunk by 50 percent. My blood test results were also much better. I felt much better. I looked much better. My oncologist was very surprised. He told me, "Lothar, you are not so crazy after all. I think I would like to learn a little from Master Sha."

I continued to chant for eight to ten hours per day. In October, I met Master Sha in Switzerland, and he gave me another divine soul healing. Afterward, the pain was completely gone.

I still continued to chant, and in November 2008, I went for another MRI and CT scan. My doctor was even more surprised, because my tumor had shrunken to one centimeter.

In February 2009, I had tests done again. My cancerous tumor had shrunken to four millimeters. I felt that everything in my body had returned to normal. I had great energy and vitality. My doctor told me, "I will come to learn soul healing from Master Sha in his retreat in Frankfurt in May of this year."

In late April 2009, I received the results of my latest recheck. My cancerous tumor has completely disappeared. There is no sign of cancer or, for that matter, any unhealthy condition in my body.

My recovery has totally proven the power of Divine Soul Transplants and the power of soul self-healing. I'm so grateful to the Divine and to Master Sha. My life has been saved. I cannot thank you enough, Divine and Master Sha. I cannot thank all the saints in Heaven and all of my friends enough for your love and blessing.

Now I am a Divine Healer and a Worldwide Representative of Master Sha. I give soul blessings regularly to more than thirty people per day. My soul blessings have greatly helped these people who are suffering. I am honored to serve. The more I serve, the happier I am. I am honored to be a servant of humanity.

Lothar's heart-moving story proves three important facts:

- A Divine Order to remove soul, mind, and body blockages in Lothar's pancreas worked.

- Divine Soul Mind Body Transplants work.
- Soul self-healing works.

Congratulations to Lothar and to the thousands of others who have shared heart-touching and moving stories from around the world in the last several years, from receiving divine karma cleansing, removal of soul, mind, and body blockages, receiving Divine Soul Mind Body Transplants, and applying soul self-healing techniques.

REMOVE SOUL MIND BODY BLOCKAGES

The essence of this book is to share with you and humanity that in order to heal, you must first remove soul, mind, and body blockages of the affected system, organ, cells, or part of the body.

Soul blockages include:

- Personal bad karma
- Ancestral bad karma
- Relationship bad karma
- Curses
- Negative memories

Mind blockages include:

- Negative mind-sets
- Negative attitudes
- Negative beliefs
- Ego
- Attachment

Body blockages include:

- Energy blockages
- Matter blockages

I will explain soul, mind, and body blockages in detail in the next chapter.

RECEIVE DIVINE SOUL MIND BODY TRANSPLANTS

After removing soul, mind, and body blockages for a system, an organ, cells, DNA and RNA, a part of the body, or an unhealthy condition, I, as a servant of humanity and of the Divine, could transmit Divine Soul Mind Body Transplants.

Divine Soul Mind Body Transplants change the souls, consciousness, energy, and tiny matter of the recipient system, organ, cells, or part of the body.

Divine Soul Mind Body Transplants carry divine frequency and vibration, with divine love, forgiveness, compassion, and light for divine soul, mind, and body healing.

I will also explain Divine Soul Mind Body Transplants further in the next chapter.

INVOKE AND PRACTICE WITH DIVINE SOUL
MIND BODY TRANSPLANTS

To receive Divine Soul Mind Body Transplants does not mean one has recovered or healed. A recipient of these divine treasures must invoke and practice with them to restore health. Lothar's story is a great example of the benefits of dedicated practice.

In general, practice three to five minutes per time, three to five times per day. For chronic and life-threatening conditions, practice a total of at least two hours per day. There are no time limits. The longer you practice, the better.

I am introducing the Divine Soul Mind Body Healing and Transmission System to humanity for the first time in history. I am honored to be a vehicle and a servant to share this breakthrough divine healing system with humanity. I wish the Divine Soul Mind Body Healing and Transmission System will serve you, your loved ones, and all humanity well.

> *God gives his heart to me*
> *God gives his love to me*
> *My heart melds with his heart*
> *My love melds with his love*

How Does the Divine Soul Mind Body Healing and Transmission System Work?

*T*HE DIVINE SOUL Mind Body Healing and Transmission System includes three vital steps:

1. Divine Order to remove soul, mind, and body blockages for your unhealthy condition in the physical, emotional, mental, and spiritual bodies
2. Divine Orders to offer Divine Soul Mind Body Transplants
3. Practice by invoking and chanting Divine Soul Mind Body Transplants to heal you, your loved ones, humanity, Mother Earth, and all universes

Remove Blockages

According to Soul Mind Body Medicine, there are three major blockages that cause all sicknesses and other unhealthy conditions. These three blockages are soul blockages, mind blockages, and body blockages.

SOUL BLOCKAGES

Soul blockages are karmic blockages. Karma is the record of your services in all of your many lifetimes, present and past. When we speak of karma, we have to talk about past lives. I totally believe in reincarnation and karma. Some people may not. I do not have any intention to change your belief system. I thank you for the opportunity to share my insights with you.

Karma is also called virtue or deed. Karma can be divided between good karma and bad karma. Good karma is the record of good services, including love, forgiveness, compassion, light, generosity, kindness, purity, integrity, and more. Bad karma is the record of unpleasant services, including killing, harming, taking advantage of others, stealing, and more.

On Mother Earth, many people borrow money from a bank to purchase a house. When you have a mortgage, you must repay your loan month after month for many years. This is a physical debt that you owe to the bank.

Bad karma is your spiritual debt. This spiritual debt is recorded in your book in the Akashic Records[3] and on your soul.

---

3. The Akashic Records are a special place in Heaven where all of your lives are recorded, including all of your activities, behaviors, and thoughts. The Divine and the leaders of the Akashic Records decide how long you will stay on Mother Earth. They also decide your spiritual standing in Heaven based on the record of all of your lifetimes.

You have made mistakes in your past lives and in this life. When you kill, harm, steal, cheat, and take advantage of others in any way, you create a spiritual debt. Spiritually, you owe the souls you have harmed. Just as you must pay your mortgage to the bank, you must pay your spiritual debt.

How do you pay this spiritual debt? When you have bad karma, you are given lessons to learn. These lessons could include sickness, accidents, broken relationships, financial challenges, mental disorders, emotional imbalances, and all kinds of blockages in life. When you are faced with a challenge in your life, when your family has a challenge, when you are seriously ill, or when you feel unhappy, stressed, angry, fearful, depressed, or anxious, you may not think about karma. I would like to share my insight that significant challenges in your physical body, emotional body, mental body, and spiritual body are almost always due to karmic issues. To pay your spiritual debt is to have lessons to learn.

The Divine taught me a one-sentence secret about karma that I shared in the third book of my Soul Power Series, *The Power of Soul: The Way to Heal, Rejuvenate, Transform, and Enlighten All Life.* In chapter 2 of that book, I explained karma in some depth. I shared a great deal of wisdom about karma. The one-sentence secret about karma that I shared on page 26 of *The Power of Soul* is:

Karma is the root cause of success and failure in every aspect of life.

Because bad karma is the root cause of any blockage and challenge in life, in order to transform our life, we must clear (or cleanse, which is a different word for the same thing) our bad karma, which is our spiritual debt from all our lifetimes.

In order to heal, we must clear our bad karma.

In order to prevent sickness, we must clear our bad karma.

In order to rejuvenate, we must clear our bad karma.

In order to transform our difficult relationships, we must clear our bad karma.

In order to transform financial and business difficulties, we must clear our bad karma.

In order to avoid serious lessons and major disasters in the rest of this life and in future lives, we must clear our bad karma.

The Divine taught me very clearly that there is only one way to self-clear bad karma: *Offer unconditional universal service.*

In April 2003 at the Land of Medicine Buddha, a retreat and meditation center in Soquel, California, I held a workshop. Suddenly, the Divine came. I bowed down to honor and show spiritual courtesy to the Divine. The Divine said, "Zhi Gang, I came today to share a spiritual law with you."

I replied, "Dear Divine, I am extremely honored to receive this law."

The Divine then pointed to himself and said, "I am a universal servant." Then the Divine pointed to me and said, "You are a universal servant." Then the Divine swept his hands before everybody in the room and said, "Everyone and everything is a universal servant. A universal servant offers universal service. Universal service includes universal love, forgiveness, peace, healing, blessing, harmony, and enlightenment."

The Divine continued: "If one offers a little service, one receives a little blessing from the universe and me. If one offers more service, one receives more blessings from the universe and me. If one offers unconditional universal service, one receives unlimited blessings from the universe and me."

Then the Divine paused for a few moments before saying,

"There are unpleasant services on Mother Earth, including killing, harming, taking advantage of others, cheating, stealing, and more. If one offers a little unpleasant service, one will learn a little lesson."

I asked, "Dear Divine, what kind of lessons will one learn?"

The Divine responded, "The lessons can include sickness, broken relationships, financial challenges, mental confusion, emotional imbalances, and any kind of blockage in life."

The Divine continued, "If one offers more unpleasant service, one will learn more lessons. If one offers huge unpleasant service, one will receive huge lessons."

I was extremely grateful to receive this teaching. I understood deeply in my heart that the Divine was explaining the law of karma to me through this Law of Universal Service. This law clearly explains that when you create good karma by doing good deeds to accumulate good virtue, you are rewarded and blessed. If you create bad karma by harming others to accumulate bad virtue, you will learn lessons.

TYPES OF KARMA

People are suffering so much on Mother Earth. For health alone, there are so many sicknesses. Most people on Mother Earth have not realized that serious, chronic, and life-threatening health conditions are due to bad karma. Even less do people understand that all the major blockages in their lives are due to bad karma.

From July 2003, when I was chosen as a divine servant, vehicle, and channel, up to now, September 2009, I have dealt with more than ten thousand people's karmic issues. Thousands of heart-touching, moving, and miracle stories have proven that karma is the root blockage for every aspect of life.

In order to heal our physical, emotional, mental, and spiritual bodies, we have to learn how to self-clear our bad karma. In order to self-clear karma, we have to first understand what kinds of bad karma human beings have.

Personal Karma

You could have had hundreds or even thousands of lifetimes as a human being. Everyone makes mistakes. In some lifetimes, you could have made huge mistakes. For example, in one lifetime you may have been the leader of a country or an important general. You could have forgotten to offer love, care, and compassion. You may have harmed others, caused a war, or even been directly involved in killing others. You could have been a very wealthy and influential person who took advantage of others.

Heaven records these behaviors. The harm that you caused others creates your spiritual debt. This harm is arranged to return to you in some form in your current life and your future lives. These are the lessons you need to learn.

We often focus on healing for health. In fact, healing is needed in every aspect of our lives. You may have relationship challenges that need healing. You may have financial challenges that need healing. All of these challenges are related to your bad karma. Karma is the root cause for success and failure in every aspect of your life.

Ancestral Karma

Everyone has parents. Everyone has grandparents on both the father's and mother's side. Everyone has great-grandparents on both sides. You could have had several hundred or even thousands of lifetimes as a human being. In each of these lifetimes, you could have had a different father and mother. Therefore, you and every person has a huge number of ancestors. I am not talking about only your biological ancestors in your current lifetime; I am talking about all of your millions of ancestors in all of your soul's lifetimes.

It is a law of karma that some of your ancestors' karma affects your present and future lifetimes. This is your ancestral karma. When I speak of ancestral karma, I am speaking about only those unpleasant services of your ancestors that affect you. I am not talking about all of your ancestors' personal karma, only about the part that affects and influences your soul journey as one of their descendants.

There is a secret about ancestral karma. The vital wisdom to know is that your grandfathers' and grandmothers' karma, and your great-grandfathers' and great-grandmothers' karma affect your life much more than your father's and mother's karma. Your parents' personal karma affects your children and grandchildren more.

If you have great blessings in your health, relationships, and finances, you are blessed by your personal good karma as well as the good karma of your grandparents and great-grandparents especially. If you have major challenges in your health, relationships, and finances, your personal bad karma has affected your life, as well as the bad karma of your grandparents and great-grandparents especially.

Everyone makes mistakes in life. Since your soul has probably had millions of ancestors, your ancestral karma could be very heavy. Some people are free of personal karma, but I have only met one person who came to me free of ancestral karma. Ancestral karma is a major blockage for one's health, relationships, and finances. Clearing ancestral karma is vital for healing and blessing your health, relationships, finances, and every aspect of your life.

Relationship Karma

Human beings have all kinds of relationships. There are husband and wife, girlfriend and boyfriend, children and parents, grandchildren and grandparents, friends, co-workers, bosses and employees, and more. There are all kinds of relationships.

If our relationships are smooth and pleasant, we are blessed. However, people have all kinds of challenges and problems in their relationships. Some people have a very hard time finding a true love. They may marry three or four times and still cannot find a true love. Some people make the same mistakes over and over again in relationships. There are all kinds of relationship issues.

I can share with you that relationships are closely related to karma. If you are related in this life, you were most likely related in a previous life or lives. Whether girlfriend and boyfriend, husband and wife, or parent and child, all have most likely been together before. If you were never related in a previous life, you would most likely not be related in this life.

Some families have very pleasant relationships. Why? It is very simple. Spiritual wisdom teaches us that they had very pleasant relationships in past lifetimes.

Some husbands and wives, girlfriends and boyfriends, children and parents have very challenging relationships. Relationships that are very difficult are also karma-related, which means they are related to past lifetimes.

You may have had hundreds or even thousands of lifetimes.

You have shared some of these lifetimes with those souls who are with you now. For example, your spouse or partner may have been your partner in previous lifetimes as well, your daughter may have been your mother, and your closest friend may have been your brother in a previous lifetime. Throughout these many lifetimes, you may have accumulated karma between you and the other person from misdeeds to each other. Your own souls and the soul of your relationship carry this karma. It can greatly influence your current relationship.

Let me give you an example. In Japan, I had a private consultation with a woman who told me she was very upset because her husband had five girlfriends. I told her to close her eyes for a moment while I did a soul reading. I connected with the Akashic Records and asked Heaven to show me the past-life relationships between her husband and her. In about twenty seconds, I got an answer. I told her to open her eyes and told her, "The problem with your husband is due to you." She was surprised and asked, "Really? It is because of me?" I said, "Yes. I did a spiritual reading with the Akashic Records. Heaven showed me that in a past life, you were the husband and your current husband was your wife. In that lifetime, you had more than twelve girlfriends. Heaven showed them to me one by one in my Third Eye."

She was stunned, but she understood. She asked me what to do. I told her, "Forgive your husband. Give him love. Love melts all blockages and transforms all life."

This example is to tell you to remember that *if you have relationship challenges, there is a spiritual reason behind them.* You could have bad relationship karma from previous lifetimes because you abused others. For example, you may have abused your spouse or one of your parents in a previous lifetime. That is why lessons are given to you through them in this lifetime.

If you open your spiritual channels, Heaven could show you some details of your actions in past lifetimes that are the root cause of your relationship blockages and other spiritual blockages in your present lifetime. When you realize your own responsibility, you will not be angry or upset with the other person anymore. It will be easier for you to offer love, forgiveness, care, and compassion. You will be able to clear more of your own karma and to break the karmic patterns of the past. You will have the potential to enjoy freedom from these karmic bonds that have imprisoned your soul, heart, mind, and body.

Curses

Millions of people are searching for soul secrets, wisdom, knowledge, and practices to transform their lives and enlighten their souls, hearts, minds, and bodies. They pray sincerely to the Divine, holy saints, buddhas, healing angels, ascended masters, lamas, gurus, and all kinds of spiritual fathers and mothers. This is good prayer.

There is another side of spiritual practice. Some beings practice with the Dark Side. They communicate daily with demons, monsters, and other major dark souls. They honor the Dark Side. They offer food and incense to the Dark Side. They make vows to the Dark Side. They invoke the Dark Side to harm others. The Dark Side will respond.

The Dark Side could put an unpleasant message on a person's heart, brain, kidney, or Message Center.[4] This unpleasant mes-

---

4. Also known as the heart chakra, the Message Center is one of the most important energy centers in the body and is *the* most important spiritual center. Located in the middle of the chest, it is the center for love, forgiveness, compassion, emotions, healing, karma, Soul Language, soul communication, life transformation, and soul enlightenment.

sage is a curse. A curse is not a type of karma, but curses can be related with karma, directly or indirectly. In fact, you may have been a very kind and loving person in many lifetimes. That might have caused others to be jealous, angry, and resentful. When others who have a strong connection with the Dark Side feel this way, they can ask the Dark Side to harm you.

Curses can be extremely powerful blockages in one's life. A person who is cursed could become sick gradually. A person could become sick suddenly. The sickness could be very serious. In the worst case, a curse could take a person's life away. Curses can also affect your relationships and finances. Curses can affect you for many lifetimes.

In 2008 in Switzerland, I met a stroke patient who had been suffering for one year. He could walk, but not talk. He could only mumble. I saw a curse in his head. A big demon sat in his head. I asked the Divine to clear this. Heaven's generals came and took the curse—a major dark soul—out of his brain. Instantly, this person was able to speak. This happened in front of many peoples' eyes.

When I went to Maui later in 2008, I met a woman who also had a curse in her brain. She told me she was very confused and could not think properly. She had a poor memory and constant heaviness and lack of clarity in her head. I offered her a Divine Curse Removal. As with the man in Switzerland, her head felt better instantly.

That same night, her car broke down. Because she had to get her car to a repair shop the next morning, she was a little late getting to my workshop, but she told me about her car breakdown. I checked with the Akashic Records, and I was so happy with the result. I did not tell her right away. I asked Marilyn Smith, one of my Worldwide Representatives and a new Divine Channel, "Marilyn, could you do a soul reading? Last night this lady drove home from the workshop and her car broke down. Can you do a reading with Heaven to explain this?"

Marilyn's reading was that it had been arranged for this lady to have a car accident the night before due to her personal bad karma and the curse that she was carrying. According to the Akashic Records' arrangement, this car accident was to be serious, leaving her paralyzed. Because the curse had been removed and her personal karma cleansed just two hours before driving home from the first day of the workshop, the lesson of serious damage to her brain was removed. She was blessed to have suffered only engine problems. I told Marilyn, "Your reading is correct. I got the same answer."

Negative Memories

Negative memories are another type of soul blockage. These memories are held in your soul and in the souls of your systems, organs, cells, DNA and RNA. They can have different sources. For example, you may have been a great servant, perhaps a powerful healer, in a previous lifetime yet suffered greatly for acting in this way. You may have been punished or even put to death. Your soul possesses all of the wisdom you have gained in your many lifetimes. It can also retain all of the powerful negative memories. In this lifetime, these negative soul memories may cause you to have great fear and resistance toward accepting your abilities—as a healer, as a teacher, or as someone who serves others. It may cause you to lack confidence.

A very common type of negative memory is related to physical experiences you had in previous lifetimes. When you were harmed, and especially when you were traumatized, in past lives and this life, your body soul and your affected inner souls remember this harm and trauma. Human beings have had hundreds of past lifetimes or more. Some lifetimes may include major disasters. Many of you have suffered, for example, from hunger and starvation, drowning, a serious injury to the spinal cord, paralysis, heart attacks, kidney failure, or amputation of a limb in previous lives. These negative memories could deeply affect your current life and future lives.

Let me give you an example. One of my certified teachers served a client who had suffered from chronic neck pain for years. A reading of the Akashic Records revealed that in a past lifetime, this person had been executed by being beheaded. That unpleasant memory was retained by the person's soul and the soul of the person's neck. This negative memory was directly related to the chronic neck pain.

The Divine asked me to offer divine removal of negative memories. The Divine can clear the negative memory from your soul in order to remove the unpleasant effects on your mind and body. I am very honored to be a chosen servant to offer this divine service.

I share this wisdom with you to explain the different kinds of soul blockages you could experience. All kinds of karma issues can happen at the level of your systems, organs, cells, cell units, DNA and RNA, smallest matter in the cells, and spaces in the body. For example, if you killed a person in a previous lifetime by stabbing him in the heart, your heart could be deeply affected in this life. If you cut someone's throat in a past life, your throat could be affected heavily in this life.

In summary, you could understand soul blockages by these examples:

If you suffer from knee problems, you most likely hurt other peoples' knees in previous lives.

If you are very angry in this life, you most likely angered others in previous lives.

If you were abused in this life, you most likely abused others in previous lives.

If you have difficulty finding true love with a partner in this life, you most likely hurt your partners in previous lives.

If you have major financial challenges in this life, you most likely took advantage of others financially in previous lives.

In one sentence:

The kinds of challenges you experience in this life, you most likely created those kinds of challenges for others in previous lives.

The opposite is also true:

The kinds of blessings you enjoy in this life, you most likely gave others these kinds of blessings in previous lives.

There is no coincidence. Everything that happens in life is karma-related.

DIVINE KARMA CLEANSING

From July 2003 up to now, September 2009, I have offered divine karma cleansing to more than ten thousand people. I do not clear people's karma. The Divine gave me the honor to offer divine karma cleansing for humanity. People apply to have their karma cleared. The Divine approves. Then the Divine does the job. Divine curse removal and divine removal of negative memories are also accomplished through a Divine Order.

When I offer divine karma cleansing, I invoke the Divine, the leaders and workers of the Akashic Records, Heaven's generals, and Heaven's soldiers. I send a Divine Order to clear one's personal karma, ancestral karma, relationship karma, curses, or negative memories. When a person has karma, a dark soul or souls reside in the person's body to give the person karmic lessons. When I send a Divine Order for karma cleansing, Heaven's generals and soldiers will take a dark soul out of a person's body and bring the dark soul to the proper place. Dark souls related to the karma that has been cleared are no longer allowed to stay inside the person's body.

Karma cleansing is the Divine's special forgiveness. When the Divine Order is sent to clear your karma, your spiritual debt is forgiven. The Divine opens Heaven's virtue bank to give virtue to the souls you harmed to create your bad karma. The souls who were harmed receive major virtue from the Divine. This virtue blesses their future lives. Because they receive this virtue, they do not resent you anymore. They forgive you. Dark souls leave your body. Your book in the Akashic Records is filled with golden and rainbow light.

Thank you, Divine, for your karma cleansing. Karma cleansing is a complete divine service and blessing for humanity. I am honored to be a divine servant, vehicle, and channel to offer divine blessings to humanity. I am honored to be a servant of humanity. Thank you.

MIND BLOCKAGES

Mind is consciousness. Many people think the mind resides only in the brain. This is not correct. Everything has a soul. Everything also has a mind or consciousness. Mind is in every system, every organ, every cell, every DNA, every RNA, and every space.

To purify the mind is to purify consciousness. To purify the mind is to remove blockages to divine consciousness. Mind blockages include negative mind-sets, attitudes, and beliefs, as well as ego and attachment. Mind blockages are major blockages on one's healing journey. Mind blockages can be key blockages for your spiritual journey, which is your soul journey.

If your mind blocks your soul journey, every aspect of your life could be blocked. Therefore, mind blockages must be removed to fulfill your spiritual journey *and* your healing journey.

There are many teachings, books, and workshops to help people remove negative mind-sets, attitudes, and beliefs, as well as ego and attachment. I honor each teaching, each book, and each workshop that helps humanity transform the mind, or their consciousness, in order to remove negative mind-sets, attitudes, and beliefs, and ego and attachment.

In July 2003, the Divine chose me as a servant of humanity and a servant, vehicle, and channel of the Divine. To be a channel of the Divine means that the Divine gives me the honor and authority to transmit his permanent soul treasures to humanity, organizations, cities, countries, nature, and more.

The Divine asked me to transmit the Divine's souls, named Divine Soul Transplants, for systems, organs, cells, DNA and RNA. The Divine also asked me to transmit souls of businesses, as well as souls of occupations and professionals, such as a divine soul of Divine Artist.

Let me share a story about the power of a Divine Soul Transplant for Divine Occupation.

A renowned composer in Taiwan, Chun Yen Chiang, has written a lot of spiritual music. He was chosen to write music for the opening of a major Buddhist conference in 1999. In 2002, he received a Golden Melody Award, a music award presented annually in Taiwan that is sometimes called the Chinese-language Grammy.

In 2002, one of my current Worldwide Representatives, Shu Chin Hsu, and another student discovered Mr. Chiang through one of his CDs, a recording of Guan Yin's enlightenment mantra, *Weng Ma Ni Ba Ma Hong.*[5] The chanting and music on this CD are joyful, beautiful, and heart-touching.

I gave Mr. Chiang a phone call. I told him that I had listened to and admired his beautiful music for *Weng Ma Ni Ba Ma Hong.* I asked him if he could compose music for four mantras for me.

When my book *Power Healing* was published that year, I told the Divine, "I really want to create a healing tool for humanity." The Divine replied, "To make a healing tool for humanity, chant mantras and create a few CDs."

I have chanted a lot since my childhood. Guan Yin came to me when I was four years old and taught me to chant the *Da Bei Zhou.* "Da" means *big.* "Bei" means *compassion.* "Zhou" means *mantra.* So, *Da Bei Zhou* (pronounced *dah bay joe*) means *big compassion mantra.* It is one of the most renowned Buddhist mantras. I have also chanted *A Mi Tuo Fuo* (pronounced *ah mee twaw fwaw*),[6] which is also one of the most powerful Buddhist mantras, a lot.

---

5. See my book *Power Healing: The Four Keys to Energizing Your Body, Mind & Spirit* (2002, San Francisco: HarperSanFrancisco) for teaching and practice of this ancient mantra.
6. A Mi Tuo Fuo (Amitabha in Sanskrit) is the buddha who leads the Pure Land in Heaven.

I asked the Divine what mantras I should chant and record to create healing tools for humanity. The Divine chose four major mantras for me:

- *Ling Guang Pu Zhao*—Shining Soul Light
- *Dao Fa Zi Ran*—Follow Nature's Way
- *Yu Zhou Zhi Guang*—Universal Light
- *Shang Di Zhi Guang*—God's Light

I would like to share teaching about each of these mantras.

Ling Guang Pu Zhao (Shining Soul Light)

Ling Guang Pu Zhao is an ancient mantra. "Ling" means *soul.* "Guang" means *light.* "Pu" means *widely.* "Zhao" means *shines. Ling Guang Pu Zhao* is pronounced *ling gwahng poo jow.*

Ling Guang Pu Zhao can be translated as "Shining Soul Light." There are countless buddhas, holy saints, Daoist saints, Hawaiian saints, Egyptian saints, Indian saints, and many other saints. There are countless healing angels, archangels, and ascended masters. There are countless lamas, gurus, and other kinds of spiritual fathers and mothers in all layers of Heaven. They are all in the soul form.

Ling Guang Pu Zhao is the mantra that connects with all of these major souls in Heaven to give us healing, blessing, and life transformation.

A mantra is a special healing sound. Generally speaking, the most powerful mantras are created by major saints, buddhas, or other high-level spiritual fathers and mothers.

Throughout history, millions of people have chanted mantras for healing and blessing. Today, millions of people chant mantras for healing and blessing. I have chanted mantras since I was a young child. Why do people chant mantras? What is the significance of chanting mantras? What is the power of chanting mantras? Let me share the essential soul wisdom about mantras.

- *A mantra is a spiritual calling.* When you chant a mantra, the saints in Heaven hear you right away. At that moment, they may be meditating in Heaven's temple. They may simply be walking around in Heaven. It doesn't matter. When we chant, they can hear us. They will respond. They could say to each other, "Wow, people are chanting on Mother Earth. They need help. Let us go to help them." In this way, major saints will come to help you. To chant is to gather these saints, other major spiritual fathers and mothers, and other souls to give you healing, blessing, and life transformation.
- *Mantras carry a spiritual frequency and vibration that can remove blockages in your health, relationships, and finances.*
- *Mantras can bring you virtue, which enhances your spiritual journey and benefits every aspect of your life.* Chanting carries love, care, and compassion. When you chant, you are literally serving others, the environment, Mother Earth, and all universes.

Dao Fa Zi Ran (Follow Nature's Way)

The second major mantra the Divine chose for me to record was *Dao Fa Zi Ran.*

"Dao" means *The Way.* "Fa" means *method.* "Zi Ran" means

to be natural. Dao Fa Zi Ran can be translated as "Follow Nature's Way." *Dao Fa Zi Ran* is pronounced *dow fah dzi rahn.*

This is easy to understand. Think about life or nature. If you follows nature's way, then your life could flourish. If you do not follow nature's way, your life could be blocked.

There is a renowned ancient spiritual statement that expresses this concept in a different way:

Shun dao zhe chang, ni dao zhe wang

"Shun" means *follow.* "Zhe" means *person.* "Chang" means *flourish.* "Ni" means *go against.* "Wang" means *end* or *die.*

Shun dao zhe chang, ni dao zhe wang is the top philosophy for all things in all universes.

Follow the Dao, flourish; go against the Dao, finish.

A very simple example can explain this highest philosophy. In the winter in Toronto, the temperature sometimes goes below zero. Imagine wearing a T-shirt and shorts in this weather. You could not tolerate it. Your body just cannot handle such cold weather wearing so little. You will not flourish. If you try to do this for hours, you will be finished. You would die. When the weather is very cold, you must wear warm clothing. This is following the Dao. To flourish, you must follow the Dao. The four seasons follow the Dao. To dress properly according to the weather is to follow the Dao.

To *follow nature's way* is to follow the Dao. This ancient mantra is very powerful. It connects with nature in all universes.

Yu Zhou Zhi Guang (Universal Light)

"Yu Zhou" means *universe*. "Zhi" is a possessive particle; it functions like an apostrophe. "Guang" means *light*. *Yu Zhou Zhi Guang* means "universal light."

Although many people think there is only one universe, there are actually countless universes. Every universe has countless souls. Every universe has souls who are extremely powerful. Words cannot explain their power enough. When you chant *universal light*, you are literally invoking all souls of all universes to give you healing, blessing, and life transformation.

Shang Di Zhi Guang (God's Light)

In July 2000, shortly after I began to flow the book, *Power Healing: The Four Keys to Energizing Your Body, Mind & Spirit*, the Divine inspired me in the moment to create a new mantra, *God's Light*. At that moment, I realized that *God's Light* is one of the most powerful mantras in all universes. When you chant *God's Light*, you are literally invoking the Divine to give you his light to heal, bless, and transform your life.

Now I will continue the story of Mr. Chiang, the composer from Taiwan.

When I was on the phone with him, I asked, "Could you compose music for four mantras? They are *Ling Guang Pu Zhao, Dao Fa Zi Ran, Yu Zhou Zhi Guang,* and *Shang Di Zhi Guang* ['shang di' means *God*]."

He asked me, "Do you prefer western-style music or eastern-style music?" I told him, "I want you to receive the music from Heaven."

He wondered, "Receive the music from Heaven? How?"

On the spot, I offered Divine Soul Downloads to him silently. I did not have time at that moment to educate him about Divine Soul Downloads. I asked the Divine to give him a Divine Soul Transplant of Divine Soul Music Composer.

I said, "Just relax. Chant these four mantras, one after another. Suddenly, the melodies for each of them will come to you."

He listened to my guidance. He began to chant these four mantras in Chinese:

Ling Guang Pu Zhao
Ling Guang Pu Zhao
Ling Guang Pu Zhao
Ling Guang Pu Zhao . . .

Dao Fa Zi Ran
Dao Fa Zi Ran
Dao Fa Zi Ran
Dao Fa Zi Ran . . .

Yu Zhou Zhi Guang
Yu Zhou Zhi Guang
Yu Zhou Zhi Guang
Yu Zhou Zhi Guang . . .

Shang Di Zhi Guang
Shang Di Zhi Guang
Shang Di Zhi Guang
Shang Di Zhi Guang . . .

He chanted for thirty minutes but nothing happened.

The next day, he chanted for thirty minutes again, and still nothing happened.

As he chanted on the third day, suddenly an entire melody came pouring into him. He went to his piano to play and record what he had just received. He knew instantly in his heart that this was the melody for *Dao Fa Zi Ran.* The melody was also perfect for the English translation of this mantra, *Follow Nature's Way.*

Mr. Chiang was really excited. In all of his years of musical study and creation, he had never experienced an entire long melody pouring into him at once. On the following day, he caught a cold, but he continued to chant the other three mantras. Nothing happened. The next day, he chanted again and again nothing happened. He chanted a third day after receiving the melody for *Dao Fa Zi Ran.* This time, the melody for *God's Light* came to him. He received the melody for the Chinese, *Shang Di Zhi Guang,* first. Then he received the melody for the English, *God's Light.* When he played the two melodies together, he had an "Aha!" moment. These two separate melodies that he received independently, one after the other, harmonized perfectly together. He did not need to change a single note or rhythm. It was as though they were joined as one from the moment of their creation. Mr. Chiang was fascinated and totally amazed.

The next day Mr. Chiang composed melodies for *Ling Guang Pu Zhao/Shining Soul Light* and *Yu Zhou Zhi Guang/Universal Light.* He went to sleep that night peaceful and happy that he had accomplished the task I had given him. However, after waking up, he realized, "Master Sha asked me to receive the melodies. But I wrote these two melodies in my head. This is not the direction that Master Sha gave me." So, he began to chant *Ling Guang Pu Zhao* and *Yu Zhou Zhi Guang* diligently. After a few minutes, the divine melodies for these two mantras also came to him. He realized that they were completely different from the melodies he had composed. The divine melodies were simpler and more beautiful. Mr. Chiang was very grateful and appreciative for the divine ability he was given as a divine channel of divine music.

This is how a renowned composer "composed" melodies for these four soul mantras in a divine way. This is Heaven-inspired music. This is divine music. Mr. Chiang received a divine soul of Divine Soul Music Composer. He was already a professional and acclaimed composer, but this Divine Soul Transplant empowered him to open his channels to receive Heaven's music. Just as this divine book is flowing out from my channel, Heaven's music flowed out from his channel. He literally received the music. He did not write it using his mind.

Mr. Chiang used to compose in the "normal" way. That was *mind over matter.* To flow music from Heaven is *soul over matter.* They are completely different approaches. They have completely different layers of frequency and vibration. These first four divine soul mantras from Mr. Chiang are extremely powerful. He has gone on to flow many more melodies, and even an entire soul symphony, the *Soul Symphony of Yin Yang,* in this way. He is truly a Divine Composer.

I was sharing teaching about mind blockages when the story about Mr. Chiang flowed out naturally. Let me return now to mind blockages.

Every kind of mind blockage is a blockage between your consciousness, or the consciousness of your systems, organs, cells, cell units, DNA, and RNA, and divine consciousness. Mind blockages can also be present in your relationships and finances.

My total life mission is:

To transform the consciousness of humanity and all souls, and enlighten them, in order to create love, peace, and harmony for humanity, Mother Earth, and all universes.

To transform consciousness is vital for healing, rejuvenation, prolonging life, enlightenment, and transforming any aspect of life, including relationships and finances. Remove negative mind-sets, attitudes, and beliefs. Remove ego and attachment. Transform them to divine consciousness. Then healing, rejuvenation, enlightenment, and transformation of soul, heart, mind, and body can occur. Then love, peace, and harmony for all souls can happen.

Mind-sets limit your thinking. They can "square" your mind. You limit possibilities. You box yourself in.

When you add an emotional aspect, you can have a negative attitude. Your systems, organs, cells, cell units, DNA, RNA, and spaces can have an attitude. They could have attitudes of openness, enthusiasm, and gratitude. These attitudes will help you improve on all levels. They could have attitudes of overanalysis, criticism, and doubt. These attitudes will limit your possibilities and could seriously block your physical life and your soul journey.

Beliefs are also an important manifestation of the mind. Beliefs often carry a judgment of being right or good. Beliefs impact all aspects of life. They can be major blockages in any aspect.

Ego is another very powerful kind of mind blockage. With ego, one tends to focus on oneself—what one can do or, in some cases, cannot do. Ego can lead to a feeling of superiority. I tell my most advanced students, "The moment you think you are special, you are not. You got lost. You are showing ego." With ego, it is very difficult and sometimes almost impossible to connect with divine consciousness to allow the healing process to begin and continue.

With attachment, a person resists change. We often have very strong emotions that connect us to what we are familiar with and those we are close to. This emotional connection can be very difficult to release, even if the familiar is uncomfortable or even painful. This is true for every level of our being.

All kinds of mind blockages can result in challenges to your health, emotions, mental clarity, relationships, finances, and soul journey. It is very important to realize that mind blockages can influence every aspect of life and greatly impact your soul journey. Therefore, it is vital to remove mind blockages and transform your consciousness.

What is the divine way to transform consciousness and remove negative mind-sets, attitudes, and beliefs, as well as ego and attachment? The divine way is to receive Divine Soul Mind Body Transplants. Divine Soul Mind Body Transplants carry divine frequency and vibration with divine love, forgiveness, compassion, and light. They can transform the recipient's consciousness quickly. They can remove negative mind-sets, attitudes, and beliefs, as well as ego and attachment, quickly.

At this moment, I am asking the Divine, "Dear Divine, could you offer major Divine Soul Downloads to every reader? I am extremely honored to ask you to offer your major Divine Soul Mind Body Transplants to remove negative mind-sets, attitudes, and beliefs, as well as ego and attachment."

The Divine replied, "Dear Zhi Gang, I am very happy to offer these treasures. You asked me. I will do it."

I am bowing to the Divine one thousand times now.

I am honored to ask the Divine to offer the first divine treasure in this book as a gift to you and every reader. I cannot bow down to the Divine enough for this divine generosity. I am so honored to be a servant of humanity and a servant, vehicle, and channel of the Divine.

RECEIVE DIVINE TREASURES AS GIFTS FROM THE DIVINE

The first Divine Soul Download offered in this book is:

Divine Soul Transplant of Divine Golden Light Ball and Golden Liquid Spring of Divine Removing Negative Mind-sets

Prepare! Sit up straight. Put the tip of your tongue near, but not touching, the roof of your mouth. Open your heart and soul to receive this divine treasure. In the next twenty seconds, the Divine will download it to your soul.

Divine Order: Divine Golden Light Ball and Golden Liquid Spring of Divine Removing Negative Mind-sets Soul Transplant Transmission!

Hao! Hao! Hao!
Thank you. Thank you. Thank you.

Congratulations! You have just received one of the Divine's major treasures. You are extremely blessed. We are extremely honored and grateful.

Next, I will offer the second divine treasure in this book:

Divine Mind Transplant of Divine Golden Light Ball and Golden Liquid Spring of Divine Removing Negative Mind-sets

Prepare! Sit up straight. Put the tip of your tongue near, but not touching, the roof of your mouth. Open your heart and soul to receive this divine treasure. In the next twenty seconds, the Divine will download it to your soul.

Divine Order: Divine Golden Light Ball and Golden Liquid Spring of Divine Removing Negative Mind-sets Mind Transplant Transmission!

Hao! Hao! Hao!
Thank you. Thank you. Thank you.

Congratulations! You are extremely blessed. We cannot honor the Divine enough for the Divine's generosity.

I would like to emphasize that when the Divine offers his major treasures as a gift to every reader, it is not a little gift or a little issue. Each and every Divine Download brings you much divine virtue to transform your life. There are no words to express our greatest gratitude. We are extremely honored and blessed.

Next, I will offer the third divine treasure in this book:

Divine Body Transplant of Divine Golden Light Ball and Golden Liquid Spring of Divine Removing Negative Mind-sets

Prepare! Sit up straight. Put the tip of your tongue near, but not touching, the roof of your mouth. Open your heart and soul to receive this divine treasure. In the next twenty seconds, the Divine will download it to your soul.

Divine Order: Divine Golden Light Ball and Golden Liquid Spring of Divine Removing Negative Mind-sets Body Transplant Transmission!

Hao! Hao! Hao!
Thank you. Thank you. Thank you.

You are extremely blessed. We are all extremely blessed. How can we honor the Divine enough for his unconditional love? We are extremely grateful.

Now, I will give another

Divine Order: Join Divine Golden Light Ball and Golden Liquid Spring of Divine Removing Negative Mind-sets Soul Transplant, Mind Transplant, and Body Transplant as one.

He La La Yi Ya You Yi Ya You!

This is the Soul Language used to send this latest Divine Order. It translates as follows:

This is my Divine Order to join soul, mind, and body transplants of Divine Golden Light Ball and Golden Liquid Spring of Divine Removing Negative Mind-sets as one. The power of these three divine treasures must concentrate together. You are extremely blessed, my daughters and my sons.

Your beloved Divine.

To receive divine treasures is to receive the divine opportunity for divine healing, blessing, and life transformation. But simply to receive divine treasures does not mean that you have recovered or transformed. You have to practice with your divine treasures to heal, bless, and transform your life.

This is the way to practice:

Divine Practice to Remove Negative Mind-sets

Body Power. Put one palm over your Message Center (heart chakra, in the middle of your chest). Put your other palm over the top of your head (over the crown chakra).

Soul Power. Say *hello:*

> *Dear my Divine Soul Mind Body Transplants of Divine Golden Light Ball and Golden Liquid Spring of Divine Removing Negative Mind-sets,*
> *I love you, honor you, and appreciate you.*
> *Please turn on to remove my negative mind-sets.*
> *I am extremely grateful.*
> *Thank you.*

Sound Power. There is always divine flexibility. You can chant your Soul Language or sing your Soul Song. You can also chant repeatedly:

> *Divine treasures remove my negative mind-sets. Thank you, Divine.*
> *Divine treasures remove my negative mind-sets. Thank you, Divine.*
> *Divine treasures remove my negative mind-sets. Thank you, Divine.*
> *Divine treasures remove my negative mind-sets. Thank you, Divine.*

Mind Power. Visualize divine golden light and divine rainbow light radiating and resonating in your Message Center and on the top of your head.

Practice three to five minutes per time, three to five times per day. The more you practice and the longer you practice, the better.

This is the divine way to remove negative mind-sets. It is much faster than other ways.

Now, I will offer the fourth divine treasure to you and every reader of this book:

Divine Soul Transplant of Divine Golden Light Ball and Golden Liquid Spring of Divine Removing Negative Attitudes

Prepare! Sit up straight. Put the tip of your tongue near, but not touching, the roof of your mouth. Open your heart and soul to receive this divine treasure. In the next twenty seconds, the Divine will download it to your soul.

Divine Order: Divine Golden Light Ball and Golden Liquid Spring of Divine Removing Negative Attitudes Soul Transplant Transmission!

Hao! Hao! Hao!
Thank you. Thank you. Thank you.

We are extremely blessed. Thank you, Divine. We cannot thank you enough.

Next, I will offer the fifth divine treasure in this book:

Divine Mind Transplant of Divine Golden Light Ball and Golden Liquid Spring of Divine Removing Negative Attitudes

Prepare! Sit up straight. Put the tip of your tongue near, but not touching, the roof of your mouth. Open your heart and soul to receive this divine treasure. In the next twenty seconds, the Divine will download it to your soul.

Divine Order: Divine Golden Light Ball and Golden Liquid Spring of Divine Removing Negative Attitudes Mind Transplant Transmission!

Hao! Hao! Hao!
Thank you. Thank you. Thank you.

We are extremely honored. The Divine's generosity leaves us speechless.

Next, I will offer the sixth divine treasure in this book:

Divine Body Transplant of Divine Golden Light Ball and Golden Liquid Spring of Divine Removing Negative Attitudes

Prepare! Sit up straight. Put the tip of your tongue near, but not touching, the roof of your mouth. Open your heart and soul to receive this divine treasure. In the next twenty seconds, the Divine will download it to your soul.

Divine Order: Divine Golden Light Ball and Golden Liquid Spring of Divine Removing Negative Attitudes Body Transplant Transmission!

Hao! Hao! Hao!
Thank you. Thank you. Thank you.

Thank you, Divine. We are blessed beyond any words. How blessed we are!

Now, I will give another

Divine Order: Join Divine Golden Light Ball and Golden Liquid Spring of Divine Removing Negative Attitudes Soul Transplant, Mind Transplant, and Body Transplant as one.

Ya Hei Ya Hei Yi Ya Ya You!

Here is a translation of this Soul Language:

This Divine Order is to join my Soul Mind Body Transplants of Golden Light Ball and Golden Liquid Spring of Removing Negative Attitudes as one. You are blessed.

Your beloved Divine.

Remember, you must invoke and practice with this major divine treasure. Otherwise, it will just rest. It is like turning on the switch for a lightbulb. If you practice, your negative attitudes could be removed very quickly. If you do not practice, it would be such a waste and a pity. This is how to practice. Do it with me now:

Divine Practice to Remove Negative Attitudes

Body Power. Put one palm over your Message Center (heart chakra in the middle of your chest). Put your other palm on top of your head, over the crown chakra.

Soul Power. Say *hello:*

> *Dear my Divine Golden Light Ball and Golden Liquid Spring of Divine Removing Negative Attitudes Soul Mind Body Transplants,*
> *I love you, honor you, and appreciate you.*
> *Please turn on to remove my negative attitudes.*
> *I am extremely grateful.*
> *Thank you.*

Sound Power. Chant your Soul Language, sing your Soul Song, or chant repeatedly:

Divine treasures remove my negative attitudes. Thank you, Divine.

Divine treasures remove my negative attitudes. Thank you, Divine.

Divine treasures remove my negative attitudes. Thank you, Divine.

Divine treasures remove my negative attitudes. Thank you, Divine.

Mind Power. Visualize divine golden light and divine rainbow light resonating in your Message Center and on top of your head.

Practice three to five minutes per time, three to five times per day. Close each practice in the usual way:

Hao! Hao! Hao!
Thank you. Thank you. Thank you.

The more you practice and the longer you practice, the better. This is the divine way to remove negative attitudes. It is much faster than other ways.

Now I will offer the seventh divine treasure for you and every reader:

Divine Soul Transplant of Divine Golden Light Ball and Golden Liquid Spring of Divine Removing Negative Beliefs

Prepare! Sit up straight. Put the tip of your tongue near, but not touching, the roof of your mouth. Open your heart and soul to receive this divine treasure. In the next twenty seconds, the Divine will download it to your soul.

Divine Order: Divine Golden Light Ball
and Golden Liquid Spring of Divine Removing
Negative Beliefs Soul Transplant
Transmission!

Hao! Hao! Hao!
Thank you. Thank you. Thank you.

We are extremely blessed. Thank you, Divine. We cannot thank you enough.

Next, prepare for the eighth divine treasure offered as a divine gift to every reader:

Divine Mind Transplant of Divine Golden Light Ball
and Golden Liquid Spring of Divine Removing
Negative Beliefs

Sit up straight. Put the tip of your tongue near the roof of your mouth. Open your heart and soul.

Divine Order: Divine Golden Light Ball
and Golden Liquid Spring of Divine Removing
Negative Beliefs Mind Transplant
Transmission!

Hao! Hao! Hao!
Thank you. Thank you. Thank you.

We are extremely honored. We are beyond speechless.

Now I am offering the ninth Divine Download to every reader of this book. This treasure is named:

Divine Body Transplant of Divine Golden Light Ball and Golden Liquid Spring of Divine Removing Negative Beliefs

Prepare! Sit up straight. Put the tip of your tongue near, but not touching, the roof of your mouth. Open your heart and soul to receive this divine treasure. In the next twenty seconds, the Divine will download it to your soul.

Divine Order: Divine Golden Light Ball and Golden Liquid Spring of Divine Removing Negative Beliefs Body Transplant Transmission!

Hao! Hao! Hao!
Thank you. Thank you. Thank you.

Thank you, Divine. We are blessed beyond any words. How blessed we are.

Divine Order: Join Divine Golden Light Ball and Golden Liquid Spring of Divine Removing Negative Beliefs Soul Transplant, Mind Transplant, and Body Transplant as one.

Ya Hei Ya Hei Yi Ya Ya You!

Let us invoke and practice with this major divine treasure to remove our negative beliefs:

Divine Practice to Remove Negative Beliefs

Body Power. Put one palm over your Message Center. Put your other palm over the top of your head (over the crown chakra).

Soul Power. Say *hello:*

> *Dear my Divine Soul Mind Body Transplants of*
>   *Divine Golden Light Ball and Golden Liquid*
>   *Spring of Divine Removing Negative Beliefs,*
> *I love you, honor you, and appreciate you.*
> *Please turn on to remove my negative beliefs.*
> *I am extremely grateful.*
> *Thank you.*

Sound Power. As in previous practices, you can chant your Soul Language or sing your Soul Song. You can also chant repeatedly:

> *Divine treasures remove my negative beliefs. Thank*
>   *you, Divine.*
> *Divine treasures remove my negative beliefs. Thank*
>   *you, Divine.*
> *Divine treasures remove my negative beliefs. Thank*
>   *you, Divine.*
> *Divine treasures remove my negative beliefs. Thank*
>   *you, Divine.*

Mind Power. Visualize divine golden light and divine rainbow light radiating and resonating in your Message Center and on the top of your head.

Practice three to five minutes per time, three to five times per day. The more you practice and the longer you practice, the better.

This is the divine way to remove negative beliefs. It is much faster than other ways.

Now I am offering the tenth divine treasure for every reader:

Divine Soul Transplant of Divine Golden Light Ball and Golden Liquid Spring of Divine Removing Ego

Prepare! Sit up straight. Put the tip of your tongue near, but not touching, the roof of your mouth. Open your heart and soul to receive this divine treasure. In the next twenty seconds, the Divine will download it to your soul.

Divine Order: Divine Golden Light Ball and Golden Liquid Spring of Divine Removing Ego Soul Transplant Transmission!

Hao! Hao! Hao!
Thank you. Thank you. Thank you.

We are extremely blessed. Thank you, Divine. We cannot thank you enough.

Next, prepare to receive the eleventh divine treasure for every reader of this book:

Divine Mind Transplant of Divine Golden Light Ball and Golden Liquid Spring of Divine Removing Ego

Put the tip of your tongue near the roof of your mouth, without touching. Sit up straight. Open your heart and soul.

Divine Order: Divine Golden Light Ball and Golden Liquid Spring of Divine Removing Ego Mind Transplant Transmission!

Hao! Hao! Hao!
Thank you. Thank you. Thank you.

Thank you, Divine. We are extremely honored.

I will now offer the twelfth permanent divine gift in this book:

Divine Body Transplant of Divine Golden Light Ball and Golden Liquid Spring of Divine Removing Ego

Prepare! Sit up straight. Put the tip of your tongue near, but not touching, the roof of your mouth. Open your heart and soul to receive this divine treasure. In the next twenty seconds, the Divine will download it to your soul.

Divine Order: Divine Golden Light Ball and Golden Liquid Spring of Divine Removing Ego Body Transplant Transmission!

Hao! Hao! Hao!
Thank you. Thank you. Thank you.

Thank you, Divine. We are blessed beyond any words.
Now, I will send a

Divine Order: Join Divine Golden Light Ball and Golden Liquid Spring of Divine Removing Ego Soul Transplant, Mind Transplant, and Body Transplant as one.

Ya Hei Ya Hei Yi Ya Ya You!

Here is a translation of Soul Language for this last Divine Order:

> *This Divine Order is to join my Golden Light Ball and Golden Liquid Spring of Removing Ego Soul Mind Body Transplants as one. Their power and abilities will be harmonized, concentrated, and united. You are blessed.*
>
> *Your beloved Divine.*

Let us invoke and practice with this major divine treasure to remove our ego:

Divine Practice to Remove Ego

Body Power. Put one palm over your Message Center (heart chakra, in the middle of your chest). Put your other palm over the top of your head (over the crown chakra).

Soul Power. Say *hello:*

> *Dear my Divine Soul Mind Body Transplants of*
>   *Divine Golden Light Ball and Golden Liquid*
>   *Spring of Divine Removing Ego,*
> *I love you, honor you, and appreciate you.*
> *Please turn on to remove my ego.*
> *I am extremely grateful.*
> *Thank you.*

Sound Power. Chant your Soul Language or sing your Soul Song. You can also chant repeatedly:

Divine treasures remove my ego. Thank you, Divine.
Divine treasures remove my ego. Thank you, Divine.
Divine treasures remove my ego. Thank you, Divine.
Divine treasures remove my ego. Thank you, Divine.

Mind Power. Visualize divine golden light and divine rainbow light radiating and resonating in your Message Center and on the top of your head.

Practice three to five minutes per time, three to five times per day. The more you practice and the longer you practice, the better.

This is the divine way to remove ego. It is much faster than other ways.

Next I will offer the thirteenth Divine Download in this book to you and every reader. This treasure is named:

Divine Soul Transplant of Divine Golden Light Ball and Golden Liquid Spring of Divine Removing Attachment

Prepare! Sit up straight. Put the tip of your tongue near the roof of your mouth. Open your heart and soul to receive this permanent divine treasure. In the next twenty seconds, the Divine will download it to your soul. It, and all of the other Divine Downloads you are receiving in this book, will remain a yin companion of your soul for the rest of your current life and for all of your future lifetimes.

Divine Order: Divine Golden Light Ball and Golden Liquid Spring of Divine Removing Attachment Soul Transplant Transmission!

Hao! Hao! Hao!
Thank you. Thank you. Thank you.

We are extremely blessed. Thank you, Divine. We cannot thank you enough.

The fourteenth divine treasure is next. This treasure is named:

Divine Mind Transplant of Divine Golden Light Ball and Golden Liquid Spring of Divine Removing Attachment

Prepare! Sit up straight. Put the tip of your tongue near the roof of your mouth. Open your heart and soul to receive this permanent divine treasure. In the next twenty seconds, the Divine will download it to your soul.

Divine Order: Divine Golden Light Ball and Golden Liquid Spring of Divine Removing Attachment Mind Transplant Transmission!

Hao! Hao! Hao!
Thank you. Thank you. Thank you.

Thank you, Divine. There are no words anymore.

The fifteenth divine treasure is now ready to be transmitted to you and every reader. This treasure is named:

Divine Body Transplant of Divine Golden Light Ball and Golden Liquid Spring of Divine Removing Attachment

Prepare! Sit up straight. Put the tip of your tongue near the roof of your mouth. Open your heart and soul to receive this permanent divine treasure. In the next twenty seconds, the Divine will download it to your soul.

Divine Order: Divine Golden Light Ball and Golden Liquid Spring of Divine Removing Attachment Body Transplant Transmission!

Hao! Hao! Hao
Thank you. Thank you. Thank you.

Thank you, Divine. We continue to be blessed beyond any words.

Divine Order: Join Divine Golden Light Ball and Golden Liquid Spring of Divine Removing Attachment Soul Transplant, Mind Transplant, and Body Transplant as one.

Yi Ya Ya Ya Ya Hei Ya Ya Hei Hei Hei!

Let us practice with this major divine treasure to remove our attachment. This is how to do it:

Divine Practice to Remove Attachment

Body Power. Put one palm over your Message Center (heart chakra in the middle of your chest). Put your other palm over the top of your head (over the crown chakra).
Soul Power. Say *hello*:

> *Dear my Divine Soul Mind Body Transplants of*
> *Divine Golden Light Ball and Golden Liquid*
> *Spring of Divine Removing Attachment,*

I love you, honor you, and appreciate you.
Please turn on to remove all of my attachments.
I am extremely grateful.
Thank you.

Sound Power. As in previous practices, you can chant your Soul Language or sing your Soul Song. You can also chant repeatedly:

> *Divine treasures remove my attachments. Thank you,*
>   *Divine.*
> *Divine treasures remove my attachments. Thank you,*
>   *Divine.*
> *Divine treasures remove my attachments. Thank you,*
>   *Divine.*
> *Divine treasures remove my attachments. Thank you,*
>   *Divine.*

Mind Power. Visualize divine golden light and divine rainbow light radiating and resonating in your Message Center and on the top of your head.

Practice three to five minutes per time, three to five times per day. The more you practice and the longer you practice, the better.

This is the divine way to remove all attachment. It is much faster than other ways.

BODY BLOCKAGES

Body blockages includes energy blockages and matter blockages. Energy blockages occur between the cells. Matter blockages occur inside the cells.

Energy Blockages

Energy is *chi.*

In traditional Chinese medicine, there are many different kinds of chi. For example, every organ has its chi—liver chi, heart chi, spleen chi, lung chi, and kidney chi. There is *yuan chi* (original chi), *zhong chi* (respiratory chi), *qing chi* (clean chi), *zong chi* (stored in the chest, this is a combination of *qing chi* and the chi of food essence produced by the spleen and stomach), and many other types of chi.

In one sentence, *chi is the energy that radiates out from cellular vibration.* The energy that radiates out from the vibration of the liver cells is named liver chi. The energy that radiates out from the vibration of the kidney cells is named kidney chi. The energy that each organ radiates from the vibration of its cells is named the chi of that organ. Each cell radiates out its own chi, which is named the chi of the cell.

In reality, *there is only one chi.* All of the different chis are aspects of this one chi.

Chi radiates out from the vibration of the cells and flows through the meridians and the spaces in the body. Meridians are the pathways of energy.

If energy flows, one is healthy.
If energy is blocked, one is sick.

Every system, every organ, every cell, and every DNA and RNA has its own chi. If chi flows, the person is healthy. If chi is blocked in one system, that system is sick. If chi is blocked in one organ, that organ is sick. If chi is blocked in one part of the body, that part of the body is sick.

This is one of the most important philosophies in *The Yellow Emperor's Internal Classic,* the top authority book of traditional Chinese medicine. This teaching has guided the practice of traditional Chinese medicine very well for five thousand years. Millions of people have received remarkable healing results from the theory of chi flow and chi blockages in the body.

Eighty-five to 90 percent of all unhealthy conditions result from too much energy. This excess energy creates a blockage around the cells, organs, and systems. This blockage makes it difficult for energy to flow. Think about a dam in a river. The dam can limit or completely stop the flow of the river. An energy blockage builds a dam to inhibit the free flow of energy. Energy will get stuck and accumulate because it cannot flow freely. This can lead to pain, inflammation, cysts, tumors, or cancer in the area.

The healing solution for too much energy is to remove the blockage to promote energy flow.

The other 10 to 15 percent of unhealthy conditions are due to deficient energy. This can lead to degenerative conditions such as multiple sclerosis, Parkinson's disease, Alzheimer's disease, chronic fatigue, and fibromyalgia.

The healing solution for not enough energy is to boost energy to promote energy flow.

Matter Blockages

As I taught in *Soul Mind Body Medicine,* matter blockages also affect health. A matter blockage is a blockage inside the cells. There are many kinds of matter in a cell, including water, protein, a nucleus, other cell units, DNA, RNA, and the smallest matter inside the cells.

Matter blockages are very closely related to energy blockages. When cells contract, matter inside the cells transforms to energy outside the cells. When cells expand, energy outside the cells transforms to matter inside the cells. This transformation between matter inside the cells and energy outside the cells is constant. It is the process of vital energy or life force in motion. When this transformation stops, the life of the cell ends.

The transformation between matter inside the cells and energy outside the cells is also a process of balancing matter and energy. For good health, matter and energy must be in relative balance. If this balance is disrupted, sickness can occur. There can be too much energy or not enough energy around the cells. There can be too much matter or not enough matter inside the cells. Just as excess energy must be dissipated, excess matter must also be transformed and dissipated. In fact, everything that I said about energy can be applied to matter. This will help you understand the importance of removing matter blockages for healing, prevention of sickness, rejuvenation, and life transformation.

Therefore, healing is to remove all kinds of blockages in the soul, mind, and body. To remove blockages is to heal soul, mind, and body. To remove blockages is to prevent sickness in soul, mind, and body. To remove blockages is to rejuvenate and promote long life in soul, mind, and body.

In this chapter so far, I have explained the essence of soul blockages, mind blockages, and body blockages. I have offered fifteen Divine Soul Mind Body Transplants to remove your mind blockages. The generosity of the Divine leaves me speechless. Please remember that we must practice. If we do not, we are very sorry to the Divine because the Divine Soul Mind Body Transplants would be wasted.

Divine Soul Mind Body Transplants Carry Divine Frequency and Vibration with Divine Love, Forgiveness, Compassion, and Light

How do Divine Soul Mind Body Transplants work?

They carry divine frequency and vibration with divine love, forgiveness, compassion, and light.

> *Divine frequency and vibration can transform the frequency and vibration of our body's systems, organs, cells, cell units, DNA, RNA, and smallest matter inside the cells, as well as the spaces between the cells.*
> *Divine love melts all blockages and transforms all life.*
> *Divine forgiveness brings inner peace and inner joy.*
> *Divine compassion boosts energy, stamina, vitality, and immunity.*
> *Divine light heals, prevents sickness, rejuvenates, prolongs life, and transforms every aspect of life, including relationships and finances.*

This is how Divine Soul Mind Body Transplants work.

Thank you, Divine.

We are honored.

Humanity is honored.

Mother Earth is honored.

All universes are honored.

We are extremely blessed that the Divine has created this divine way, the Divine Soul Mind Body Healing and Transmission System, to heal you, humanity, Mother Earth, and all universes.

Receive Divine Soul Mind Body Transplants— Golden Light Beings

In July 2003, the Divine chose me as a divine servant, vehicle, and channel. I had made a vow to be an unconditional servant for humanity and the Divine. I have been a servant in my thousands of previous lifetimes. Therefore, the Divine chose me for this honor. The Divine said, "Zhi Gang, when you act, I act." I was extremely honored and humbled.

The Divine gave me a very special healing tool called Divine Soul Downloads. A Divine Soul Download is a new soul created from the heart of the Divine. For the physical body, this new golden light being can be for a system, organ, cells, cell units, DNA, RNA, smallest matter, and spaces in the body. Divine Soul Downloads can give new souls for relationships or finances. There is no limit to Divine Soul Downloads because there is no limit to divine creation.

The first Divine Soul Downloads that I offered from the Divine were Divine Soul Softwares and Divine Soul Transplants. For a human being, Divine Soul Transplants can replace the original souls of the systems, organs, cells, cell units, DNA, RNA, smallest matter, and spaces. It is just like a physical organ transplant, where the original physical kidney, liver, or heart is replaced by a new kidney, liver, or heart.

I have offered countless Divine Soul Transplants to humanity and all souls since 2003.

In August 2008, the Divine told me to start to transmit Divine Soul Energy Matter Transplants.

Divine Energy Transplants are new divine energy light beings created by the Divine to replace the original energy of systems, organs, cells, cell units, DNA, RNA, smallest matter, and spaces.

Divine Matter Transplants are new divine matter light beings created by the Divine to replace the original tiny matter of systems, organs, cells, cell units, DNA, RNA, smallest matter, and spaces.

I have offered thousands and thousands of Divine Soul Energy Matter Transplants to humanity since August 2008.

In May 2009, the Divine told me that Divine Soul Energy Matter Transplants would be "upgraded" to Divine Soul Mind Body Transplants. In these two sets of Divine Downloads, the Soul Transplants are the same. Divine Body Transplants include both Divine Energy Transplants and Divine Matter Transplants. Divine Mind Transplants are being given to humanity for the first time in history. You have been offered five Divine Mind Transplants as divine gifts in this chapter.

I have already transmitted thousands and thousands of Divine Soul Mind Body Transplants to humanity since May 2009.

I will further explain Divine Soul Transplants, Divine Mind Transplants, and Divine Body Transplants in the following sections.

I cannot honor and thank the Divine enough for the honor, privilege, and authority to transmit divine souls.

I cannot honor and thank the Divine enough for this divine way to serve humanity, Mother Earth, and all universes.

We cannot honor and thank the Divine enough for making this divine service available to us.

Thank you. Thank you. Thank you.

DIVINE SOUL TRANSPLANTS

When you receive a Divine Soul Transplant for your liver, for example, the original soul of your liver returns to the heart of the

Divine, and you are given a new soul for your liver. This new divine soul is very big, very strong, very bright, and karma-free. It carries divine consciousness and intelligence, with divine frequency and vibration. It offers unconditional universal service with divine love, forgiveness, compassion, and light.

Every system, every organ, every cell, every cell unit, every DNA, every RNA, every smallest matter, and every space in the body has a soul. If you are sick, the *soul* of the sick organ or area is sick. If you have an unhealthy condition in your liver, such as hepatitis B or cirrhosis, the soul of your liver is not functioning at its optimum level. It is probably small, perhaps even shriveled or deformed. It is often dark gray or black in color.

A soul in this condition cannot serve you well. It cannot serve your liver. When you receive a Divine Soul Transplant, this original soul of your liver returns to the heart of the Divine to receive blessings and teachings. This is a wonderful gift for this soul. At the same time, your liver receives a huge new divine soul that is more than eighty feet tall, karma-free, and full of divine love, forgiveness, compassion, and light. This soul is given to your liver to serve the healing, rejuvenation, and transformation of your liver.

It is easy to understand that a Divine Soul Transplant can make a huge difference for your liver. Divine souls carry divine soul frequency and vibration, which can transform the frequency of your body, systems, organs, cells, cell units, DNA, RNA, smallest matter, and spaces. The story about Walter's liver cancer in the beginning of this book has already proven the power, significance, and healing, blessing, and life transformation abilities of a single Divine Soul Transplant. It is a perfect example of the one-sentence secret in action:

Heal the soul first; then healing of the mind and body will follow.

A Divine Soul Transplant takes place in a matter of seconds. Do not worry about how such a huge soul will affect you. The new soul will reduce itself in size. In two or three days, it will shrink to the proper size to serve your liver.

Receiving a Divine Soul Transplant only starts the Divine Soul Mind Body Healing and Transmission System healing process. The vital step is what you do after you receive it. The Divine Soul Transplant (and Divine Mind Transplant and Divine Body Transplant) is the divine action. What you do to invoke and practice is the human action. Your involvement and participation in this way are vital. To benefit fully from the Divine Soul Mind Body Healing and Transmission System, you must invoke and practice with Divine Soul Mind Body Transplants.

Later in this chapter, I will further explain Divine Mind Transplants and Divine Body Transplants. I will tell you clearly what you must do to benefit from them. Earlier in this chapter, you have already received fifteen Divine Soul Mind Body Transplants. I have already led you in many practices with them. I cannot emphasize enough that practice is essential. To benefit fully, you must do your part.

We are so blessed.

I cannot thank the Divine enough for being chosen to serve humanity, Mother Earth, and all universes by transmitting Divine Soul Transplants.

I wish to serve each of you very well.

DIVINE MIND TRANSPLANTS

Divine Mind Transplants are also light beings created by the Divine. These divine light beings carry divine consciousness to replace the original consciousness of a person's body, systems, organs, cells, cell units, DNA, RNA, smallest matter, and spaces. Divine Mind Transplants can transform the negative mind-sets, attitudes, and beliefs, and remove ego and attachment of a person's body, systems, organs, cells, cell units, DNA, RNA, smallest matter, and spaces. Divine Mind Transplants also carry divine frequency and vibration with divine love, forgiveness, compassion, and light.

Millions of people in Mother Earth are on a spiritual journey. Negative mind-sets, attitudes, beliefs, ego, and attachment are the major blockages for one's spiritual journey. People do all kinds of spiritual practices to remove these. Divine Mind Transplants are the divine way to remove negative mind-sets, attitudes, beliefs, ego, and attachment.

I cannot honor and thank the Divine enough for giving Divine Mind Transplants to humanity. We are extremely honored and blessed.

DIVINE BODY TRANSPLANTS

Divine Body Transplants are also light beings created by the Divine. These light beings carry divine energy and divine matter to replace the existing energy and tiny matter of a person's body, systems, organs, cells, cell units, DNA, RNA, smallest matter, and spaces. Divine Body Transplants also carry divine frequency and vibration with divine love, forgiveness, compassion, and light.

Like Divine Soul Transplants and Divine Mind Transplants, Divine Body Transplants are also very big and brilliant. They are also karma-free unconditional universal servants. Divine Body Transplants at the level of energy are also fluid. They flow freely. Blockages to the free flow of energy are removed and replaced by divine light that has a fluid quality of liquid. As *The Yellow Emperor's Internal Classic* told us five thousand years ago:

If chi flows, one is healthy.

Everything that I have taught about energy is also true for matter. Think about it. Matter that is deformed, deficient, or excessive can receive new light beings that are the proper shape, size, and function. Receiving Divine Body Transplants on the level of matter is also very important for healing, rejuvenation, and transformation.

I am extremely honored to have been chosen as a servant, vehicle, and vessel of the Divine to offer the Divine's Soul Mind Body Transplants to you, humanity, and all souls. I have trained my top teachers and healers to be Divine Servants as I am. From February 2009 through July 2009, I have trained and created twelve Divine Servants who are authorized to download Divine Soul Mind Body Transplants to humanity as new Divine Channels:

Marilyn Smith
Francisco Quintero
Joyce Brown
Lothar Zahler

Michael Stevens

Peggy Werner

Shu Chin Hsu

David Lusch

Patricia Smith

Patty Baker

Petra Herz

Allan Chuck

These Divine Servants have received a Divine Order and divine authority to be a vessel, vehicle, channel, and servant of the Divine. They are now traveling worldwide to offer the Divine Soul Mind Body Healing and Transmission System to humanity. I am continually training and preparing many more Divine Servants, vessels, vehicles, and channels to serve you, humanity, Mother Earth, and all universes. I am honored and grateful to have been given this divine task.

Invoke and Practice with Divine Soul Mind Body Transplants

The Divine Soul Mind Body Healing and Transmission System is a unique combination of yin and yang. This is the first time in history that such a combination has existed. The yin aspect is the Divine Order to remove soul mind body blockages and the Divine Orders to transmit Divine Soul Mind Body Transplants.

People have prayed to the Divine throughout the ages. Prayer is powerful, healing, and transforming. Now, people have the possibility of calling upon the Divine Soul Mind Body Transplants that have been transmitted to their souls. This is a unique and powerful divine presence that has not been given to humanity before. It is a most profound yin presence. There are no words to adequately express how blessed we are to have the Divine present in this way.

The yang aspect is our practice. Both yin and yang are essential. To practice is to self-heal. Everything I teach has its foundation in self-healing. It is one of the three empowerments that support my total life mission. The message of healing is:

I have the power to heal myself.
You have the power to heal yourself.
Together, we have the power to heal the world.

Invoking ("turning on") and practicing with your divine treasures is the divine way to do self-healing. The Divine Soul Mind Body Healing and Transmission System moves self-healing to the divine level.

When you turn on your divine treasures, you are consciously connecting with divine presence. There is nothing more powerful or transforming. As you practice, you are literally in the presence of the Divine. You can *be* the presence of the Divine. Think about it. What an honor and privilege! Your frequency and vibration are uplifted. Your soul standing is uplifted. The benefits radiate from you to all humanity, Mother Earth, and beyond.

When you practice, you are also expressing your total GOLD (gratitude, obedience, loyalty, and devotion) to the Divine. You are living your gratitude. You are responding with obedience to the Divine's request that each person who receives these treasures practice. You are showing your loyalty and devotion. You are becoming more of a total GOLD universal servant.

These are some of the main benefits of practicing with your

divine treasures. As you practice more, you will gain wisdom and insights and receive sacred secrets. You will discover ways to practice that are specific to you. Every divine treasure carries healing, blessing, and transformation. Every divine treasure also carries sacred wisdom, teachings, and practices. The more you practice, the more you will have access to them.

I cannot remind you enough and I cannot emphasize enough how important your practice is. Receiving Divine Soul Mind Body Transplants does not mean you have recovered or transformed. You *must* practice. Divine Soul Mind Body Transplants are a most extraordinary gift. They carry divine love, forgiveness, compassion, and light. They have the power to heal, bless, and transform. However, if you do not turn them on, they cannot serve you. They are like perfect lightbulbs that will never burn out. However, you *must* turn them on.

After receiving Divine Soul Mind Body Transplants, invoke them and practice with them to restore your health in your physical, emotional, mental, and spiritual bodies.

I wish you will practice well.

I wish you will receive great benefits from the Divine Soul Mind Body Healing and Transmission System.

Hao!

ONE-SENTENCE SECRET FORMULA

Very few people would ignore the light switch in their home and choose to walk around in the dark. Yet many people receive Divine Soul Mind Body Transplants and ignore the "light switch." They do not turn on their divine treasures! This is not a good choice. It is very simple to turn on the treasures you have received. First, say *hello:*

Dear my divine treasures,
I love you, honor you, and appreciate you.
Please turn on to heal and rejuvenate me.
Thank you, Divine.

Then chant the one-sentence secret repeatedly, silently or aloud:

Divine treasures heal and rejuvenate me.
Divine treasures heal and rejuvenate me.
Divine treasures heal and rejuvenate me.
Divine treasures heal and rejuvenate me.

After three to five minutes (there is no time limit; the longer you chant, the better, especially for chronic and life-threatening conditions), close your practice:

Hao! Hao! Hao!
Thank you. Thank you. Thank you.

That is all you need to do.

SACRED AREAS FOR PRACTICING WITH DIVINE SOUL MIND BODY TRANSPLANTS

Dao (or Tao) is "the Way." In Daoist teachings there is a highest philosophy and principle that explains everything in all universes:

Dao produces one.
One produces two.

Two produces three.
Three produces everything.

Millions of people throughout history have studied and applied this highest philosophy to guide every aspect of their lives. Many have tried to explain this highest philosophy. There are too many explanations. People really have a difficult time explaining this highest philosophy. Let me share the essence of my understanding.

Dao produces one.

To say that "Dao produces one" means Dao *is* one. Dao and one are the same. Many people are confused about this part.

One produces two.

Two represents Heaven and Earth. Heaven is yang. Earth is yin. To say that "one produces two" means one produces yin and yang.

Two produces three.

Dao, yin, and yang together are three. Dao, yin, and yang are a triangle. Dao is at the top of the triangle. Yin and yang are at the bottom of the triangle.

Three produces everything.

Dao, yin, and yang can produce and transform everything in a being and in all universes.

In Christian teaching, God, Jesus, and the Holy Spirit form a triangle.

In Daoist teaching, three saints, Yuan Shi Tian Zun (the Universal Lord of the Primordial Beginning), Dao Te Tian Zun (the Universal Lord of The Way and Its Virtue), and Ling Bao Tian Zun (the Universal Lord of the Numinous Treasure) form the triangle.

In Buddhist teaching, three buddhas, Shi Jia Mo Ni Fuo

(Shakyamuni), A Mi Tuo Fuo (Amitabha), and Yao Shi Fuo (the Medicine Buddha) are the triangle.

These few examples all follow *Dao produces one, One produces two, Two produces three, and Three produces everything.*

I am not teaching religion. I have studied Daoism deeply in my life. I have also studied Buddhism and Confucianism. I honor each teaching.

I am sharing the profound wisdom and secrets within this highest teaching of Daoism. In fact, the Divine is using these four brief sentences to teach me divine secrets for soul self-healing.

In July 2003, I was chosen as a servant of humanity and the Divine. The Divine teaches me daily. Whatever profound wisdom, secrets, and practical techniques I receive from the Divine, I share immediately with humanity.

As I flowed this book in early May 2009, the Divine gave me a new teaching for soul self-healing. This new wisdom is so profound that I became speechless. I am delighted and extremely honored to share that teaching with you in this book.

Divine wisdom, secrets, and practical treasures come into my Ling Gong. "Ling" means *soul.* "Gong" means *temple.* The Ling Gong is the soul temple in the body. It is located between the heart and the Message Center. Let me review the significance and power of the Message Center. I have done this in almost all of my books because the Message Center is a vital energy center and spiritual center.

The Message Center is the key energy and spiritual center in the body for:

- *Soul communication.* The Message Center is the key for opening your four major spiritual communication channels: the Soul Language Channel, Direct Soul Communication Channel, Third Eye Channel, and Direct Knowing Channel.

- *Soul Language.* Open your Message Center and your Soul Language will flow out. Develop your Soul Language further and you will be able to translate your Soul Language into any human language you know.

- *Healing.* The Message Center is the soul healing center. It carries soul healing power. It can offer soul healing for your physical body, emotional body, mental body, and spiritual body.

- *Emotions.* The Message Center is the emotional center. To cleanse and purify the Message Center can balance your emotions, including depression, anxiety, worry, grief, fear, guilt, anger, and more.

- *Love, forgiveness, and compassion.* The Message Center is the love center. It radiates love within and without. Love melts all blockages and transforms all life. The Message Center is also the forgiveness center. Forgiveness brings inner joy and inner peace. The Message Center is also the compassion center. Compassion boosts energy, stamina, vitality, and immunity.

- *Life transformation.* The Message Center is the center for transforming your life. Life transformation includes transformation of your relationships and finances.

- *Karma.* The Message Center stores a record of your karma from all of your lifetimes. To clear bad karma, one must cleanse the Message Center.

- *Soul enlightenment.* If your body soul sits in the Message Center, your soul is considered to be enlightened.

The Ling Gong is the soul temple. The sacred wisdom about the Ling Gong is that when a human being is born, the Akashic Records sends a special soul to the newborn's Ling Gong. This special soul is named the Tian Ming. "Tian" means *Heaven.* "Ming" means *order.* The Tian Ming is Heaven's special soul that is sent to your Ling Gong to lead and guide your entire life. Your Tian Ming carries Heaven's orders for you.

Above all, your Tian Ming wants to make sure that you accomplish the Divine's tasks for you in this lifetime. If you or your soul listen to the guidance of your Tian Ming, your life could be very smooth, happy, and successful. If you or your soul ignore or go against the directions from your Tian Ming, your life could be a big mess. Up to now, very few human beings have known this sacred wisdom.

There is a renowned ancient spiritual statement that, for thousands of years, has explained the importance of the Tian Ming and guided many spiritual beings to follow the Tian Ming's guidance from Heaven and the Divine:

Follow Heaven's idea and flourish.
Go against Heaven's idea and face big blockages.

Because the Tian Ming resides in the Ling Gong, the Ling Gong is the most important area for soul transformation.

Now, it is my great honor to share with you the sacred areas of the body for practicing with Divine Soul Mind Body Transplants.

In a human's body, where is Dao? **Dao is the Ling Gong,** which is located between your Message Center and heart. Where are yin and yang? **Yin is the Message Center. Yang is the Snow Mountain Area.** (The Snow Mountain Area is an important foundational energy center. It is located toward the back of the torso, slightly above the tailbone. It is a key for quality of life and long life. It is the source of energy for the kidneys and the reproductive organs. It also nourishes the energy of the brain and the Third Eye. In other traditions and practices, the Snow Mountain Area is known as Kundalini.) To heal yourself, your loved ones, or humanity, pay attention to these three areas.

Any sickness could be healed in a special way. Focus on Dao (the Ling Gong), and you could heal any sickness quickly. Focus on yin (the Message Center) and yang (the Snow Mountain Area), and you could heal yourself even faster. To focus on the Dao and the yin and yang of the body is the divine way to heal yourself faster.

Let me summarize this new divine sacred and secret wisdom in one sentence:

**The Ling Gong, Message Center, and Snow Mountain
Area can heal, prevent sickness, rejuvenate, prolong life,
and transform every aspect of life,
including relationships and finances.**

Now, let me show you practical exercises that apply this highest universal truth, which is the way to heal and transform every aspect of your life.

First, let me show you how to do self-healing:

Ling Gong Practice to Self-heal

Body Power. Put one palm or fist over your Ling Gong. Do Soul Tapping on your Ling Gong continuously during the practice.
   Soul Power. Say *hello:*

> *Dear soul, mind, and body of my Ling Gong,*
> *I love you.*
> *You have the power to heal my* _____ [make
>   your requests for healing].
> *Do a good job.*
> *Thank you.*

Sound Power. Chant repeatedly, silently or aloud:

> *Ling Gong heals my* [name the areas or conditions].
>   *Thank you.*
> *Ling Gong heals my* [name the areas or conditions].
>   *Thank you.*
> *Ling Gong heals my* [name the areas or conditions].
>   *Thank you.*
> *Ling Gong heals my* [name the areas or conditions].
>   *Thank you.*

Mind Power. Visualize golden or rainbow light shining in the area or areas of sickness.

Practice three to five minutes per time, three to five times per day. The longer and the more often you practice, the better.

Next, let us practice the Ling Gong to prevent sickness. *The Yellow Emperor's Internal Classic,* the authoritative text of traditional Chinese medicine for five thousand years, states: *Shang gong zhi wei bing, bu zhi yi bing.* "Shang gong" means *best doctor.* "Zhi" means *treat.* "Wei" means *not appeared.* "Bing" means *sickness.* "Bu" means *not.* "Zhi" means *treat.* "Yi bing" means *sickness already.*

This one sentence can be translated as:

The best doctor is one who teaches people to prevent sickness, not one who treats sickness after it has appeared.

If we can prevent sickness, we do not need to have sickness. Nobody wants to be sick.

Let me share the divine sacred way to prevent all sicknesses:

Ling Gong Practice to Prevent Sickness

Body Power. Put one palm or fist over your Ling Gong. Do Soul Tapping on your Ling Gong continuously during the practice.

Soul Power. Say *hello:*

> *Dear soul, mind, and body of my Ling Gong,*
> *I love you, honor you, and appreciate you.*
> *You have the power to prevent all sicknesses.*
> *Please prevent all sicknesses.*
> *I am very grateful.*
> *Thank you.*

Sound Power. Chant repeatedly, silently or aloud:

> *Ling Gong prevents all sicknesses. Thank you.*
> *Ling Gong prevents all sicknesses. Thank you.*

Ling Gong prevents all sicknesses. Thank you.
Ling Gong prevents all sicknesses. Thank you.

Mind Power. Visualize golden or rainbow light shining from head to toe, skin to bone.

Practice three to five minutes per time, three to five times per day. The longer and the more often you practice, the better.

Next, let me share with you how to receive rejuvenation for your soul, heart, mind, and body from your Ling Gong.

Ling Gong Practice to Rejuvenate Soul, Heart, Mind, and Body

Body Power. Put one palm over your Lower Dan Tian. (As I have explained in every book of my Soul Power Series, the Lower Dan Tian is another important foundational energy center in your abdomen just below the navel. It is key for energy, stamina, vitality, immunity, and long life. For most of humanity, it is also the seat of the soul. The Lower Dan Tian is the postnatal energy center, while the Snow Mountain Area is the prenatal energy center.) Put the other palm over the Ling Gong. Do Soul Tapping of both areas continuously during the practice.

Soul Power. Say *hello:*

> *Dear soul, mind, and body of my Ling Gong and*
> *Lower Dan Tian,*
> *I love you.*
> *You have the power to rejuvenate my soul, heart,*
> *mind, and body.*
> *Do a good job.*
> *Thank you.*

Sound Power. Chant repeatedly, silently or aloud:

Ling Gong rejuvenates my soul, heart, mind, and
  body. Thank you, Divine.
Ling Gong rejuvenates my soul, heart, mind, and
  body. Thank you, Divine.
Ling Gong rejuvenates my soul, heart, mind, and
  body. Thank you, Divine.
Ling Gong rejuvenates my soul, heart, mind, and
  body. Thank you, Divine.

Mind Power. Visualize golden or rainbow light radiating and vibrating from head to toe, skin to bone.

Practice for three to five minutes, three to five times per day. The longer and the more often you practice, the better.

Your Ling Gong has the power to prolong your life. You must practice diligently:

Ling Gong Practice to Prolong Life

Body Power. Put one palm over the Snow Mountain Area. Put the other palm over the Ling Gong. Do Soul Tapping on both of these areas at the same time.

Soul Power. Say *hello*:

Dear soul, mind, and body of my Ling Gong and
  Snow Mountain Area,
I love you, honor you, and appreciate you.
You have the power to prolong my life.
Do a good job.
Thank you.

Sound Power. Chant repeatedly, silently or aloud:

Ling Gong prolongs my life. Thank you, Divine.
Ling Gong prolongs my life. Thank you, Divine.
Ling Gong prolongs my life. Thank you, Divine.
Ling Gong prolongs my life. Thank you, Divine.

Mind Power. Visualize golden or rainbow light radiating and vibrating from head to toe, skin to bone.

Practice for three to five minutes, three to five times per day. The longer and the more often you practice, the better.

Next, let us transform relationships through a Ling Gong practice:

Ling Gong Practice to Transform Relationships

Body Power. Put your left palm over your Ling Gong. Put your right palm over your Message Center. Do Soul Tapping on both areas simultaneously.

Soul Power. Say *hello:*

> *Dear soul, mind, and body of my Ling Gong and Mes-*
> *   sage Center,*
> *I love you, honor you, and appreciate you.*
> *You have the power to transform my relationship with*
> *   _____ [name a person].*
> *Do a good job.*
> *Thank you.*

Sound Power. Chant repeatedly, silently or aloud:

Ling Gong transforms my relationship. Thank you,
  Divine.
Ling Gong transforms my relationship. Thank you,
  Divine.
Ling Gong transforms my relationship. Thank you,
  Divine.
Ling Gong transforms my relationship. Thank you,
  Divine.

Mind Power. Visualize golden or rainbow light shining between you and the person with whom you are requesting a relationship blessing.

Practice for three to five minutes, three to five times per day. The longer and the more often you practice, the better.

Next, I will show you how to transform finances through a Ling Gong practice:

Ling Gong Practice to Transform Finances

Body Power. Put your left palm over your Ling Gong. Put your right palm over your Message Center. Do Soul Tapping on both areas simultaneously.

Soul Power. Say *hello:*

Dear soul, mind, and body of my Ling Gong and Message Center,
I love you, honor you, and appreciate you.
You have the power to transform my finances.
Do a good job.
Thank you.

Sound Power. Chant repeatedly, silently or aloud:

> *Ling Gong transforms my finances. Thank you,*
>   *Divine.*
> *Ling Gong transforms my finances. Thank you,*
>   *Divine.*
> *Ling Gong transforms my finances. Thank you,*
>   *Divine.*
> *Ling Gong transforms my finances. Thank you,*
>   *Divine.*

Mind Power. Visualize golden or rainbow light shining between you and the soul of your finances.

Practice for three to five minutes, three to five times per day. The longer and the more often you practice, the better.

In summary, Ling Gong is the Dao for a human being. You can apply this Dao to receive anything you need. Following is the sacred and secret practice to transform every aspect of life:

Ling Gong Practice to Transform Every Aspect of Life

Body Power. Put one palm over the Ling Gong. Put your other palm over the Snow Mountain Area. Do Soul Tapping on both of these areas at the same time.

Soul Power. Say *hello*:

> *Dear soul, mind, and body of my Ling Gong and*
>   *Snow Mountain Area,*
> *I love you, honor you, and appreciate you.*
> *You have the power to heal, prevent sicknesses, rejuve-*

*nate, prolong life, and transform every aspect of life,
   including relationship and finances.*
Please bless me.
Do a good job.
Thank you.

Sound Power. Chant repeatedly, silently or aloud:

*Ling Gong heals, prevents sickness, rejuvenates,
   prolongs life, and transforms every aspect of my life,
   including relationships and finances. Thank you,
   Divine.*
*Ling Gong heals, prevents sickness, rejuvenates,
   prolongs life, and transforms every aspect of my life,
   including relationships and finances. Thank you,
   Divine.*
*Ling Gong heals, prevents sickness, rejuvenates,
   prolongs life, and transforms every aspect of my life,
   including relationships and finances. Thank you,
   Divine.*
*Ling Gong heals, prevents sickness, rejuvenates,
   prolongs life, and transforms every aspect of my life,
   including relationships and finances. Thank you,
   Divine.*

Mind Power. Visualize golden or rainbow light shining in your Ling Gong and Snow Mountain Area.

Practice for three to five minutes, three to five times per day. The longer and the more often you practice, the better.

This is one practice that can benefit every aspect of your life.

If you can speak Soul Language or sing your Soul Song, you may begin this practice by chanting four times:

> *Ling Gong heals, prevents sickness, rejuvenates, pro-*
> *longs life, and transforms every aspect of my life,*
> *including relationships and finances.*
> *Thank you, Divine.*

After chanting four times, speak Soul Language or sing your Soul Song for as long as you can.

The benefits are beyond comprehension. Soul Language and Soul Song are advanced soul treasures to transform every aspect of your life. Doing Ling Gong practices together with your Soul Language and Soul Song will accelerate and enhance the transformation of every aspect of your life.

The Divine Soul Mind Body Healing and Transmission System teaches humanity the divine way to heal sicknesses in the physical, emotional, mental, and spiritual bodies. Every sickness is due to soul, mind, and body blockages. To heal any sickness, first remove soul, mind, and body blockages in the unhealthy systems, organs, cells, cell units, DNA, RNA, smallest matter in the cells, and spaces between cells.

To remove soul blockages is to remove blockages in the Ling Gong. Karma is stored in the Akashic Records and in the Ling Gong. To remove soul blockages also includes removing soul blockages at the levels of the systems, organs, and cells.

To remove mind blockages is to remove blockages in the Message Center. The Message Center is the key for consciousness, not the brain. To remove mind blockages also includes removing mind blockages at the levels of the systems, organs, and cells, but the key is to remove the blockages in the Message Center.

To remove body blockages is to remove blockages in the Snow Mountain Area. Body blockages include energy blockages and matter blockages. To remove body blockages also includes removing energy and matter blockages at the levels of the systems, organs, and cells.

You can remove your soul blockages by yourself. How? The Divine made a spiritual law for humanity and for all souls. This spiritual law can be summarized in one sentence:

To remove your soul blockages by yourself, you must offer good service to others.

In other words, to clear your bad karma, you must accumulate good karma. Let me share with you one of the most powerful and practical ways to remove your soul blockages. I am honored to share this sacred divine practice with you and humanity. Let's do it now:

Ling Gong Practice to Self-clear Soul Blockages

Body Power. Put one fist or palm over the Ling Gong and do Soul Tapping there.
Soul Power. Say *hello:*

> *Dear soul, mind, and body of my Ling Gong,*
> *Dear Divine Soul Song* Love, Peace and Harmony,
> *I love you, honor you, and appreciate you.*
> *Please remove my soul blockages for _____* [name the unhealthy system, organ, or condition].

Dear all my Divine Soul Mind Body Transplants,
I love you, honor you, and appreciate you.
Please turn on.
Please remove my soul blockages for _____ [repeat
    the unhealthy system, organ, or condition].
Thank you. Thank you. Thank you.

Sound Power. Sing the Divine Soul Song *Love, Peace and
Harmony* repeatedly:

Lu La Lu La Li
Lu La Lu La La Li
Lu La Lu La Li Lu La
Lu La Li Lu La
Lu La Li Lu La

I love my heart and soul
I love all humanity
Join hearts and souls together
Love, peace and harmony
Love, peace and harmony

After singing for at least three to five minutes, close the practice:

Hao! Hao! Hao!
Thank you. Thank you. Thank you.

The longer and the more often you sing, the better. There are
no time limits for this practice. It does take time and effort to

clear the related soul blockages for serious and chronic conditions.

TIME REQUIREMENTS FOR PRACTICING WITH
DIVINE SOUL MIND BODY TRANSPLANTS

When I became a Divine Channel and started to transmit divine souls in July 2003, the Divine taught me that Divine Transplants are permanent divine treasures, but a recipient is required to invoke them and chant. The Divine gives a healing treasure to a person. The person must do homework.

Divine Soul Mind Body Transplants are light beings. These light beings are unique. They are like lightbulbs. They have to be turned on. If you invoke the Divine Transplants or you chant, the lightbulb is turned on. If you do not invoke them or chant, the lightbulb is off.

When you practice with the divine treasures, do so for at least three to five minutes. The longer you practice, the better. If you have a chronic or life-threatening condition, you must practice for a total of at least two hours per day. If you go into a dark room and turn on the light switch, but then turn it off quickly, the benefits you receive from the lightbulb will be very limited. This is also true for the divine treasures. If you just turn them on briefly and call that your practice, the benefits you receive will be very limited. The longer you turn them on, the greater the benefits. Even if you do not have a chronic or life-threatening condition, you will still benefit by practicing longer. You can receive very special blessings of rejuvenation and longevity.

Chanting itself brings great benefits. Divine Soul Downloads will assist you further. Together, they are a most powerful team.

Remember the story of Lothar. He reversed pancreatic cancer, which is almost always a terminal illness. He did this by chanting with his divine treasures for hours every day. His healing became his job. If you have chronic or life-threatening conditions, I wish you will also think of your healing as your job.

You can practice sitting down. If that is too difficult for you, you can practice lying down. The only thing to remember is that you must chant silently when lying down. Chanting aloud when you lie down drains your energy.

If you fall asleep while you practice, that is quite all right. Before you begin to practice, ask your beloved soul to continue chanting. That way, if you fall asleep, your practice will continue. Your divine treasures will continue to be turned on. When you return to wakefulness, reconnect with the divine treasures and begin chanting consciously again.

Even if you do not have a chronic or life-threatening condition, you can benefit from these suggestions. For example, if you are going to work, ask your soul to continue to chant and practice with your divine treasures while you are working. Whenever you have a break in your activities throughout the day, consciously connect with your divine treasures and chant.

To receive a Divine Soul Download does not mean you have recovered. I repeat this sentence again and again in this book to emphasize to you and every reader that you *must* invoke Divine Soul Mind Body Transplants you have received and chant. There are no time limits. The longer you chant, the better. Again, Lothar's story of his seventeen-centimeter pancreatic cancer tumor shrinking and shrinking until it completely disappeared is perfect to explain the three vital steps for healing with the Divine Soul Mind Body Healing and Transmission System:

1. Divine Order to remove soul mind body blockages
2. Divine Orders to offer Divine Soul Mind Body Transplants
3. Invoke Divine Soul Mind Body Transplants and chant to do divine soul mind body self-healing

In many cases, recipients feel immediate improvement after the first two steps. They must continue to invoke and chant for complete recovery. How long does recovery take? Each case is unique. Thousands of cases have demonstrated that recovery time varies. But you can be sure that how long and how often you practice is vital for recovery.

Remember, the Divine Soul Mind Body Transplants you receive are with you permanently. Even after you recover, you must continue to invoke them and chant. These Divine Soul Mind Body Transplants can then help prevent the sickness from reoccurring. They can also rejuvenate your soul, mind, body, systems, organs, cells, cell units, DNA, RNA, and smallest matter. We are further blessed to know that these divine treasures can prolong our lives.

Divine treasures can bless us beyond words and comprehension.

Practice more and more.

Receive healing, prevention of sickness, rejuvenation, and prolongation of life more and more.

Thank you, Divine, for giving the Divine Soul Mind Body Healing and Transmission System to humanity.

*Soul Song and Soul Dance—Practical Soul Treasures to
Assist Divine Treasures*

Soul Song and Soul Dance are major healing gifts the Divine has given humanity at this time. Practicing Soul Song and Soul Dance with your Divine Soul Mind Body Transplants can accelerate and enhance your healing and transformation beyond imagination.

Soul Song is a very high level of Soul Language. I have given a complete teaching on Soul Language in the first two books of my Soul Power Series, *Soul Communication* and *Soul Wisdom.* I will summarize some important points here.

Soul Language is the language of the Soul World and of your soul. It does not sound like ordinary language. It is a very pure and direct connection with the Divine and the Soul World. Since everyone and everything has a soul, Soul Language is a truly universal language.

Soul Song is the song of your soul. It is your Soul Language expressed in melody. Soul Language and Soul Song are both powerful healing tools, but Soul Song carries an even higher frequency and vibration than Soul Language does.

The message of Soul Song is:

> *I have the power to sing Soul Song.*
> *You have the power to sing Soul Song.*
> *Together, we have the power to sing Soul Song with*
> *the souls of all humanity, Mother Earth, and all*
> *universes.*

It will be a beautiful chorus of healing and blessing.

Soul Dance is another special gift from the Divine at this

special time. My book *Soul Wisdom* has sections on Soul Song and Soul Dance. The one-sentence secret about Soul Dance is:

Soul Dance is soul-guided dance.

Soul Dance follows the guidance of your soul. Your body will move in the specific ways needed to remove blockages and to boost energy. Your Soul Dance can heal, rejuvenate, and transform every aspect of your being.

After receiving the first two steps of the Divine Soul Mind Body Healing and Transmission System (Divine Orders to remove soul, mind, and body blockages and to receive Divine Soul Mind Body Transplants), the third step is vital to restore your health. The third step is to invoke and chant—to practice with your Divine Soul Mind Body Transplants, sing Divine Soul Songs, and do Divine Soul Dancing.

Soul Song and Soul Dance are major self-healing treasures. When you include Soul Song and Soul Dance in your practice and connect with all the divine treasures you have received, your Soul Song and Soul Dance will become divine. Turning on Divine Soul Mind Body Transplants, singing Divine Soul Songs, and doing Divine Soul Dancing together are the divine way to restore your health as quickly as possible.

This is how to invoke Divine Soul Mind Body Transplants together with singing Divine Soul Songs and doing Divine Soul Dancing:

> *Dear all my Divine Soul Mind Body Transplants,*
> *I love you.*
> *You have the power to heal and rejuvenate me.*
> *Please turn on.*

I am extremely honored and grateful.
Thank you.

Dear all Divine Soul Songs and Divine Soul Dance,
I love you.
You have the power to heal and rejuvenate me.
I am extremely honored and grateful.
Thank you.

Then sing Soul Song and do Soul Dancing, the longer, the better.

This is the divine way to heal you, your loved ones, humanity, Mother Earth, and all universes.

LIVING WITH THE DAO

Dao is the universal law and principle. Dao is The Way. There is a renowned ancient teaching:

Shun dao zhe chang, ni dao zhe wang

"Shun" means *follow*. "Zhe" means *the person*. "Chang" means *flourish*. "Ni" means *go against*. "Wang" means *die*.

Follow the Dao, follow nature's way, and you will flourish in every aspect of life. You will have good health, good relationships, and financial abundance.

Go against the Dao, do not follow nature's way, and you will have blockages in every aspect of life.

I will share how to live with the Dao.

There are several times during the day when it is especially important to live with the Dao. When and how do you do it? I am honored to share this wisdom with you.

Upon Awakening

It is very important to live with the Dao immediately after you awaken. Spend fifteen minutes doing the following four practices in succession and the benefits will be beyond your comprehension.

PRACTICE IN LYING POSITION (THREE MINUTES)

The moment that you awaken, say *hello* silently:

> *Good morning, Divine.*
> *Good morning, Dao.*
> *I love you, honor you, and appreciate you.*
> *Thank you so much for your teaching, blessing, and*
>   *nourishment for my life.*
> *I am very grateful.*

Then put one palm on your Ling Gong. Say silently:

> *Dear my Ling Gong, you are the Dao of my body.*
> *Tian Ming sits inside.*
> *Tian Ming is the messenger of the Divine or Dao.*
> *Thank you for your guidance, blessing, and nourish-*
>   *ment.*
> *I am very grateful.*

Then do Soul Tapping on your Ling Gong as you silently chant Soul Language or sing a Soul Song for one minute. Visualize divine light or Dao light vibrating in your Ling Gong.

Next, put one palm on your Message Center and the other palm on your Snow Mountain area. Say:

> *Dear soul, mind, and body of my Message Center and*
>   *Snow Mountain Area,*
> *I love you.*
> *You are the yin and yang of my body. Your balance is*
>   *vital for my life.*
> *Please bless and nourish my life.*
> *I am very grateful.*

Then do Soul Tapping on your Message Center and Snow Mountain Area as you silently chant Soul Language or sing a Soul Song silently for one minute. Visualize divine light or Dao light vibrating in your Message Center and Snow Mountain Area.

Here is another practice to help you awaken and prepare for a new, vibrant, and successful day:

Body Power. Put one palm on your Ling Gong right away. Do Soul Tapping and sing a Soul Song silently for three minutes in order to awaken with the Dao.

Soul Power. Say *hello* silently:

> *Dear Divine,*
> *Dear all of my spiritual fathers and mothers in all lay-*
>   *ers of Heaven and in the physical world,*
> *Dear my ancestors,*
> *Dear all humanity,*
> *Dear all souls in all universes,*
> *I love you, honor you, and appreciate you.*
> *I am your servant.*

Bless me for a new day.
I am very grateful.
Thank you.

Sound Power. Silently chant four times:

The Divine creates and fulfills a new day for me.
The Divine creates and fulfills a new day for me.
The Divine creates and fulfills a new day for me.
The Divine creates and fulfills a new day for me.

Then sing a Soul Song silently for three minutes.

Mind Power. Visualize your Ling Gong filled with divine golden light. Then visualize your whole body filled with divine golden light, from head to toe, skin to bone.

PRACTICE IN SITTING POSITION (THREE MINUTES)

Slowly sit up in bed. Tap your Ling Gong again. Sing a Soul Song or chant your Soul Language for one minute. Visualize divine light or Dao light in your Ling Gong.

Then tap your Message Center and Snow Mountain Area at the same time. Sing a Soul Song or chant your Soul Language. Visualize divine light or Dao light in your Message Center and Snow Mountain Area.

PRACTICE IN STANDING POSITION (THREE MINUTES)

Stand up. Tap your Ling Gong again. Sing a Soul Song or chant your Soul Language for one minute. Visualize divine light or Dao light in your Ling Gong.

Then tap your Message Center and Snow Mountain Area at the same time. Sing a Soul Song or chant your Soul Language.

Visualize divine light or Dao light in your Message Center and Snow Mountain Area.

PRACTICE IN MOVING POSITION (THREE MINUTES)

Start to do Soul Dance and Soul Song. Continue tapping your Ling Gong for one minute. Then do Soul Tapping on the Message Center and Snow Mountain Area with Soul Song and Soul Dance together.

Let me explain this profound wisdom. In the morning, the sun rises. Yang increases. When you have just awakened, your body is in the yin condition. Your body must transform from the yin condition to the yang condition.

Do not jump out of bed right away. There are many cases where people suddenly jump out of bed and collapse with a heart attack or stroke. When people have heart problems, blood pressure problems, or poor circulation, blood supply to the body can be unbalanced when the body suddenly changes position. That is why it can be very dangerous to get up too quickly.

After waking up, do not get up right away. Immediately communicate with the Divine. Show your greatest gratitude for the Divine's guidance, nourishment, and blessing for your life. After showing your appreciation to the Divine, connect with your Ling Gong, Message Center, and Snow Mountain Area to show your gratitude to them and to invoke and practice with them.

As I have explained, you are practicing Dao and yin yang within your body. You are following the highest philosophy and principle in the universe. When you do this, Dao produces one. One produces two. Two produces three. Three produces everything. When you do this, you are literally practicing Dao yin yang. These three produce everything.

This practice in the lying position awakens the souls, minds, and bodies of all your systems, organs, cells, cell units, DNA, RNA, smallest matter in the cells, and spaces between cells. Every part of your body is alive, vibrating, and resonating. Energy and blood circulation are instantly stimulated.

After three minutes in the lying position, sit up. The sitting position is more yang than the lying position. Yin moves toward yang. This is in alignment with the Dao of the morning.

After about three minutes of practice in the sitting position, move to the standing position, which is one step further toward yang. Energy and blood circulation move more. They become more yang.

The moving position is even more yang. Energy and blood circulation move even more. You have prepared your energy and blood circulation for a new day.

Dao is within every part of your body and in every activity of your life. How you wake up is one important step for the day.

The next important time to live with the Dao is at breakfast. Some people do not like to eat breakfast. I suggest that you do not neglect breakfast. Breakfast is very important. Your body absolutely needs the support of food when you begin a new day.

Before, During, and After Meals

Here are important practices for living with the Dao before, during, and after breakfast and every meal.

PRACTICE BEFORE MEALS

Before a meal, it is very important to prepare your whole digestive system. Digestive liquids and enzymes must be prepared for best digestion and absorption of nutrients. How do you prepare your digestive system? This is the way to do it while seated at your dining table:

Body Power. Put one palm over your Ling Gong. Put your other palm over your stomach. Do Soul Tapping on both areas simultaneously for two minutes.

Soul Power. Say *hello:*

> *Dear soul, mind, and body of my Ling Gong and my stomach,*
> *I love you, honor you, and appreciate you.*
> *You have the power to prepare my digestive system.*
> *Please prepare my digestive system.*
> *I am very grateful.*
> *Thank you.*

Sound Power. As you tap your Ling Gong and stomach, sing a Soul Song for two minutes.

You also can sing the Divine Soul Song for the Earth Element[7] for two minutes because the stomach is the yang organ connected with this element:

> *Gong Ya Gong Ya Gong Ya You*
> *Gong Ya Gong Ya You*
> *Gong Ya Gong Ya Gong Ya You*
> *Gong Ya Gong Ya Gong Ya Gong Ya You*

---

7. For the entire Divine Soul Song of Five Elements, see the fourth book in my Soul Power Series, *Divine Soul Songs: Sacred Practical Treasures to Heal, Rejuvenate, and Transform You, Humanity, Mother Earth, and All Universes* (2009, New York/Toronto: Atria Books/Heaven's Library).

Mind Power. Visualize golden light or rainbow light vibrating in your Ling Gong and stomach area.

Here is an alternative practice:

Body Power. Put one palm on your Message Center. Put your other palm on your Snow Mountain Area. Do Soul Tapping on both areas and sing Soul Song for three minutes to prepare your whole digestive system. Then continue with the rest of the practice:

Soul Power. Say *hello:*

> *Dear soul, mind, and body of my Message Center and Snow Mountain Area,*
> *Dear soul, mind, and body of my whole digestive system, including organs, cells, cell units, DNA, RNA, smallest matter in the cells, and spaces between the cells,*
> *I love you all.*
> *You have the power to prepare yourselves for great digestion.*
> *I am very grateful.*
> *Thank you.*

Sound Power. Chant four times:

> *Prepare my digestive system for food. Thank you.*
> *Prepare my digestive system for food. Thank you.*
> *Prepare my digestive system for food. Thank you.*
> *Prepare my digestive system for food. Thank you.*

Then sing a Soul Song for three minutes.

Mind Power. Visualize your Message Center, Snow Mountain Area, and digestive system shining with divine golden light.

PRACTICE WHILE EATING

While you are eating, it is most important to chew your food well. There is a renowned Japanese doctor who suggests chewing each mouthful twenty-four times before swallowing your food.

This number comes from the Divine. The Divine told me just now that this number carries a secret. Every number carries messages. To chew twenty-four times before swallowing is the best practice that you can do for digestion and absorption.

PRACTICE AFTER MEALS

The Divine told me that doing the following practice for living with the Dao for about eight minutes following meals will help you to digest and absorb food well:

Body Power. Put one palm on your Ling Gong. Put your other palm on your stomach. Tap both areas gently.

Soul Power. Say *hello:*

> *Dear soul, mind, and body of my Ling Gong, stomach,*
>   *and digestive system,*
> *I love you, honor you, and appreciate you.*
> *Please help me digest well and absorb well.*
> *I am very grateful.*

Sound Power. Chant:

> *Digest well. Absorb well. Thank you.*
> *Digest well. Absorb well. Thank you.*

Digest well. Absorb well. Thank you.
Digest well. Absorb well. Thank you.

This practice uses a direct Soul Order, assisted by Soul Tapping on the Ling Gong and stomach. It will help you tremendously. If you digest well and absorb well, many sicknesses will be prevented. Digesting well and absorbing well are a vital part of life.

Here is a variation of this practice:

Body Power. Put one palm on your Message Center, and the other palm on your Snow Mountain Area and digestive system. Do Soul Tapping of both areas while you sing a Soul Song for three minutes to prepare your entire digestive system to digest and absorb your meal well.

Soul Power. Say *hello:*

> *Dear soul, mind, and body of my Message Center and*
>   *Snow Mountain Area,*
> *Dear soul, mind, and body of my whole digestive*
>   *system, including organs, cells, cell units, DNA,*
>   *RNA, smallest matter in the cells, and spaces be-*
>   *tween the cells,*
> *I love you all.*
> *You have the power to prepare yourself for great*
>   *digestion.*
> *I am very grateful.*
> *Thank you.*

Sound Power. Chant four times:

> *Digest well and absorb well. Thank you.*
> *Digest well and absorb well. Thank you.*

Digest well and absorb well. Thank you.
Digest well and absorb well. Thank you.

Then sing a Soul Song for three minutes.

Mind Power. Visualize your Message Center, Snow Mountain Area, and digestive system shining with golden light.

Do these practices before and after every meal. Between lunch and dinner, you could also add ten to fifteen minutes of Soul Dancing together with Soul Tapping on your Ling Gong, Message Center, and Snow Mountain Area, with or without Soul Song as well.

Before Sleeping

The best time to go to sleep is no later than 11:00 PM. 11:00 PM to 1:00 AM is *zi* time. *Zi* time is the time of yin yang exchange. During these two hours, rest is best for the body. If you cannot be asleep in this period of time, then doing spiritual and energy practice is best.

Fifteen minutes before you go to sleep, do the following practice to move from yang to yin with the Dao:

- Soul Dance for about three minutes while Soul Tapping your Ling Gong, Message Center, and Snow Mountain Area together.
- Stand for about three minutes while Soul Tapping your Ling Gong, Message Center, and Snow Mountain Area together.
- Sit for about three minutes while Soul Tapping your Ling Gong, Message Center, and Snow Mountain Area together.

- Lie down for about three minutes while Soul Tapping your Ling Gong, Message Center, and Snow Mountain Area together.

After the fourth step, say *thank you* three times.

The first *thank you* is to the Divine for another day of service, blessing, and nourishment from the Divine.

The second *thank you* is to your spiritual fathers and mothers in all layers of Heaven for another day of service, blessing, and nourishment from them.

The third *thank you* is to your own soul, mind, and body for another day of service, blessing, and nourishment from nature, from all of the people, and from all the things you came in contact with throughout your day.

Finally, say *hello* to your own soul, your spiritual fathers and mothers, and the Divine:

> *Dear my beloved soul,*
> *Dear my beloved spiritual fathers and mothers in all*
> *layers of Heaven,*
> *Dear nature, Mother Earth, and Heaven,*
> *Dear Divine,*
> *I am extremely grateful for today's activities and*
> *success.*
> *During my sleep, please boost my energy, vitality, stamina, and immunity, and balance my physical, emotional, mental, and spiritual bodies.*
> *Purify my soul, heart, mind, and body to prepare me*
> *to be a better servant for humanity.*
> *I am extremely grateful.*
> *Thank you.*

This Say Hello practice just before you go to sleep will help you tremendously during the whole night. The benefits for your soul, heart, mind, and body are beyond words and thoughts.

These are very important practices from awakening until going to sleep. Each practice is very important. Do not ignore them. These practices are very important for healing, prevention of sickness, rejuvenation, and prolonging life, as well as transforming relationships and finances. The more dedicatedly you practice, the better the results you could receive.

How can you practice living with the Dao to heal the physical body, emotional body, mental body, and spiritual body? Practice Dao inside the body in this way:

Practice for Self-healing with the Dao

Body Power. Put one palm or fist over your Ling Gong and continue to do Soul Tapping there.

Sound Power. Sing or chant the words to the Divine Soul Song *Love, Peace and Harmony.*

Mind Power. Visualize golden light cleansing and purifying your Ling Gong.

Soul Power. Invoke all of your Divine Soul Mind Body Transplants to heal you, to prevent sickness, to rejuvenate you, and to prolong your life, as well to transform your relationships, finances, and every aspect of your life.

Let's do an example together that focuses on healing. Put one fist or one palm over your Ling Gong. Say *hello:*

> *Dear soul, mind, and body of my Ling Gong,*
> *I love you.*

You have the power to heal my _____ [name an
   issue or issues for which you wish healing].
I am very grateful.
Dear all my Divine Soul Mind Body Transplants,
I love you.
Turn on, please.
You have the power to heal my _____ [repeat
   the issue or issues].
I am very grateful.

Sound Power. Chant repeatedly as you do Soul Tapping:

Divine Soul Mind Body Transplants heal me.
My Ling Gong heals me.
Thank you, Divine Soul Mind Body Transplants.
Thank you, my Ling Gong.

Continue to chant these four sentences for at least three to
five minutes. The longer you practice and the more times you
practice per day, the better. There are no time limits to practicing
this soul self-healing with the Dao.

*Practice for Balancing and Harmonizing Yin and Yang of the Body
with the Dao*

As I explained earlier in this chapter, yin in the body is the Message Center; yang is the Snow Mountain Area. Do the following
practice to balance and harmonize yin and yang:

Body Power. Put your right palm over your Message Center.
Put your left palm over your Snow Mountain Area.

Soul Power. Say *hello:*

Dear soul, mind, and body of my Message Center and
  my Snow Mountain Area,
I love you, honor you, and appreciate you.
You have the power to balance and harmonize my yin
  and yang.
Dear all my Divine Soul Mind Body Transplants,
I love you, honor you, and appreciate you.
Please turn on.
Please balance and harmonize my yin and yang.
I am very grateful.
Thank you.

Mind Power. Visualize golden light cleansing and purifying your Message Center and Snow Mountain Area.

Sound Power. Chant repeatedly:

My Message Center and my Snow Mountain Area bal-
  ance and harmonize my yin and yang.
Divine Soul Mind Body Transplants balance and har-
  monize my yin and yang.
Thank you all.
Thank you. Thank you. Thank you.

After chanting for at least three minutes, close the practice:

Hao! Hao! Hao!
Thank you. Thank you. Thank you.

The longer and the more often you practice, the better.
All practices can be summarized in one sentence. This one-

sentence secret of soul healing, soul prevention of sickness, soul rejuvenation, soul longevity, and soul transformation practice is:

Request what you need in your life by tapping your Ling Gong or tapping your Message Center and Snow Mountain Area, together with invoking your divine treasures, doing Soul Dance, and singing Soul Song or chanting Soul Language.

For example, if you want to heal your knee, here is a way to do it:

Dear my Ling Gong,
Dear my Message Center and Snow Mountain Area,
Dear my Soul Tapping,
Dear my Soul Song and Soul Dance,
I love you, honor you, and appreciate you.
You have the power to heal my knee.
Do a good job.
Thank you.
Dear all my Divine Soul Mind Body Transplants,
I love you, honor you, and appreciate you.
Turn on, please.
Please heal my knee.
Thank you.

Again, this most important practice is to tap your Ling Gong, Message Center, and Snow Mountain Area and to sing a Soul Song and do Soul Dance together with applying your divine treasures. It will enhance the transformation of every aspect of your life.

This is the sacred divine practice for healing, prevention of sickness, rejuvenation, and longevity, as well as transformation of every aspect of life, including relationships and finances. It may be too simple to believe.

I wish that this new divine wisdom and practice will transform your life.

Remember to practice. Even practicing for one minute, you could receive great results. Better, practice at least three to five minutes per time, three to five times per day. Always remember, the longer you practice, the better.

When you can live fully with the Dao, you are living *in* the Dao. To live in the Dao is to live in the condition of love, peace, and harmony all the time. To live in the Dao, you must practice love, forgiveness, peace, healing, blessing, and harmony all the time.

Practice daily. Make it a habit. The benefits for all aspects of your life are immeasurable.

Hao!

Receive the Divine Soul Mind Body Healing and Transmission System to Heal All Life, Including You, Humanity, Mother Earth, and All Universes

*I*N THIS CHAPTER, it is my honor and privilege to download more Divine Soul Mind Body Transplants to you and every reader of this book to heal all life, including you, humanity, Mother Earth, and all universes. Some of these Divine Soul Downloads have never been given before. To receive these divine treasures, you only need to read and follow the directions on the following pages.

Remember everything I have taught about clearing blockages and receiving new souls. Remember especially my teachings on the importance of practice. By receiving the Divine Soul Mind Body Transplants and following the teachings and practices in this book, you will be empowered to help yourself, all humanity, Mother Earth, and all universes. *All you have to do is practice.*

People often wish they could help others. All of you want this. Many of you want to assist Mother Earth. Some of you are aware of the need to help all universes. By practicing with these Divine Soul Mind Body Transplants, you can do exactly that. It is an honor and privilege to be able to serve in this way. It is an extraordinary opportunity to offer total GOLD universal service.

Your participation through practice is essential for bringing about the healing of any issue that receives Divine Soul Mind Body Transplants.

If you, hundreds of people, thousands of people, and millions of people practice from their hearts and souls, great healing and transformation can occur for each of them, for humanity, Mother Earth, and all universes. Mother Earth is experiencing challenging times. We are in the process of transformation and purification. This process can be softened significantly when enough people commit themselves to doing the practices connected with these Divine Soul Mind Body Transplants.

I cannot thank the Divine enough for my being chosen as a servant, vehicle, and channel to offer these divine treasures to humanity.

Receive Gifts of Divine Soul Mind Body Transplants

Now I am going to offer major Divine Soul Mind Body Transplants to you and every reader.

The sixteenth major treasure offered as a gift in this book is:

Divine Soul Transplant of Divine Golden Light Ball and Golden Liquid Spring of Divine Love

Prepare to receive this priceless divine treasure. Sit up straight. Put the tip of your tongue close to the roof of your mouth without touching. Totally relax. Open your heart and soul to receive one of the greatest honors:

Divine Order: Divine Golden Light Ball and Golden Liquid Spring of Divine Love Soul Transplant Transmission!

Congratulations! You have just received this priceless divine treasure. You are extremely blessed.

This major divine treasure is a divine golden light being that is more than five hundred feet high and more than two hundred feet wide. It will take two to three days to shrink down to its final size to serve you. Its final size will be about three times bigger than your body. If your Third Eye is open, you could see this soul. If you meet an advanced spiritual being with an advanced Third Eye, you could hear this person say, "Wow, you are such a big golden light being!" You will know that this big golden light being is what you just received as a Divine Soul Download.

We are honored beyond words.

Thank you. Thank you. Thank you.

Now prepare to receive the seventeenth Divine Soul Download offered to you as a gift:

Divine Order: Divine Golden Light Ball and Golden Liquid Spring of Divine Love Mind Transplant Transmission!

You have received another priceless divine treasure. You are extremely blessed.

This major divine treasure is approximately the same size as the Soul Transplant. It will also take two to three days to shrink down to its final size, which will also be about three times bigger than your body.

Millions of people worldwide are searching for soul secrets, wisdom, knowledge, and practices. Millions of people want to remove their negative mind-sets, attitudes, and beliefs, as well as ego and attachment. Many books, workshops, and television programs teach humanity how to remove negative mind-sets, attitudes, and beliefs, as well as ego and attachment. All of them are great. I deeply appreciate all teachings and all practices.

The Divine Mind Transplant you just received is a golden light being created by the Divine that carries divine consciousness. This Divine Mind Transplant can remove negative mind-sets, attitudes, and beliefs, as well as ego and attachment. This divine treasure offers you the divine way to remove these mind blockages. The divine way is so simple. The divine way is to receive this Divine Soul Download and then invoke and practice with it. The divine way may be too simple for you to believe. Your negative mind-sets, attitudes, and beliefs, and your ego and attachment, could be removed so fast that you cannot believe it.

Let's do it now. I do not want to wait another minute. I am honored and delighted to lead you in the following practice to help you remove your negative mind-sets, attitudes, beliefs, ego and attachment:

Practice to Remove Negative Mind-sets, Attitudes, and Beliefs, As Well As Ego and Attachment

Sit up straight!

Body Power. Put your right palm over your Message Center. Put your left palm over your heart.

Soul Power. Say *hello:*

> *Dear my Divine Golden Light Ball and Golden*
>   *Liquid Spring of Divine Love Mind Trans-*
>   *plant,*
> *I love you.*
> *You have the power to remove my negative mind-*
>   *sets, attitudes, and beliefs, as well as my ego and*
>   *attachment.*
> *Please turn on.*
> *I am very grateful.*
> *Thank you.*

Sound Power. Then chant repeatedly, silently or aloud:

> *Divine Love Mind Transplant removes my negative*
>   *mind-sets, attitudes, beliefs, ego, and attachment.*
>   *Thank you.*
> *Divine Love Mind Transplant removes my negative*
>   *mind-sets, attitudes, beliefs, ego, and attachment.*
>   *Thank you.*
> *Divine Love Mind Transplant removes my negative*
>   *mind-sets, attitudes, beliefs, ego, and attachment.*
>   *Thank you.*

> *Divine Love Mind Transplant removes my negative*
> *mind-sets, attitudes, beliefs, ego, and attachment.*
> *Thank you.*

The best way to practice is to combine chanting with Soul Tapping. As you chant, tap your heart with your left palm or fingertips, and tap your Message Center with your right palm or fingertips. Do not use your mind. Let your soul guide your tapping. This is Soul Tapping. Doing Soul Tapping and chanting simultaneously could produce benefits faster, because Soul Tapping is an advanced soul healing treasure.[8]

If for some physical reason you cannot do Soul Tapping, that is totally fine. When you are cooking, walking, or doing some other activity, you can simply chant:

> *Divine Love Mind Transplant removes my negative*
> *mind-sets, attitudes, beliefs, ego, and attachment.*
> *Thank you.*
> *Divine Love Mind Transplant removes my negative*
> *mind-sets, attitudes, beliefs, ego, and attachment.*
> *Thank you.*
> *Divine Love Mind Transplant removes my negative*
> *mind-sets, attitudes, beliefs, ego, and attachment.*
> *Thank you.*
> *Divine Love Mind Transplant removes my negative*
> *mind-sets, attitudes, beliefs, ego, and attachment.*
> *Thank you.*

---

8. The first book of my Soul Power Series, *Soul Wisdom: Practical Soul Treasures to Transform Your Life* (2008, New York/Toronto: Atria Books/Heaven's Library) has an entire section on the soul secrets, wisdom, knowledge, and practice of Soul Tapping.

Chanting alone works well. You can always chant silently or aloud. Chanting silently is yin chanting. Chanting aloud is yang chanting. *The key wisdom is that when you invoke and chant, the Divine Love Mind Transplant vibrates and shines.* Divine Mind Transplants carry divine frequency and vibration with divine love, forgiveness, compassion, and light. They can remove negative mind-sets, attitudes, and beliefs, as well as ego and attachment.

Practice three to five minutes per time, three to five times per day. The longer you practice, the better. There is no time limit. The divine treasure is a huge divine golden light being. Every divine golden light being is like a lightbulb in a room. When you enter a dark room, you turn the light switch on. When the switch is on, the light is on. When you go to sleep or leave the room, you turn the switch off and the light is off. To say "Please turn on" is to invoke the divine treasure to vibrate and shine. It is just like the light switch. If you invoke, the divine treasure shines. If you do not invoke, it rests. Like a human being, the divine treasure also needs rest. A good way to close this and every practice with Divine Soul Downloads is to say:

> *Hao! Hao! Hao!*
> *Thank you. Thank you. Thank you.*
> *Dear my divine treasure(s), please rest.*

Now prepare to receive the eighteenth Divine Soul Download offered in this book:

Divine Order: Divine Golden Light Ball and Golden Liquid Spring of Divine Love Body Transplant Transmission!

This is another priceless divine treasure. You are extremely blessed.

This major divine treasure is the same size as the Soul Transplant and Mind Transplant. It will also take two to three days to shrink down to its final size. Its final size will also be the same as the Soul Transplant and the Mind Transplant.

This Divine Body Transplant is another golden light being created by the Divine. It carries divine energy and divine matter. This Divine Body Transplant can boost your energy, stamina, vitality, and immunity. It can also boost your matter.

Everybody wants energy. Everybody wishes for stamina. Everybody enjoys vitality. Everybody desires strong immunity. Here is how to practice with your Divine Love Body Transplant:

Practice to Boost Energy, Stamina, Vitality, and Immunity

Body Power. Put one palm over your Lower Dan Tian, just below your navel. Put your other palm over your Snow Mountain Area, above your tailbone.

The Lower Dan Tian and Snow Mountain Area are the two most important centers for energy, stamina, vitality, and immunity, as well as long life. Building the power of these two energy centers is the key for energy and long life.

Soul Power. Say *hello*:

> *Dear my Divine Golden Light Ball and Golden Liquid Spring of Divine Love Body Transplant,*
> *I love you.*
> *You have the power to boost my energy, stamina, vitality, and immunity.*
> *Please turn on.*

I am very grateful.
Thank you.

Then chant repeatedly, silently or aloud:

Divine Love Body Transplant boosts my energy, stamina, vitality, and immunity, and prolongs my life.
Thank you.
Divine Love Body Transplant boosts my energy, stamina, vitality, and immunity, and prolongs my life.
Thank you.
Divine Love Body Transplant boosts my energy, stamina, vitality, and immunity, and prolongs my life.
Thank you.
Divine Love Body Transplant boosts my energy, stamina, vitality, and immunity, and prolongs my life.
Thank you.

When you chant, it is best to also do Soul Tapping of your Lower Dan Tian and Snow Mountain Area at the same time.

Let us do three minutes of practice together:

Divine Love Body Transplant boosts my energy, stamina, vitality, and immunity, and prolongs my life.
Thank you.
Divine Love Body Transplant boosts my energy, stamina, vitality, and immunity, and prolongs my life.
Thank you.
Divine Love Body Transplant boosts my energy, stamina, vitality, and immunity, and prolongs my life.
Thank you.

Divine Love Body Transplant boosts my energy, stamina, vitality, and immunity, and prolongs my life. Thank you.

Always remember that the longer you practice, the better. I will send another important Divine Order now:

Divine Order: Join Divine Love Soul Mind Body Transplants as one.

Hei Ya Ya You!
Hei Ya Ya You!
Hei Ya Ya You!
Hei Ya Ya You!

Hao! Hao! Hao!
Thank you. Thank you. Thank you.

Hei Ya Ya You is Soul Language to give the Divine Order. It can be translated as follows:

This is a Divine Order to join the Divine Love Soul Transplant, Divine Love Mind Transplant, and Divine Love Body Transplant as one. Join as one now!

This Divine Order enables the Divine Love Soul Mind Body Transplants that you have just received to instantly become one. The power and service of these three golden light beings is concentrated and integrated.

Now I am offering the nineteenth Divine Soul Download to you:

Divine Soul Transplant of Divine Golden Light Ball and Golden Liquid Spring of Divine Forgiveness

Prepare. Sit up straight. Put the tip of your tongue close to the roof of your mouth without touching. Totally relax. Open your heart and soul to receive another one of the Divine's highest treasures:

Divine Order: Divine Golden Light Ball and Golden Liquid Spring of Divine Forgiveness Soul Transplant Transmission!

You are *extremely* blessed.

This major divine treasure is a golden light being more than six hundred feet high and more than three hundred feet wide. It will take two to three days to shrink down to its final size. The final size of this divine soul will be four times bigger than your body. Like all of the Divine Soul Downloads you receive in this book, it is a permanent gift to your soul. It will remain with you for the rest of your life. It will remain with you and your soul for all of your future lives. This honor could be beyond your imagination. We are honored beyond imagination.

Now prepare for the twentieth permanent divine gift and treasure:

Divine Mind Transplant of Divine Golden Light Ball and Golden Liquid Spring of Divine Forgiveness

Sit up straight. Put the tip of your tongue close to the roof of your mouth without touching. Totally relax. Open your heart and soul to receive another of the Divine's highest treasures:

Divine Order: Divine Golden Light Ball and Golden Liquid Spring of Divine Forgiveness Mind Transplant Transmission!

You are extremely blessed.

This divine treasure is the same size as the Divine Forgiveness Soul Transplant. It will also take two to three days to shrink down to size. Its final size will also be the same as the Divine Forgiveness Soul Transplant. We are extremely honored, beyond comprehension.

Now I am offering the twenty-first Divine Soul Download to you:

Divine Body Transplant of Divine Golden Light Ball and Golden Liquid Spring of Divine Forgiveness

Prepare. Sit up straight. Put the tip of your tongue close to the roof of your mouth without touching. Totally relax. Open your heart and soul to receive another of the Divine's highest treasures:

Divine Order: Divine Golden Light Ball and Golden Liquid Spring of Divine Forgiveness Body Transplant Transmission!

This major divine treasure is the same size as the Divine Forgiveness Soul Transplant and Mind Transplant. It will also take two to three days to shrink down to its final size, which will also be four times bigger than your body.

We are extremely blessed.

I will now send a Divine Order to join these Soul Mind Body Transplants as one:

Divine Order: Join Divine Forgiveness Soul Mind Body Transplants as one.

Hei Ya Hei Ya Hei Ya You!
Hei Ya Ya You!
Hei Ya Hei Ya!
You! You! You!

Hao! Hao! Hao!
Thank you. Thank you. Thank you.

This Divine Order has instantly joined your Divine Forgiveness Soul Mind Body Transplants together as one golden light being. Thank you, Divine.

Divine forgiveness brings inner joy and inner peace. Its power is heart-touching. Practice now with me:

Practice to Bring Inner Joy and Inner Peace

Body Power. Put one palm over your heart. Put your other palm over one of your kidneys.

The heart represents fire. The kidneys represent water. To balance the heart and kidneys is to balance fire and water. Fire represents yang and water represents yin. To balance yin and yang is to bring inner joy and inner peace.

Soul Power. Say *hello:*

Dear my Divine Golden Light Ball and Golden Liq-
uid Spring of Divine Forgiveness Soul Mind Body
Transplants,
I love you.
You have the power to bring inner joy and inner peace
to my soul, heart, mind, and body.
Please turn on.
I am very grateful.
Thank you.

Then chant repeatedly, silently or aloud:

Divine Forgiveness Soul Mind Body Transplants bring
me inner joy and inner peace. Thank you.
Divine Forgiveness Soul Mind Body Transplants bring
me inner joy and inner peace. Thank you.
Divine Forgiveness Soul Mind Body Transplants bring
me inner joy and inner peace. Thank you.
Divine Forgiveness Soul Mind Body Transplants bring
me inner joy and inner peace. Thank you.

Practice three to five minutes per time, three to five times per day. The longer and the more often you practice, the better.

I am extremely honored to offer the twenty-second major divine treasure in this book:

Divine Soul Transplant of Divine Golden Light Ball and Golden Liquid Spring of Divine Compassion

Prepare. Sit up straight. Put the tip of your tongue close to the roof of your mouth without touching. Totally relax. Open your heart and soul to receive another one of the Divine's highest treasures:

Divine Order: Divine Golden Light Ball and Golden Liquid Spring of Divine Compassion Soul Transplant Transmission!

You are extremely blessed.

This major divine major treasure is a golden light being that is more than seven hundred feet high and more than four hundred feet wide. It will take two to three days to shrink down to its final size. Its final size will be five times bigger than your body. If your Third Eye is open, you could see this soul. When you meet an advanced spiritual being with an advanced Third Eye, the person could say, "Wow, you have many big golden light beings around you!"

We are *extremely* honored and blessed.

Now, you will receive the twenty-third Divine Soul Download offered as a divine gift in this book:

Divine Mind Transplant of Divine Golden Light Ball and Golden Liquid Spring of Divine Compassion

Prepare. Sit up straight. Put the tip of your tongue close to the roof of your mouth without touching. Totally relax. Open your heart and soul to receive another one of the Divine's highest treasures:

Divine Order: Divine Golden Light Ball and Golden Liquid Spring of Divine Compassion Mind Transplant Transmission!

You are extremely blessed.

This major divine treasure is the same size as the Divine Compassion Soul Transplant. It will also take two to three days to shrink down to its final size, which will also be the same as the Divine Compassion Soul Transplant. We are deeply honored and touched.

Now I am offering the twenty-fourth Divine Soul Download to you:

Divine Body Transplant of Divine Golden Light Ball and Golden Liquid Spring of Divine Compassion

Prepare. Sit up straight. Put the tip of your tongue close to the roof of your mouth without touching. Totally relax. Open your heart and soul to receive another one of the Divine's highest treasures:

Divine Order: Divine Golden Light Ball and Golden Liquid Spring of Divine Compassion Body Transplant Transmission!

You are extremely blessed.

This major divine treasure is the same size as the Divine Compassion Soul Transplant and Mind Transplant. It will also take two to three days to shrink down to its final size. Its final size is also five times bigger than your body. We are extremely blessed.

Let me send the Divine Order to join the last three divine golden light beings you have received as one:

Divine Order: Join Divine Compassion Soul Mind Body Transplants as one.

Hei Ya Ya You!
Hei Ya Ya You!
Hei Ya Ya You!
Hei Ya Ya You!

Hao! Hao! Hao!
Thank you. Thank you. Thank you.

Divine compassion boosts energy, stamina, vitality, and immunity, and prolongs life. Its power is heart-moving. Practice now with me:

Practice to Boost Energy, Stamina, Vitality, and Immunity and to Prolong Life

Body Power. Put one palm over your Lower Dan Tian. Put your other palm over your Snow Mountain Area.
Soul Power. Say *hello*:

> *Dear my Divine Golden Light Ball and Golden Liquid Spring of Divine Compassion Soul Mind Body Transplants,*
> *I love you.*
> *You have the power to boost my energy, stamina, vitality, and immunity, and prolong my life.*
> *Please turn on.*
> *I am very grateful.*
> *Thank you.*

Then chant repeatedly, silently or aloud:

*Divine Compassion Soul Mind Body Transplants boost
my energy, stamina, vitality, and immunity, and
prolong my life. Thank you.*

*Divine Compassion Soul Mind Body Transplants boost
my energy, stamina, vitality, and immunity, and
prolong my life. Thank you.*

*Divine Compassion Soul Mind Body Transplants boost
my energy, stamina, vitality, and immunity, and
prolong my life. Thank you.*

*Divine Compassion Soul Mind Body Transplants boost
my energy, stamina, vitality, and immunity, and
prolong my life. Thank you.*

Practice three to five minutes per time, three to five times per day. The longer and the more often you practice, the better.

A SPECIAL GIFT FOR ALL MOTHERS

At this moment, I am in San Francisco. It is 2:22 AM on May 10, 2009, which is Mother's Day. Happy Mother's Day to every mother in the world!

I am speaking with the Divine.

*Dear Divine, may I request another treasure from you
for all mothers in the whole world? I would like
you to offer Soul Mind Body Transplants of Divine
Golden Light Ball and Golden Liquid Spring of
Divine Mother's Love.*

The Divine replies:

> *Dear my son, I am very moved by your total GOLD*
> *service to humanity and to me. Your total GOLD*
> *has deeply touched my heart and soul. You speak; I*
> *act. You ask; I give.*

The love and generosity that the Divine gives to humanity leaves me speechless. I ask the Divine further:

> *Dear Divine, could you offer this major treasure to all*
> *mothers on Mother Earth now? This book will be*
> *published near the end of this year. Could you offer*
> *this major treasure to all mothers on Mother Earth*
> *now, on Mother's Day?*

The Divine replies:

> *Dear my son, you ask; I give. You can send my Divine*
> *Order now.*

Dear soul, mind, body of all mothers on Mother Earth,
I love you, honor you, and appreciate you.
I am currently with thirty-four people at this moment in the Pavilion Room at the Cathedral Hill Hotel in San Francisco, California.
Nine of them are mothers.
They are witnessing and receiving this major divine treasure. This treasure is not only for them; it is for all mothers on Mother Earth.
It is now 2:36 AM Pacific Daylight Time on May 10, 2009. I am sending a Divine Order now:

Divine Order: Divine Golden Light Ball and Golden Liquid Spring of Divine Mother's Love Soul Transplant to all mothers on Mother Earth Transmission!

Joyce Brown, one of my Worldwide Representatives and a new divine servant, vehicle, and channel, is here with us. I am asking her to share Third Eye images and direct soul communication about this transmission to all mothers in the whole world.

Joyce:

> *The Divine gave to all mothers on Mother Earth a very special gift. From the heart of the Divine came a beautiful golden light. This light came in two ways: as a Golden Light Ball and as a Golden Liquid Spring. They merged together to create a perfect light of love, compassion, and joy. Within this light were the most exquisite flowers. They were shaped like hearts and lotuses. This gift has come to every mother's heart to provide nourishment; to give every mother pure love; to sustain and support every mother through Mother Earth's transition time.*
> *All mothers will receive this as part of the foundation for their Lower Dan Tian, Snow Mountain Area, and Message Center. This treasure will give to them strength, stamina, and vitality, and prolong their lives. It will open their hearts to love and to forgive. It will help rebuild relationships, bringing families back together. It is a gift to help ease the mother's pain from losses; to clear memories and release great sorrow and sadness. It helps to heal their souls,*

minds, and bodies. It is a gift for their souls' journeys
forever.
You are so extremely blessed.
Happy Mother's Day to all mothers everywhere.
I am the Divine.
Thank you. Thank you. Thank you.

Thank you, Joyce, for your divine soul communication. My Worldwide Representatives are also Certified Divine Direct Soul Communicators. They have received training from me. They have practiced direct soul communication with the Divine for years. Now they teach many students worldwide how to open their soul communication channels.

Michael Stevens, another of my Worldwide Representatives and a new divine servant, vehicle, and channel, now shares his spiritual reading about this treasure:

> *When Master Sha gave the Divine Order, a beautiful*
> *golden light came down from Heaven and covered*
> *Mother Earth. It was as if there were a shower of*
> *what looked like hearts. They were rose or pink and*
> *they had faces that were smiling beautifully. They*
> *went to every mother's Message Center and opened*
> *their hearts to allow them to share greater love.*
> *That one blessing did much to improve the general*
> *quality of life on Mother Earth because so much*
> *stems from the love of the mother, especially in the*
> *early years. Notwithstanding the many difficulties*
> *being experienced on Mother Earth at this time,*
> *and which may increase in the next few years, this*
> *blessing will allow mothers to continue to give*

greater love to their children and create a new hu-
manity for tomorrow. We were all very blessed by
that Divine Soul Transplant. Hao!

Thank you, Michael, for your spiritual reading. We are truly blessed. I am so happy for all mothers on Mother Earth who have received this priceless treasure that can transform every aspect of their lives.

At this moment, all of the people in this room are joining me to bow to the floor one thousand times to the Divine to show our greatest gratitude to the Divine.

I understand in my heart how much love the Divine gives to all mothers and to me. There are huge numbers of mothers on Mother Earth. Each and every one of them received this priceless treasure. Each of these Divine Mother's Love Soul Transplants carries a huge amount of virtue.

Virtue is spiritual currency. It is divine flowers. On Mother Earth, money is exchanged. In Heaven, virtue is exchanged. To receive virtue is to receive huge blessings. The Divine Mother's Love Soul Transplant gifted to all mothers has brought countless virtue from the Divine's virtue bank to Mother Earth.

How blessed I am that the Divine responded to my request with unconditional generosity to offer this priceless treasure to all mothers. I am speechless. I have full gratitude in my heart. The Divine's words "You ask; I give" totally touched me and blessed me. How can I honor the Divine enough?

I will make another vow to the Divine. I bow to the floor. This is my vow:

Dear Divine,
My name is Zhi Gang Sha.
I am bowing down to you now.

I am your total GOLD servant.
I am a total GOLD servant of humanity.
I am honored to serve you.
I am honored to serve all humanity and all souls.
My life is yours.
My life belongs to humanity and all souls.
I give my total life for service.
I am extremely honored.

Now I am bowing down one thousand times again to express my total GOLD to the Divine, humanity, and all souls. How can I bow down enough for the virtue that the Divine gave to all mothers through the Divine Soul Transplant of Divine Mother's Love?

In July 2003, I was chosen as a divine servant, vehicle, and channel. I have offered countless Divine Soul Transplants, Divine Mind Transplants, and Divine Body Transplants to humanity. I have no words to express my greatest gratitude to the Divine. All I can do is to give my total life to be a servant.

I am now bowing down another one thousand times for the honor of being chosen as a servant for humanity and the Divine. To be a servant and channel of the Divine means that the Divine has given me the honor to transmit permanent Divine Soul Mind Body Transplants to heal, prevent sickness, rejuvenate, prolong life, and transform every aspect of life, including relationships and finances, for humanity, Mother Earth, and all universes. I cannot bow down enough.

If I were to bow down continuously from now to the end of my physical life, it would not be enough for the honor that the Divine has given to me. I am extremely honored. I am totally humble. I am speechless.

Let me bow down one thousand times more just to show my gratitude to the Divine.

Now I am going to offer the Divine Mind Transplant and Divine Body Transplant of Divine Golden Light Ball and Golden Liquid Spring of Mother's Love to all mothers on Mother Earth:

Divine Order: Divine Golden Light Ball and Golden Liquid Spring of Divine Mother's Love Mind Transplant to all Mothers on Mother Earth Transmission!

Divine Order: Divine Golden Light Ball and Golden Liquid Spring of Divine Mother's Love Body Transplant to all Mothers on Mother Earth Transmission!

Divine Order: Divine Golden Light Ball and Golden Liquid Spring of Divine Mother's Love Soul Mind Body Transplants join as one.

He La La La La Lu!
He La La La La Lu!
He La La La La Lu!
He La La La La Lu!

These Divine Soul Mind Body Transplants of Divine Mother's Love have been transmitted to all mothers on Mother Earth on the spot. Every mother on Mother Earth has received these treasures without being aware of it in their conscious minds, except for the nine mothers present with me now. This is far beyond the

Divine Soul Mind Body Transplants offered to every reader of this book.

Now, the Divine has agreed to give these treasures to you and all readers of this book. If you were a mother at 2:36 AM Pacific Time on May 10, 2009, you have already received the Divine Soul Mind Body Transplants of Divine Mother's Love. You will not receive a second set of them now. However, you will receive a boost.

Other readers, prepare to receive the twenty-fifth, twenty-sixth, and twenty-seventh permanent divine gifts offered in this book. Sit up straight. Put the tip of your tongue close to the roof of your mouth without touching. Totally relax. Open your heart and soul.

Divine Order: Divine Golden Light Ball and Golden Liquid Spring of Divine Mother's Love Soul Transplant Transmission!

Divine Order: Divine Golden Light Ball and Golden Liquid Spring of Divine Mother's Love Mind Transplant Transmission!

Divine Order: Divine Golden Light Ball and Golden Liquid Spring of Divine Mother's Love Body Transplant Transmission!

Divine Order: Divine Golden Light Ball and Golden Liquid Spring of Divine Mother's Love Soul Mind Body Transplants join as one.

Hei Ya Hei Ya You!
Hei Ya You!

Hei Ya You!
Hei! Hei ! Hei!

Thank you, Divine.
We cannot thank you enough.
We are honored and blessed.
We are in awe and speechless at your love and generosity.

RECEIVE ADDITIONAL DIVINE TREASURES AND PRACTICE

Now let me continue to offer permanent divine gifts to you and every reader.

The twenty-eighth Divine Soul Download is:

Divine Soul Transplant of Divine Golden Light Ball and Golden Liquid Spring of Divine Light

Prepare. Sit up straight. Put the tip of your tongue close to the roof of your mouth without touching. Totally relax. Open your heart and soul to receive another one of the Divine's highest treasures in the next twenty seconds:

Divine Order: Divine Golden Light Ball and Golden Liquid Spring of Divine Light Soul Transplant Transmission!

You are extremely blessed.

This permanent divine treasure is more than eight hundred feet high and more than five hundred feet wide. This divine golden light being will shrink over the next two to three days to its final size, which will be six times bigger than your body.

Prepare now to receive the twenty-ninth treasure as a gift from the Divine in this book:

Divine Mind Transplant of Divine Golden Light Ball and Golden Liquid Spring of Divine Light

Sit up straight. Put the tip of your tongue close to the roof of your mouth without touching. Totally relax. Open your heart and soul.

Divine Order: Divine Golden Light Ball and Golden Liquid Spring of Divine Light Mind Transplant Transmission!

You are extremely blessed.

This divine treasure is the same size as the Divine Light Soul Transplant. It will also take two to three days to shrink down to its final size, which will be the same size as the Divine Light Soul Transplant. We are extremely touched and moved.

Next, I will offer the thirtieth Divine Soul Download in this book:

Divine Body Transplant of Divine Golden Light Ball and Golden Liquid Spring of Divine Light

Prepare. Sit up straight. Put the tip of your tongue close to the roof of your mouth without touching. Totally relax. Open your heart and soul to receive another priceless treasure from the Divine:

Divine Order: Divine Golden Light Ball and Golden Liquid Spring of Divine Light Body Transplant Transmission!

You are extremely blessed.

This major divine treasure is the same size as the Divine Light Soul Transplant and Mind Transplant. It will also take two to three days to shrink down to its final size (six times bigger than your body). We are extremely blessed.

I am ready to send the next Divine Order:

Divine Order: Join Divine Golden Light Ball and Golden Liquid Spring of Divine Light Soul Mind Body Transplants as one.

Ya Hei Ya Hei!
Ya Hei Ya Hei!
Ya Hei Ya Hei!
Ya Hei Ya Hei!

Hao! Hao! Hao!
Thank you. Thank you. Thank you.

Divine light heals, prevents sickness, rejuvenates, prolongs life, and transforms every aspect of life, including relationships and finances.

Let us practice right away for healing:

Practice for Soul Self-healing

Body Power. Put one palm over an area of the body for which you need healing. Put your other palm over another area of your body for which you need healing.

Soul Power. Say *hello:*

> *Dear my Divine Golden Light Ball and Golden Liquid Spring of Divine Light Soul Mind Body Transplants,*
> *I love you.*
> *You have the power to heal me.*
> *Please turn on.*
> *I am very grateful.*
> *Thank you.*

Then chant repeatedly, silently or aloud:

> *Divine Light Soul Mind Body Transplants heal me.*
>   *Thank you, Divine.*
> *Divine Light Soul Mind Body Transplants heal me.*
>   *Thank you, Divine.*
> *Divine Light Soul Mind Body Transplants heal me.*
>   *Thank you, Divine.*
> *Divine Light Soul Mind Body Transplants heal me.*
>   *Thank you, Divine.*

Practice three to five minutes per time, three to five times per day. The longer and the more often you practice, the better.

Now let us practice to offer healing to others:

Practice for Soul Healing of Others

Soul Power. Say *hello* to the person to whom you are offering healing:

> *Dear* _____ [name the person],
> *I love you, honor you, and appreciate you.*
> *Could you please come in front of me?*
> *You have the power to heal yourself.*
> *Do a good job.*
> *Thank you.*

If your Third Eye is open, you will see the soul of the person in front of you. If your Third Eye is not open, imagine or visualize that the person is in front of you.

Next, say *hello* to your divine treasures:

> *Dear my Divine Light Soul Mind Body Transplants,*
> *I love you, honor you, and appreciate you.*
> *You have the power to heal* _____ [name the
>   person and make a healing request].
> *Please turn on.*
> *I am very grateful.*
> *Thank you.*

Body Power. Point the fingers of one hand at the soul of the person in front of you. Point at the area for which you are requesting healing. If there is more than one area, point at the person's Message Center.

Mind Power. Visualize divine golden light radiating and vibrating in the person's area of sickness or in the person's whole body, from head to toe, skin to bone.

Sound Power. Chant repeatedly for three to five minutes, silently or aloud:

> *Divine Light Soul Mind Body Transplants heal* _____
> [name the person]. *Thank you.*
> *Divine Light Soul Mind Body Transplants heal* _____
> [name the person]. *Thank you.*
> *Divine Light Soul Mind Body Transplants heal* _____
> [name the person]. *Thank you.*
> *Divine Light Soul Mind Body Transplants heal* _____
> [name the person]. *Thank you.*

Now let us practice for prevention of sickness:

Practice for Prevention of Sickness

Body Power. Put one palm below the navel, over the Lower Dan Tian. Put your other palm over the Message Center.

Soul Power. Say *hello:*

> *Dear my Divine Light Soul Mind Body Transplants,*
> *I love you.*
> *You have the power to prevent sickness.*
> *Please turn on.*
> *I am extremely honored.*
> *Thank you.*

Then chant repeatedly for at least three minutes, silently or aloud:

> *Divine Light Soul Mind Body Transplants prevent*
> *sickness. Thank you, Divine.*
> *Divine Light Soul Mind Body Transplants prevent*
> *sickness. Thank you, Divine.*
> *Divine Light Soul Mind Body Transplants prevent*
> *sickness. Thank you, Divine.*
> *Divine Light Soul Mind Body Transplants prevent*
> *sickness. Thank you, Divine.*

On Mother Earth, new infectious diseases have appeared. People are scared. Pandemics have been declared. More, and more serious ones, could come. This is the way to practice with these divine treasures to prevent contracting an infectious disease. Do it with me now:

> *Divine Light Soul Mind Body Transplants prevent in-*
> *fectious disease. Thank you, Divine.*
> *Divine Light Soul Mind Body Transplants prevent in-*
> *fectious disease. Thank you, Divine.*
> *Divine Light Soul Mind Body Transplants prevent in-*
> *fectious disease. Thank you, Divine.*
> *Divine Light Soul Mind Body Transplants prevent in-*
> *fectious disease. Thank you, Divine.*

Now let me lead you to apply your Divine Light Soul Mind Body Transplants to rejuvenate:

Practice for Rejuvenation

Body Power. Put one palm over your Lower Dan Tian. Put your other palm over the thyroid.

Soul Power. Say *hello:*

> *Dear my Divine Light Soul Mind Body Transplants,*
> *I love you, honor you, and appreciate you.*
> *You have the power to rejuvenate me.*
> *Turn on, please.*
> *I am very grateful.*
> *Thank you.*

Then chant repeatedly for at least three minutes, the longer, the better:

> *Divine Light Soul Mind Body Transplants rejuvenate my soul, heart, mind, and body. Thank you, Divine.*
> *Divine Light Soul Mind Body Transplants rejuvenate my soul, heart, mind, and body. Thank you, Divine.*
> *Divine Light Soul Mind Body Transplants rejuvenate my soul, heart, mind, and body. Thank you, Divine.*
> *Divine Light Soul Mind Body Transplants rejuvenate my soul, heart, mind, and body. Thank you, Divine.*

Now let us practice to prolong our lives by applying the Divine Light Soul Mind Body Transplants:

Practice for Prolonging Life

Body Power. Put one palm over the Lower Dan Tian. Put your other palm over the Ling Gong. [Recall that the *Ling Gong* is the soul temple in your body. "Ling" means *soul*. "Gong" means *temple*. The Ling Gong is located between the Message Center and heart.]

Soul Power. Say *hello:*

> *Dear soul, mind, and body of my Divine Light Soul*
>   *Mind Body Transplants,*
> *I love you, honor you, and appreciate you.*
> *Please turn on to prolong my life.*
> *I am very grateful.*
> *Thank you.*

Sound Power. Chant repeatedly:

> *Divine Light Soul Mind Body Transplants prolong my*
>   *life. Thank you, Divine.*
> *Divine Light Soul Mind Body Transplants prolong my*
>   *life. Thank you, Divine.*
> *Divine Light Soul Mind Body Transplants prolong my*
>   *life. Thank you, Divine.*
> *Divine Light Soul Mind Body Transplants prolong my*
>   *life. Thank you, Divine.*

Practice three to five minutes per time, three to five times per day. The longer and the more often you practice, the better.

Now, let me lead you in a practice to transform relationships by applying the Divine Light Soul Mind Body Transplants:

Practice for Transforming Relationships

Body Power. Put one palm over your Message Center. Put your other palm over a kidney.

Soul Power. Say *hello:*

> *Dear soul, mind, and body of my Divine Light Soul*
>   *Mind Body Transplants,*
> *I love you, honor you, and appreciate you.*
> *You have the power to transform the relationship*
>   *between me and* [person's name].
> *Please turn on.*
> *I am very grateful.*
> *Thank you.*

Chant silently or aloud for at least three minutes:

> *Divine Light Soul Mind Body Transplants transform*
>   *the relationship between* [give the other person's
>   name] *and me. Thank you, Divine.*
> *Divine Light Soul Mind Body Transplants transform*
>   *the relationship between* [give the other person's
>   name] *and me. Thank you, Divine.*
> *Divine Light Soul Mind Body Transplants transform*
>   *the relationship between* [give the other person's
>   name] *and me. Thank you, Divine.*
> *Divine Light Soul Mind Body Transplants transform*
>   *the relationship between* [give the other person's
>   name] *and me. Thank you, Divine.*

Your priceless divine treasures can be applied to transform your finances. Here is how to do it:

Practice for Transforming Finances

Body Power. Put one palm over the Message Center. Put the other palm above the crown chakra at the top of your head.

Soul Power. Say *hello:*

> *Dear my Divine Light Soul Mind Body Transplants,*
> *I love you, honor you, and appreciate you.*
> *You have the power to transform my finances.*
> *Please turn on.*
> *I am very grateful.*
> *Thank you, Divine.*

Chant repeatedly, silently or aloud:

> *Divine Light Soul Mind Body Transplants transform*
>   *my finances. Thank you, Divine.*
> *Divine Light Soul Mind Body Transplants transform*
>   *my finances. Thank you, Divine.*
> *Divine Light Soul Mind Body Transplants transform*
>   *my finances. Thank you, Divine.*
> *Divine Light Soul Mind Body Transplants transform*
>   *my finances. Thank you, Divine.*

Practice as much as you can. The more, the better.

We are so blessed.

You have now received thirty Divine Soul Mind Body Transplants in this book, including Soul Mind Body Transplants of

Divine Love, Divine Forgiveness, Divine Compassion, Divine Light, and Divine Mother's Love.

These priceless Divine Soul Mind Body Transplants give you the divine way to heal and transform every aspect of your life.

Each treasure is beyond words, thoughts, comprehension, and explanation.

Practice more and more.

Receive the benefits more and more.

Heal you, your loved ones, humanity, and all universes.

Prevent sickness for you, your loved ones, humanity, and all universes.

Rejuvenate you, your loved ones, humanity, and all universes.

Prolong life for you, your loved ones, humanity, and all universes.

Transform relationships for you, your loved ones, humanity, and all universes.

Transform finances for you, your loved ones, humanity, and all universes.

Transform every aspect of life for you, your loved ones, humanity, and all universes.

We are extremely honored and blessed to receive these totally heart-touching and moving Divine Soul Mind Body Transplants.

We cannot thank the Divine enough.

Hao! Hao! Hao!

Thank you. Thank you. Thank you.

How to Receive Customized Divine Soul Mind Body Transplants for Yourself and Your Loved Ones

If you suffer from any unhealthy condition in your physical, mental, emotional, or spiritual body, you can receive customized Divine Soul Mind Body Transplants for that condition. You can do this in two ways.

One is to visit a Divine Channel at a Love Peace Harmony Center or a Soul Healing Center to receive Divine Soul Mind Body Transplants in a physical place. You can also find Divine Channels on my website, www.drsha.com, and make an appointment to receive Divine Soul Mind Body Transplants from them. Because the transmissions are at the soul level, you can receive them remotely, just as you have received them by reading this book. There is no time, no space for Divine Soul Downloads.

The other way is to receive Divine Soul Mind Body Transplants is in my Sunday Divine Blessings teleconference. Every Sunday, fifty-two weeks a year, I hold this teleconference from 5:00–7:00 PM Pacific Time. During this regular session, I offer Divine Soul Mind Body Transplants. You can register in advance on my website to receive Divine Soul Mind Body Transplants for your systems, organs, cells, cell units, DNA, RNA, smallest matter inside the cells, and spaces between the cells; or for a specific condition; as well as for your relationships, business, finances, and more. If you can be present during the teleconference when I transmit the divine treasures, that is wonderful. Even if you are not present during the teleconference, your soul will still receive the divine treasures as long as you are properly registered.

I have offered hundreds of thousands of Divine Soul Mind Body Transplants to humanity. This divine service is continuous.

Now twelve new Divine Channels can offer Divine Soul Mind Body Transplants for your requests worldwide. I am so happy that these Divine Channels, who have received the divine honor and authority to offer Divine Soul Mind Body Transplants, are available to serve humanity. We are extremely blessed.

Summary

I have taught that the Divine Soul Mind Body Healing and Transmission System has three steps to deal with a sickness, unhealthy condition, or unbalanced situation in a divine way. For example, if a person has breast cancer, the following steps will occur.

Step 1. The Divine will remove the person's soul, mind, and body blockages related to the breast cancer. The person could have major soul blockages, which are bad karma. Bad karma could include personal karma, ancestral karma, and relationship karma. Other issues that could be closely related with karma are curses and negative memories. Each of these five types of blockages could be the root cause of the breast cancer. The Divine will send a Divine Order to clear the bad karma, curses, and negative memories related to the breast cancer.

The Divine has told me that Divine Orders can be sent only by those chosen by the Divine to be given this honor and authority. You and every reader must remember that you *cannot* send a Divine Order. As I write this, there are now twelve Divine Channels on Mother Earth who have been given the divine honor and authority to send a Divine Order to clear soul, mind, and body blockages for a person. You can learn more about them on my website, www.drsha.com. They can serve you in the divine way I am teaching in this book. They can serve you with the Divine Soul Mind Body Healing and Transmission System, the divine way to heal you, humanity, Mother Earth, and all universes.

I was honored to be chosen as a divine servant, vehicle, and channel in July 2003. I have trained and certified twelve new divine servants, vehicles, and channels for the Divine. I am training and will certify many more. If you are not formally given the divine honor and authority, please do *not* try to send a Divine Order. *That is not allowed* and, according to spiritual law, it could cause serious difficulties for you.

The same is true for karma cleansing. If you are not given the honor and authority by the Divine to cleanse karma and yet you try to clear someone's karma, the results could be very serious for you. If, for example, the person has a life-threatening condition with one or two years of physical life left, that condition could be given to you. You will carry the spiritual debt, or bad karma, of that person. You could learn the lessons that were meant for that person. If you want to try cleansing karma, the consequences can be very serious like this. You may not believe me. That is fine. I am simply sharing what the Divine has told me through direct soul communication. This is a most serious spiritual law.

I am not the Divine. I am the chosen divine servant, vehicle, and channel to offer Divine Orders, to offer Divine Karma Cleansing, and to offer Divine Soul Mind Body Transplants to serve humanity and all souls. I was given a formal order from the Divine to do all of this. The twelve Divine Channels who are my Certified Worldwide Representatives have also received a formal Divine Order to offer divine treasures for humanity. Thank you, Divine, for choosing these Divine Channels to offer the Divine Soul Mind Body and Healing Transmission System. They are the ones to offer divine treasures. This is **Step 2** of the Divine Soul

Mind Body Healing and Transmission System: Receive Divine Soul Mind Body Transplants.

In step 2, a person with breast cancer will receive the Divine Soul Mind Body Transplants that are appropriate for her condition. She could receive these Divine Soul Downloads for her breasts and for her breast cells, breast cell units, breast DNA and RNA, smallest matter in the breasts, and spaces between the breast cells. She could receive them for her lymphatic system. If, for example, the breast cancer has started to spread to her lungs— even if it is not yet detectable by conventional medicine—she could receive Divine Soul Mind Body Transplants for her lungs. If she has curses or negative memories related to her breast cancer, they will be removed. What she receives will be customized for her. She could receive five, ten, or more Divine Soul Downloads. Each person who has breast cancer is unique. What each person receives from the Divine Soul Mind Body Healing and Transmission System could be unique.

More than forty divine treasures are preprogrammed in this book as divine gifts for you and every reader. You are extremely blessed to receive these permanent divine souls. You will be much more blessed when you apply (which means invoke and practice with) these divine treasures to heal, rejuvenate, and transform you and your loved ones. The benefits are beyond any words, thoughts, and comprehension. We are extremely honored to receive the Divine's unconditional generosity. Pause for a moment to think about it: the Divine preprogrammed more than forty major Divine Soul Mind Body Transplants within this book to bless every reader. How generous the Divine is! There are no words to describe this book's value from these Divine Soul Downloads.

The permanent divine treasures given to you from these

pages give you the divine way to heal, rejuvenate, and transform you and your loved ones. There is only one requirement: you have to open the book and read the appropriate paragraphs to receive the divine treasures. If you do not read the paragraph, you will not receive the divine treasure. After receiving the treasures, remember to practice. This is **Step 3** of healing and rejuvenating the divine way.

To receive Divine Soul Mind Body Transplants does not mean that you are recovered. It only means that you have received divine treasures. Remember, they are light beings. Like a lightbulb in a room, you have to turn them on. You have to practice with the divine treasures by turning them on and chanting; otherwise the divine treasures are resting. When turned on, the divine treasures shine, and all kinds of blockages could be removed. Life-threatening and chronic conditions could have hope of recovery. They could recover very fast.

How do you practice? It is not difficult at all. I have led you in many examples. Here is the essence of an example for a person with breast cancer:

> *Dear my beloved Divine Soul Mind Body Transplants*
>   or simply
> *Dear my divine treasures,*
> *I love you, honor you, and appreciate you.*
> *Please turn on.*
> *Please heal my breast cancer.*
> *I am very grateful.*
> *Thank you.*

Then chant repeatedly:

Divine treasures heal my breast cancer. Thank you,
    Divine.
Divine treasures heal my breast cancer. Thank you,
    Divine.
Divine treasures heal my breast cancer. Thank you,
    Divine.
Divine treasures heal my breast cancer. Thank you,
    Divine.

Practice for three to five minutes per time, several times a day. There is no time limit. **For serious, chronic, and life-threatening conditions, such as breast cancer, practice for a total of two hours or more per day.** The more you practice and the longer you practice, the better.

When you are done with your practice session, close like this:

Hao. Hao. Hao.
Thank you. Thank you. Thank you.
Dear my divine treasures, please rest.
I am very grateful.

Since July 2003, Divine Soul Downloads have created thousands of heart-touching and moving stories. In Mother Earth's language they are called miracle stories. Examples include Lothar's story of healing of pancreatic cancer, healing of liver cancer, lymphatic cancer, lung cancer, breast cancer, bone cancer, serious arthritis where the person needed a knee transplant, kidney failure, stroke, heart attack, uncontrollable bleeding in a lung, genetic sickness in newborn twins who were given little chance of survival, many slipped disks, depression with suicidal thoughts, schizophrenia, and many more. These moving and heart-touching stories have proven the effectiveness of the Divine Soul Mind Body Healing and Transmission System.

Because the Divine Soul Mind Body Transplants are extremely powerful and many peoples' hearts have been deeply touched by their results, the Divine guided me to release this book at this time. In the last few years, my divine healing service has demonstrated the divine way to heal. This book is being released now to spread divine healing to humanity. I am extremely honored.

The Divine made it happen. The Divine has offered divine treasures since July 2003. The Divine offers more and more divine treasures. More Divine Channels have been produced. More Divine Channels are on the way. How blessed humanity is that the Divine chose servants and channels to offer divine treasures, such as Divine Soul Mind Body Transplants, to heal you, your loved ones, and humanity. We are honored beyond any words. We are humbled. We are blessed. Thank you, Divine.

I have offered Divine Soul Transplants for more than six years. Now I continually offer Divine Soul Transplants, Divine Mind Transplants, and Divine Body Transplants. Now twelve Divine Channels are offering Divine Soul Mind Body Transplants for your needs and for the needs of your loved ones. You could have challenges with your physical body, emotional body, mental body, or spiritual body. Divine Channels offer the Divine Soul Mind Body Healing and Transmission System to humanity to transform health challenges and more.

You have experienced many practices in this book. The steps are easy to follow. They can be summarized as follows:

Body Power. Place one palm or fist on your Message Center.

Place the other palm or fist on your lower back. Tap these areas constantly as you chant during your practice.

Soul Power. Say *hello:*

> *Dear soul, mind, and body of my Message Center,*
> *Dear soul, mind, and body of my Snow Mountain*
> *Area,*
> *I love you, honor you, and appreciate you.*
> *You have the power to heal and rejuvenate me.*
> *I am very grateful.*
> *Dear my Divine Soul Mind Body Transplants,*
> *I love you, honor you, and appreciate you.*
> *Please turn on to heal me and rejuvenate me.*
> *I am extremely grateful and honored.*
> *Thank you.*

Mind Power. Visualize divine golden light or divine rainbow light radiating in your Message Center, your Snow Mountain Area, and any part of your body where you need healing or want rejuvenation.

Sound Power. Chant repeatedly:

> *Divine Soul Mind Body Treasures heal and rejuvenate*
> *me. Thank you, Divine.*
> *Divine Soul Mind Body Treasures heal and rejuvenate*
> *me. Thank you, Divine.*
> *Divine Soul Mind Body Treasures heal and rejuvenate*
> *me. Thank you, Divine.*
> *Divine Soul Mind Body Treasures heal and rejuvenate*
> *me. Thank you, Divine.*

Alternatively, you can visualize divine golden light and divine rainbow light radiating and vibrating from head to toe, skin to bone. In this way, you will not miss any area that needs healing. You will also receive prevention of sickness for your entire body. If your Third Eye is not open, you cannot see dark areas in your body. You do not know whether the souls of any of your systems or organs are sick. When you visualize divine light in your entire body, Divine Soul Mind Body Transplants will transform the soul's condition to prevent sickness.

I shared the soul secret with humanity in my book *The Power of Soul*. When a person gets sick, the soul gets sick first. Before conventional medicine can diagnose you with a liver sickness, the soul of liver changes first. How? The color of the soul changes. A healthy soul of the liver is a bright golden light being. The soul of an unhealthy liver turns gray or dark. The size of the soul also changes when your liver is sick. It shrinks. It can look tired. After seeing this condition in many cases, I realized this secret, which I released to humanity:

When a person becomes sick, the soul became sick first.

Based on this finding, I released the one-sentence soul healing secret:

**Heal the soul first; then healing of the
mind and body will follow.**

The Divine Soul Mind Body Healing and Transmission System is more than "healing the soul first." This system goes one step further and literally offers Divine Soul Mind Body Transplants to change the original soul, mind, and body of the system, organ, or part of the body that is unhealthy.

A Soul Transplant changes the soul. A Mind Transplant changes the consciousness. A Body Transplant changes the energy and tiny matter. This Divine Soul Mind Body Healing and Transmission System can be summarized in one sentence. (I started to give one-sentence secrets in *The Power of Soul*. People are searching for wisdom, techniques, and solutions. People could read hundreds of books and still not figure out the essence of the teachings. From what and how the Divine and my spiritual fathers and mothers have taught me, plus my insights from "Aha!" moments, I have figured out one-sentence secrets.) I share this one-sentence secret with every reader. I hope this wisdom will serve you well. I am honored to be a servant to you, humanity, and the Divine.

This is the one-sentence secret for this whole book:

Remove soul, mind, and body blockages;
receive Divine Soul Mind Body Transplants;
and apply these transplants to heal you, humanity,
Mother Earth, and all universes.

A simpler way to state the essence is:

Receive Divine Transplants of Soul Mind Body first;
then all layers of healing will follow.

The Divine Soul Mind Body Healing and Transmission System is the divine way to heal you, humanity, Mother Earth, and all universes. This divine way has never happened before in history. This divine way is very clear. The Divine gives the authority and honor to chosen ones to offer divine healing.

How blessed we and all humanity are that the Divine is formally offering healing to us. Pause a moment and think about what kind of honor—and what kind of opportunity—humanity has at this moment.

We are extremely blessed and honored.

Thank you, Divine.

Thank you is not enough to express our greatest gratitude to the Divine for offering a divine healing and transmission system to humanity through chosen servants, vehicles, and channels.

Thank you. Thank you. Thank you.

Purify Your Soul, Heart, Mind, and Body to Receive Divine Treasures for Healing and Transforming Every Aspect of Your Life

ON THE SPIRITUAL journey, a spiritual being wants to transform him- or herself. There could be many issues that need transformation. For example, some people want to open their hearts because they feel their hearts are closed. Some people wish to heal their anger and learn to forgive. Some people have jealousy issues and can never find inner peace and inner joy. Some people have relationship blockages and cannot find a true love. Some people have extreme financial difficulties. Spiritual beings search for ways to transform these issues. They want to be free to move forward on their spiritual journeys.

Throughout history, there have been many teachings about transformation. Spiritual beings worldwide practice countless techniques for transformation. All of these teachings and practices are important. I honor every teacher, every teaching, and every practice. I am honored to share my insights on how to transform every aspect of your life.

The one-sentence secret for transforming your life is:

Purification is the key for transforming every aspect of life, including health, relationships, and finances.

Purification is key when you have a chronic or life-threatening condition such as arthritis or cancer; emotional imbalances such as depression, anger, or fear; mental blockages such as confusion or mental disorders; relationship blockages; financial blockages; or spiritual blockages, such as lack of direction on the spiritual journey.

All blockages, including those in health, relationships, and finances, can be removed through the purification process. If your life blockages are removed, your life is transformed. Purification is vital to transform every aspect of life. Divine Soul Mind Body Transplants can give you divine assistance for purification of your soul, heart, mind, and body.

Clean the Room to Welcome the Special Guest

You would not bring a special guest to your home without some preparation, would you? If your home is cluttered and disordered, you would clean and put things away. If the guest is going to stay for several days, your preparation is even greater. You do this to show honor and respect to your guest. You want to let the guest know how welcome he or she is.

A spiritual being wants to do something similar to receive a special guest from the Divine. Divine Soul Mind Body Transplants are special guests from the Divine. Clean the room to receive them. Remove blockages on the levels of soul, heart, mind, and body. When you remove these blockages, the guests know that they are respected, welcomed, and treasured.

Every aspect of our being can be purified. Removing the soul, mind, and body blockages begins the process of purification in a very special way. The purification process is never totally complete. It is ongoing. Issues that need to be transformed may continue to manifest. As soon as you think, "I have purified this issue," you know the issue is far from being purified. It will move to a deeper level, and its manifestation could be more subtle. For example, negative mind-sets, attitudes, and beliefs, as well as ego and attachment have usually been present for a long time. If you think you have dealt completely with one of these issues, you will be surprised by its manifestation. You may even be discouraged, thinking, "I have already dealt with this issue so many times." It is true you have dealt with the issue, but just as weeds in a garden have very deep roots, issues that need purification go very deep. Transforming them takes time, blessings, chanting, and practices. I will lead you in purification practices now:

Practices for Purification

Soul Power. Say *hello:*

> *Dear soul, mind, and body of* [name your issue],
> *I love you.*

You have the power to transform.
Do a good job.
Thank you.

Sound Power. Chant your Soul Language or sing a Divine Soul Song or your own Soul Song for at least three minutes, the longer, the better. Practice at least three times per day, the more, the better.

Another practice is to call on your divine treasures:
Soul Power. Say *hello:*

Dear my divine treasures,
I love you, honor you, and appreciate you.
Please transform my [name your concern; I will use
    anger as an example].
I am very grateful.
Thank you.

Sound Power. Chant repeatedly, silently or aloud:

Divine treasures transform my anger. Thank you,
    Divine.
Divine treasures transform my anger. Thank you,
    Divine.
Divine treasures transform my anger. Thank you,
    Divine.
Divine treasures transform my anger. Thank you,
    Divine.

Continue chanting for three to five minutes. Do this three to five times per day, the longer and the more often, the better.

You can also chant:

Divine treasures purify my anger. Thank you, Divine.
Divine treasures purify my anger. Thank you, Divine.
Divine treasures purify my anger. Thank you, Divine.
Divine treasures purify my anger. Thank you, Divine.

Since anger is connected with the liver, you can also chant:

Divine treasures heal my liver. Thank you, Divine.
Divine treasures heal my liver. Thank you, Divine.
Divine treasures heal my liver. Thank you, Divine.
Divine treasures heal my liver. Thank you, Divine.

Hao! Hao! Hao!
Thank you. Thank you. Thank you.

I have given you several examples of how you can purify a particular issue, in this case, anger. You can adapt these practices for any issue that needs purification.

It is a good idea to vary your practices. One day, use one practice. The next day, use a different practice. Varying your practice is divine flexibility in action. There is no single right way to practice. The only guideline regarding practice is that you *must* practice.

Where you practice, when you practice, how long you practice, and the way you practice are all flexible. They can change from day to day. They can change within the same day. Flexibility is essential. It is a key practice for purification. Think about it. The times when you have needed to be very flexible are prob-

ably times when you have experienced great purification. This is
no coincidence.

There are countless opportunities throughout the day to
apply the practices I have suggested. Practice can remove barriers
to divine light. The more you practice, the more you benefit. You
can accelerate the purification process tremendously.

To assist you in being more flexible, you can practice like
this:

Practice for Flexibility

Soul Power. Say *hello:*

> *Dear my divine treasures,*
> *I love you, honor you, and appreciate you.*
> *Please purify my lack of flexibility.*
> *Thank you.*

Sound Power. Chant repeatedly for at least three minutes:

> *My divine treasures purify my lack of flexibility.*
>   *Thank you, Divine.*
> *My divine treasures purify my lack of flexibility.*
>   *Thank you, Divine.*
> *My divine treasures purify my lack of flexibility.*
>   *Thank you, Divine.*
> *My divine treasures purify my lack of flexibility.*
>   *Thank you, Divine.*

If you are brave, you will use this practice often. It could accelerate your purification process beyond your imagination.

Think about what you are asking, which is why I said "If you are brave." The Soul World will respond to your request. Your lack of flexibility will be tested and purified in every aspect of life. You will be very blessed. Your soul standing will be uplifted. Your soul journey will accelerate.

It is not a great risk to use this practice. Know that there are teams of saints to assist you. Know that the Divine will never give you more purification than you can handle. Know that whatever tests you are given, you also receive ten, twenty, one hundred, perhaps even one thousand times more blessings to make it possible for you to pass through the purification. The Divine always blesses us more than we need.

All of the practices in this chapter are ways to continue the process of "cleaning the room in order to welcome the special guest."

Love and Forgiveness Are the Keys for Purification

Any sickness or unhealthy condition, whether it is in your physical body, emotional body, mental body, or spiritual body, is due to soul, mind, and body blockages. Applying love and forgiveness can remove all blockages. Love and forgiveness are the keys for purification.

LOVE

Love removes all blockages and transforms all life. You can apply divine love to melt any blockage. This is the way to practice. I am releasing one of the simplest ways for healing all sickness.

Practice for Self-healing All Sicknesses

Body Power. Put one palm on the area of the sickness or the unhealthy condition. Do gentle Soul Tapping there continuously during the practice. Give your total love to that area.

Soul Power. Say *hello:*

> *Dear divine love,*
> *I cannot honor you enough.*
> *Please heal my _____ [name the condition].*
> *I am very grateful.*
> *Thank you.*

Mind Power. Visualize divine love as golden or rainbow light removing all blockages in the unhealthy area.

Sound Power. Chant repeatedly, silently or aloud:

> *Divine love heals me. Thank you.*
> *Divine love heals me. Thank you.*
> *Divine love heals me. Thank you.*
> *Divine love heals me. Thank you.*

Chant for three to five minutes per time, three to five times per day. The longer you chant, the better.

Words are limited to describe the power of divine love. The Divine is the creator, the source. Divine love can melt all blockages and transform every aspect of life.

You may do this practice diligently, chanting *divine love* five times a day for a week, and still not notice any improvement in your health issues, relationship blockages, or financial blockages. You may think that this practice does not work. It is important to understand that your health challenges, relationship challenges, and financial challenges are due to soul, mind, and body blockages. All kinds of blockages in life are due to soul, mind, and body blockages. It takes time to remove soul, mind, and body blockages. You must be persistent, patient, and confident.

For example, if you killed, hurt, or cheated many people in a past life, you could have accumulated heavy bad karma. You could chant *divine love* for two hours every day for a month. You could even chant for a few days straight. If you have heavy karma, it will not be enough. People do not realize that one has to chant *divine love* a lot to remove one's soul, mind, and body blockages. It could take you five hundred hours or more to see significant changes. Not many people have the patience to chant for five hundred hours. Therefore, many people stop practicing before they receive significant benefits, because they feel the practice does not work. I will tell you very directly: it works beyond your comprehension.

If you trust divine love and practice seriously, you will see results more quickly. Many people chant *divine love* three to five minutes per time a few times per day, as I suggested above, and they do feel better. We are in a special time. Mother Earth is in transition. In this transition, Mother Earth is facing major challenges, including natural disasters, conflicts between nations and religions, economic challenges, sicknesses, and more. Many people are depressed, anxious, fearful, and upset. Divine love will show its divine power to help humanity. Therefore, at this historic period, chanting *divine love* could produce results in a short time. I reveal this simple technique to assist humanity in Mother Earth's transition time. Pay attention to it, even if it may be too simple to believe.

People may think: *If this works, why do I need to study to be a healer or a healthcare professional?* Studying to be a healer or a healthcare professional is very important. The wisdom and techniques that you learn can really help humanity. I honor all healers and all healthcare professionals. At the same time I also share with and ask humanity to *trust divine love.* Simple chanting works because divine love has power beyond words, thoughts, and comprehension.

I always say, *if you want to know if a pear is sweet, taste it.* If you want to know if chanting *divine love* is powerful, experience it.

If chanting *divine love* works for you right away, congratulations! If you see no improvement, it does not mean that it does not work. Trusting divine love is very important. You may experience significant results after you practice a little more. Trust, practice, confidence, and persistence are very important for spiritual healing. I wish you will really understand this simple teaching of chanting *divine love* consistently to self-heal your chronic and life-threatening conditions.

If you really understand my teaching here, I congratulate you from the bottom of my heart. Why do I congratulate you? Because you understand that the best technique is the simplest technique. True power is within the simplest technique. My wish is that you will really understand it.

Love melts all blockages. I have said this many times in connection with physical healing. What love can do on the physical level, it can do on every other level—emotional, mental, and spiritual. Unconditional love is one of the keys to the purification process. It opens the door to forgiveness, compassion, kindness, peace, and harmony. It opens the door to service. It opens the door to the Divine. It opens the door to staying in the condition throughout your day.

When I talk about *staying in the condition*, I mean that you *are* divine presence. You *are* the presence of a particular highest saint. You *are* the presence of a particular mantra. You *are* the presence of unconditional love. You *are* the presence of divine love.

Love melts all blockages. This means that anything that is an obstacle to your journey can be removed. This means you can see the final goal of your journey. You are not stopped by small problems along the way. You can see the big picture.

When you focus on the goal or the big picture, things that seem very big at the moment are seen in their proper size. Many people ask themselves: *How important will this be in one hundred years?* For most issues, you can honestly say it will not be important at all. You do not even have to think in terms of one hundred years. Often, you can think in terms of one hundred days. In some cases, you can ask: *How important will this be in one hundred hours?* This helps to keep things in perspective.

You get my point. Unconditional love is very gentle. It is also very strong. It has a yin aspect. It also has a yang aspect. Both are needed for purification.

Let me lead you to practice *going into the condition* so you can experience *being* divine love.

Practice to Go into the Condition of Divine Love

Find a quiet space. Turn off your phone and other potential distractions and interruptions. You can sit on a chair. Make sure your feet are flat on the floor. Keep your back straight and not touching the chair. You can also sit on the floor in a full lotus, half-lotus, or with simply crossed legs.

Body Power. Put your left palm over your heart and your

right palm over your Message Center. Do Soul Tapping of those two areas continuously during this practice.

Soul Power. Say *hello*:

Dear divine love,
I love you, honor you, and appreciate you.
Please sit inside my Message Center and my heart.
Thank you.

You are inviting the soul of divine love to sit inside your Message Center and your heart.

Sound Power. Chant repeatedly, silently or aloud:

Divine love
Divine love
Divine love
Divine love

Chant *divine love*. *Be* divine love. Keep your focus on your Message Center. If this mantra becomes a song, that is fine. Otherwise, simply chant *divine love*.

Do this practice for at least five minutes. It would be much better to practice for twenty minutes if possible.

When you have experienced *being* divine love, you have gone into the condition. You may notice a shift occurring. Allow the peace, the emptiness, the images, the messages to present themselves and flow. In the condition, you will experience purification.

You could be amazed and delighted by this simple practice. The more you do this practice, the more your day will become filled with times when you are in the condition. Eventually, your entire day will be lived in the condition of divine love. This is a blessing beyond words.

FORGIVENESS

In addition to love, forgiveness is another key to purification and healing. Forgiveness and love are two sides of the same key. You cannot have unconditional love without unconditional forgiveness. You cannot have unconditional forgiveness without unconditional love. Forgiveness brings inner joy and inner peace. Many sicknesses, relationship blockages, financial challenges, and other challenges in life are due to a lack of forgiveness.

Let me give you an example. Say a husband and wife or a girlfriend and boyfriend are upset with each other about something. If the man blames the woman, the woman often fights back. They say unpleasant things to each other. The fighting gets stronger. It seems impossible to find a solution. The conflict could escalate quickly.

If the woman tells the man: *Something is wrong with you,* the man should really think about it and check himself from the bottom of his heart. If he realizes that he really did something wrong, he should apologize sincerely and ask to be forgiven. If he knows that he did nothing wrong, he should tell his partner: *Please calm down.* Sometimes there is misunderstanding or miscommunication. If one side is very upset, which is yang, the other side should be calm, or yin. Yin and yang are easy to balance. If both sides took the yang approach, they would bump into each other, making it very hard to be balanced.

To forgive someone is like erasing a whiteboard. The board may be filled with many unpleasant actions, behaviors, words, and thoughts. When you forgive unconditionally, you are erasing the whiteboard. This removes heavy burdens from the other person. Think about a time when you made a mistake and you were forgiven. Maybe you did something wrong as a child. When your mother forgave you with her unconditional mother's love, didn't you feel great relief? When you forgive someone, you give that person this gift and blessing. You also receive a great gift and blessing. You may have been really bothered by the other person's actions or words. You may have had angry thoughts every day about revenge. When you erase the whiteboard, you are erasing this burden for yourself also.

Forgiveness is very important for purification. It is very important for your physical journey and your spiritual journey.

If everyone forgave themselves, many health, relationship, and financial issues would be solved.

If everyone forgave each other—spouse, boyfriend, girlfriend, colleague, boss, friend, and all kinds of relationships—there would be no fighting.

If everyone applied forgiveness in the work environment, there would be harmony in the work environment.

If forgiveness was applied between nations, there would be no fighting and no war. World peace could come much faster.

In chapter 5 of *Soul Mind Body Medicine,* I taught a Universal Meditation practice for cleansing karma by giving forgiveness and receiving forgiveness. This practice is very powerful and life-transforming. Let me give you an example:

One of the Divine Healers I trained had a client whose husband left her after twenty years. It was a big shock to her. She had all kinds of emotions, including intense anger. When she was very angry, she had a physical response. Her eyes became very swollen—almost completely closed. Her entire face became swollen. This made her very scared.

She came to my Divine Healer for a soul healing blessing and learned some Soul Mind Body Medicine self-healing techniques for healing and balancing her anger. My Divine Healer also taught her the Universal Meditation for forgiveness.

The client did the practice faithfully. Her co-workers asked her one day what she had been doing because she was so peaceful and calm. They saw a dramatic transformation and had received the benefit of her deep peace and inner joy. They assumed she had been receiving some kind of therapy. It never occurred to them that she was simply practicing forgiveness.

This is just one example of how powerful and life-transforming forgiveness is. There are countless stories. Many books could be written about the power of forgiveness.

Practice to Go into the Condition of Divine Forgiveness

Body Power. Put your left palm over your heart and your right palm over your Message Center. Do Soul Tapping of those two areas continuously during this practice.

Soul Power. Say *hello:*

> *Dear divine forgiveness,*
> *I love you, honor you, and appreciate you.*
> *Please sit inside my Message Center and my heart.*
> *Thank you.*

You are inviting the soul of divine forgiveness to sit inside your Message Center and your heart.

Sound Power. Chant repeatedly, silently or aloud:

> *Divine forgiveness*
> *Divine forgiveness*

Divine forgiveness
Divine forgiveness

Chant *divine forgiveness. Be* divine forgiveness. Keep your focus on your Message Center. If this mantra becomes a song, that is fine. Otherwise, simply chant *divine forgiveness.*

Do this practice for at least five minutes. It would be much better to practice for twenty minutes if possible.

When you have experienced *being* divine forgiveness, you have gone into the condition. You will notice a shift occurring. Allow the peace, the emptiness, the images, the messages to present themselves and flow. In the condition, you will experience purification.

If your Third Eye is open, you may see images of what needs purification. The Soul World may show you situations or people whom you need to forgive or to whom you need to offer forgiveness. If you receive direct soul communication, you may receive teachings from your guides on what needs purification. You may also receive direct communication from the souls of those who have hurt you or whom you have hurt. Invite those souls to chant *divine forgiveness* with you. Invite them to ask divine forgiveness to sit inside their hearts and Message Centers. Invite them to *become* divine forgiveness also.

This practice can transform you and all the others who have become part of your practice. This forgiveness will allow you and others to begin a new chapter in your physical journeys and your soul journeys. It will purify you at the deepest levels of your being. It will bless you, humanity, Mother Earth, and beyond.

You could be amazed and delighted by this simple practice. The more you do this practice, the more your day will become filled with times when you are in the condition. Eventually, your entire day will be lived in the condition of divine forgiveness. This is a blessing beyond words.

How to Apply Forgiveness (A Practice)

Applying forgiveness is very simple. With any challenges in life, whether in health, relationships, finances, or other aspects of life, know that you have contributed to this blockage in some way, either in past lifetimes or in this lifetime. You can ask for forgiveness. If you can talk with the person, that is great. If you cannot, you can still communicate with them at the soul level. This is the way to do it:

Soul Power. Say *hello:*

> *Dear soul of* _____ [name the person with
>   whom there is conflict],
> *I love you, honor you, and appreciate you.*
> *I ask you to come.*
> *There are issues between you and me.*
> *I would like to ask you to forgive my mistakes.*
> *At the same time, I will forgive you for your mistakes.*
> *Let us forgive each other.*
> *Thank you.*

Sound Power. Chant repeatedly, silently or aloud:

> *Forgiveness. Forgiveness. Forgiveness. Forgiveness.*
> *Forgiveness. Forgiveness. Forgiveness. Forgiveness.*
> *Forgiveness. Forgiveness. Forgiveness. Forgiveness.*
> *Forgiveness. Forgiveness. Forgiveness. Forgiveness.*

Chant *forgiveness* sincerely from the bottom of your heart for three to five minutes. Do this practice three to five times per day. If there is a serious issue between you and the other person, chant longer and more often.

Unconditional forgiveness is very powerful. It is important to know that your life can be much smoother if you sincerely forgive those who have hurt, harmed, or taken advantage of you and by asking for forgiveness from those souls you have hurt, harmed, or taken advantage of. Forgiveness brings inner joy and peace. Inner joy and peace are huge blessings for a person's life.

Purify Soul

Soul is the boss for a human being. There are many ways to purify the soul. I am sharing with you one of the most important ways to purify your soul. This way is to offer you a priceless divine treasure to purify your soul. This is the thirty-first divine treasure offered to every reader of this book. This treasure is:

Divine Soul Transplant of Divine Golden Light Ball and Golden Liquid Spring of Divine Purification

Put the tip of your tongue near the roof of your mouth, without touching. Relax. Open your heart and soul and close your eyes for twenty seconds to receive this major divine soul treasure. Prepare!

Divine Order: Divine Golden Light Ball and Golden Liquid Spring of Divine Purification Soul Transplant Transmission!

Hao! Hao! Hao!

Thank you. Thank you. Thank you.

You are extremely blessed.

You can apply this treasure immediately to purify your soul. I will lead you to practice:

Divine Practice to Purify the Soul

Body Power. Put one palm or fist over your Ling Gong (your soul temple, located between your Message Center and heart). Do Soul Tapping there constantly during the practice.

Soul Power. Say *hello:*

> *Dear my Ling Gong,*
> *I love you, honor you, and appreciate you.*
> *You have the power to purify my soul.*
> *Dear my Divine Purification Soul Transplant,*
> *I love you, honor you, and appreciate you.*
> *Please turn on to purify my soul.*
> *Thank you.*

Mind Power. Visualize divine golden light vibrating in your Ling Gong.

Sound Power. Chant repeatedly, silently or aloud:

> *Divine Purification Soul Transplant purifies my soul.*
>   *Thank you, Divine.*
> *Divine Purification Soul Transplant purifies my soul.*
>   *Thank you, Divine.*
> *Divine Purification Soul Transplant purifies my soul.*
>   *Thank you, Divine.*

Divine Purification Soul Transplant purifies my soul.
Thank you, Divine.

Chant three to five minutes per time, three to five times per day; the longer, the better.

This divine treasure can work to purify every soul of the body, every soul of a business, and every soul of a relationship. Its power is beyond comprehension. You must apply it to benefit from it. Practice more. You are extremely blessed. We are extremely honored that the Divine has given this major treasure to every reader.

For many highly developed spiritual people, negative memories are an important concern. When negative memories are cleared, you are free to behave differently. If you experience yourself returning to certain behaviors that were associated with your negative memories, it is very simple to transform those behaviors. Simply say to the negative memories: *Welcome. I love you. Please join me. Let us chant* God's Light *together. Let us both become God's light.* All negative memories can become God's light. When that happens, all that has been associated with the negative memories can be transformed to light.

It is also possible to give an order to the negative memories. I gave one of my students an assignment to flow a very powerful and significant teaching. Every time she began to flow, she developed a sore throat. The first time it happened, she could barely whisper, much less speak. This happened several times. She gave herself plenty of rest. She did all the right things to heal her sore throat.

After allowing six weeks for healing, she tried to flow the assignment again. Within less than a minute, her throat began to hurt. This time, she had a different response. Immediately, she said out loud, "Oh, no you don't. You are not going any place. You cannot get sore. You must speak. You are going to do this job. This is a new chapter, a new page, and a new part of my journey, and you are going to finish the job. Do a good job!" Within another minute, the pain in her throat subsided significantly. She was able to complete her task soon afterward.

When curses have been removed, it is important to keep your Divine Light Wall[9] strong and active. Some people have had their curses removed only to discover later that they carry more curses. This can be very puzzling. What I have learned from the Divine is that some curses could have been placed upon you to be released at a certain time. You could say they are like a time-release capsule. Do not let this worry you or discourage you. You can do a great deal to minimize the effect of the curses by offering total GOLD universal service and by chanting.

I have given you a divine treasure and techniques to *clean the room to welcome the special guest*. You must also keep the room clean to continue to welcome guests. Do the practices to keep your soul journey full of love, forgiveness, compassion, and light. In this way, you will continue to welcome divine gifts. You will continue to welcome the Divine Soul Mind Body Transplants and receive optimum benefits from them.

Purify Heart

Traditional Chinese medicine teaches that the heart houses the mind and soul. The heart is one of the most important organs

---

9. A Divine Light Wall is a special kind of Divine Soul Download. It is literally a protective shield or barrier of divine light that protects you from spiritual incursions by dark souls that would harm you. There are different layers of Divine Light Wall to protect one from different layers of dark souls.

for a human being. Purifying one's heart is vital for one's life and soul journey.

Expanding the wisdom, everyone and everything has a soul, heart, mind, and body. I am going to offer one of the most powerful treasures to purify every reader's heart. This is the thirty-second divine treasure offered to you and every reader of this book. This divine treasure is named:

Divine Heart Transplant of Divine Golden Light Ball and Golden Liquid Spring of Divine Purification

Prepare! Put the tip of your tongue near the roof of your mouth without touching. Open your heart and soul and close your eyes for twenty seconds to receive this major divine treasure.

Divine Order: Divine Golden Light Ball and Golden Liquid Spring of Divine Purification Heart Transplant Transmission!

Hao! Hao! Hao!
Thank you. Thank you. Thank you.
You are extremely blessed.
You can apply this treasure instantly to purify your heart. I will lead you to practice:

Divine Practice to Purify the Heart

Body Power. Put one palm or fist over your heart. Do Soul Tapping there constantly during the practice.
Soul Power. Say *hello*:

Dear soul, mind, and body of my heart,
I love you, honor you, and appreciate you.
You have the power to purify yourself.
Dear my Divine Purification Heart Transplant,
I love you, honor you, and appreciate you.
Please turn on to purify my heart.
Thank you.

Mind Power. Visualize divine golden light vibrating in your heart.

Sound Power. Chant repeatedly, silently or aloud:

Divine Purification Heart Transplant purifies my
*   heart. Thank you, Divine.*
Divine Purification Heart Transplant purifies my
*   heart. Thank you, Divine.*
Divine Purification Heart Transplant purifies my
*   heart. Thank you, Divine.*
Divine Purification Heart Transplant purifies my
*   heart. Thank you, Divine.*

Chant three to five minutes per time, three to five times per day; the longer, the better.

This divine treasure can purify a human being's heart, the heart of an organization, the heart of a relationship, and more. Its power is immeasurable. Every reader is very blessed to receive this divine priceless treasure. We are all extremely honored and blessed.

Practice more. The benefits are unlimited.

The heart is the boss of all the systems, organs, cells, cell units, DNA, RNA, smallest matter, and spaces in the body.

When the boss is purified, everything else is transformed. Think about your own work life. If the boss of your company wants things done a particular way, everyone needs to follow, or there will be consequences. Since the heart is the boss of the body, focusing on purifying the heart will have many benefits for the entire body.

The one-sentence secret about purifying the heart is:

Purify the heart; then purification of the body's systems, organs, cells, cell units, DNA, RNA, smallest matter, and spaces will follow.

Purifying your heart benefits everything else. This is a key wisdom to remember. In *The Power of Soul*, I gave teachings and practices about this. Use this information. Live this teaching. Let it transform your life.

The heart is the boss of all other organs. The cardiovascular system is the boss of all other systems. The heart cells are the boss of all other cells. The heart cell units are the boss of all other cell units. The heart DNA and RNA are the boss of all the other DNA and RNA. The smallest matter in the heart is the boss of all the other smallest matter. The spaces in the heart are the boss of all other spaces. This means that when you call upon the cells of your heart to purify, you are calling upon all the cells in your entire body to purify. This is true for every other level: systems, organs, cell units, DNA, RNA, smallest matter, and spaces.

Let me lead you to practice:

Additional Practices to Purify the Heart

Body Power. Put one palm or fist over your heart. Do Soul Tapping there continuously during the practice.

Soul Power. Say *hello:*

> *Dear soul, mind, and body of my heart cells,*
> *I love you, honor you, and appreciate you.*
> *You have the power to purify yourselves and all of my*
> *   cells.*
> *Do a good job.*
> *Thank you.*

Sound Power. You can give a Soul Order.[10] Let me lead you in this practice. Since your heart cells are the boss of all your cells, you can chant repeatedly for three to five minutes:

> *Souls of my heart cells order all my cells to purify.*
> *Souls of my heart cells order all my cells to purify.*
> *Souls of my heart cells order all my cells to purify.*
> *Souls of my heart cells order all my cells to purify.*

The best practice would be to give Soul Orders at all levels of your body:

> *Soul of my heart orders all my organs to purify.*
> *Soul of my cardiovascular system orders all my systems*
> *   to purify.*

---

10. See chapter 4 of my book *The Power of Soul* (2009, New York/Toronto: Atria Books/ Heaven's Library) for fundamental soul secrets, wisdom, knowledge, and practices of Soul Orders.

Souls of my heart cells order all my cells to purify.

Souls of my heart cell units order all my cell units to purify.

Souls of my heart DNA and RNA order all my DNA and RNA to purify.

Souls of my heart smallest matter order all my smallest matter to purify.

Souls of my heart spaces order all my spaces to purify.

Repeat each Soul Order at least ten times; the more, the better.

If you know you have an issue at a particular level, spend more time on that level.

Do this three to five times per day. Benefit from this practice. It will serve you well.

This practice is such an efficient way to purify your entire body. It is a perfect way to continue the process that started with the removal of soul, mind, and body blockages.

Because the heart houses the soul and the mind, when you continue to purify your heart, you will continue to purify your soul and mind at the same time.

By now you understand how important the heart is for your healing and purification journey. Pay great attention. Follow these teachings. Benefit well.

Hao!

Purify Mind

Mind means consciousness. To purify the mind is to purify the consciousness. To purify the mind is to remove negative mind-sets, attitudes, beliefs, ego, and attachment. To completely purify the mind is to have divine consciousness.

Purification of the mind is needed at every level of your being. It is not just the mind for your entire body, but it is also the mind of every system, organ, cell, cell unit, DNA, RNA, smallest matter, and space in your body. The first step of the Divine Soul Mind Body Healing and Transmission System removes mind blockages for a system, organ, cells, cell units, DNA, RNA, smallest matter, or spaces.

After blockages have been removed, patterns may still need to be changed. Certain patterns have been present in your life because of the mind blockages. You may ask, "How do I change the patterns?" The answer is simple: *just do it.* You do not need a complicated plan. You do not need many steps. You simply need to make a decision. You need to follow that decision with action.

Let me lead you in some simple practices to support your decision:

Practices to Purify the Mind and Transform Mind Patterns

You can say *hello* like this:

> *Dear the beloved minds of my systems, organs, cells,*
>   *cell units, DNA, RNA, smallest matter, and spaces,*
> *I love you.*
> *You have the power to be purified.*
> *You have the power to purify yourselves.*
> *Do a good job.*
> *Thank you.*

Or, you can chant this one-sentence secret, silently or aloud:

Every mind pattern of my soul, mind, and body trans-
forms and purifies.
Thank you.

Chant for at least three minutes per time, the longer, the better.

These practices are very simple and very powerful. They will benefit your healing journey and your soul journey. You can do these practices anywhere, anytime.

This is the divine way to purify the mind: receive a priceless divine treasure and apply it to purify the mind. No technique can be better than this divine technique.

I am offering the thirty-third major divine treasure in this book so that you can apply this divine technique with it:

Divine Mind Transplant of Divine Golden Light Ball and Golden Liquid Spring of Divine Purification

Prepare!

Put the tip of your tongue near the roof of your mouth, without touching. Open your heart and soul and close your eyes for twenty seconds to receive this major treasure.

Divine Order: Divine Golden Light Ball and Golden Liquid Spring of Divine Purification Mind Transplant Transmission!

Hao! Hao! Hao!
Thank you. Thank you. Thank you.
You are extremely blessed.

You can apply this treasure instantly to purify your mind. I will lead you to practice:

Divine Practice to Purify the Mind

Body Power. Put one palm or fist over your Message Center. Put the other palm or fist over your crown chakra, at the top of your head. Do Soul Tapping constantly in those two areas during the practice.

Soul Power. Say *hello:*

> *Dear soul, mind, and body of my Message Center and*
> *   brain,*
> *I love you, honor you, and appreciate you.*
> *You have the power to purify my mind.*
> *Do a good job.*
> *Dear my Divine Purification Mind Transplant,*
> *I love you, honor you, and appreciate you.*
> *Please turn on to purify my mind.*
> *Thank you.*

Mind Power. Visualize divine golden light vibrating in your Message Center and brain.

Sound Power. Chant repeatedly, silently or aloud:

> *Divine Purification Mind Transplant purifies my*
> *   mind. Thank you, Divine.*
> *Divine Purification Mind Transplant purifies my*
> *   mind. Thank you, Divine.*
> *Divine Purification Mind Transplant purifies my*
> *   mind. Thank you, Divine.*

Divine Purification Mind Transplant purifies my
mind. Thank you, Divine.

Chant three to five minutes per time, three to five times per day; the longer, the better.

This divine treasure can purify a human being's mind, the mind of an organization, the mind of a relationship, the minds of your organs, systems, and cells, and more. Its power is heart-touching and moving.

Issues of the mind on the levels of the systems, organs, cells, cell units, DNA, RNA, smallest matter, and spaces are major blockages to your healing journey. Purification on these levels will accelerate every aspect of your healing journey. Mind blockages are major blockages for one's life, especially for the spiritual journey. Negative mind-sets, attitudes, beliefs, ego, and attachment are the vital blockages for every aspect of your life. This priceless divine treasure and the Divine Soul Mind Body Healing and Transmission System can transform these issues very quickly. We cannot honor the Divine enough.

Purify Body

A human being's body includes systems, organs, cells, cell units, DNA, RNA, smallest matter inside the cells, and spaces between the cells. Purifying the body includes purifying all of them.

I am offering a divine way to purify your body. This is the thirty-fourth divine treasure to every reader. This incredible divine treasure is named:

Divine Body Transplant of Divine Golden Light Ball and Golden Liquid Spring of Divine Purification

Prepare!

Put the tip of your tongue near the roof of your mouth without touching. Open your heart and soul to receive this major treasure.

Divine Order: Divine Golden Light Ball and Golden Liquid Spring of Divine Purification Body Transplant Transmission!

Hao! Hao! Hao!

Thank you. Thank you. Thank you.

You are extremely blessed.

You can instantly apply this treasure to purify your body. I will lead you to practice:

Divine Practice to Purify the Body

Body Power. Put one palm or fist over your Message Center. Put your other palm or fist over your Snow Mountain Area. Do Soul Tapping constantly in those areas during the practice.

Soul Power. Say *hello*:

> *Dear soul, mind, and body of my Message Center and*
>   *Snow Mountain Area,*
> *I love you, honor you, and appreciate you.*
> *You have the power to purify my body.*
> *Do a good job.*
> *Dear my Divine Purification Body Transplant,*
> *I love you, honor you, and appreciate you.*
> *Please turn on to purify my body.*
> *Thank you.*

Mind Power. Visualize divine golden light vibrating in your Message Center and Snow Mountain Area.

Sound Power. Chant repeatedly, silently or aloud:

> *Divine Purification Body Transplant purifies my body.*
> *Thank you, Divine.*
> *Divine Purification Body Transplant purifies my body.*
> *Thank you, Divine.*
> *Divine Purification Body Transplant purifies my body.*
> *Thank you, Divine.*
> *Divine Purification Body Transplant purifies my body.*
> *Thank you, Divine.*

Chant three to five minutes per time, three to five times per day; the longer, the better.

This divine treasure can purify a human being's body, the body of an organization, and the body of a relationship. Its power is heart-touching and moving.

Body blockages are also major blockages for one's life. Apply this powerful treasure to purify your body. There are no words to express our gratitude for the Divine's generosity.

Purification of the body includes purifying energy and matter. For energy, blockages to energy flow are removed. Then, you must make sure there are no new blockages. There are many ways to do this. Practicing with your divine treasures is the best way. Chanting continually is another.

When you are aware of the need for purification, you can do the things needed to avoid creating more blockages and to prevent the old blockages from returning. Sometimes people do nothing. The old blockages return, and they say this healing did not work. This misses the point. This is a self-healing system. You must do something. The Divine has given you powerful, priceless treasures. You must be part of the healing process.

By now, you certainly understand the importance of practice. I have emphasized it throughout this book. I have made comparisons to turning on a lightbulb. I have led you in numerous practices. All of these are ways of telling you practice is essential. *There is no second way.*

Some of you may experience miraculous results instantly, but practice is still important. With the changes you experience when your blockages are removed or your energy is boosted, remember you must still do your part and continue to practice.

If you do not feel better right away, it does not mean that the divine treasures do not work. You need to practice more to remove your soul, mind, and body blockages. You have learned that the Divine Soul Mind Body Healing and Transmission System has three steps. The Divine does the first two steps. You are responsible for step 3: practice. Results *will* come.

Remember Lothar's story. Let me share another story. I met a woman in Europe who suffered from a rare sickness that was similar to multiple sclerosis. For more than ten years, she had suffered from pain so severe that she had to go to a hospital several times a year for relief. In one of my workshops in 2008, she received karma cleansing and many Divine Soul Mind Body Transplants. She heard my teaching: *To receive karma cleansing and Divine Soul Mind Body Transplants does not mean you will recover right away. Some people do receive amazing results instantly. Some people do feel significantly better right away. Some people feel a little better. Some people feel no improvement at all. Whatever result you receive, it is important to invoke and apply your Soul Mind*

Body Transplants to continue your healing. She went home and chanted and chanted very hard, as much as six hours per day on weekends. One month passed, and her pain was the same. She believed in my teaching, so she chanted for a second month, for at least two hours each day. At the end of the second month, she still had no improvement. She continued to chant. Within one more month, her pain suddenly and completely disappeared. Her specialist was totally surprised. She has remained completely pain-free to this day. She shared: *I am the rare case to receive major divine blessings but not feel any improvement for two months even though I practiced diligently. But I believe in and continued to follow Master Sha's teaching. I continued to practice and received remarkable results after three months of chanting. I am extremely grateful. I want everyone to know how much I suffered for ten years. It was absolutely awful. I cannot thank the Divine and Master Sha enough for their teaching and blessing.*

The stories of Lothar and this woman tell us that if you do not feel benefits right away from Divine Soul Mind Body Transplants, do not feel disappointed. Do not complain. Please trust divine power. Please trust that you *can* receive remarkable healing results. In some cases, results will come only after very persistent practice. This is to emphasize how important step 3 is. Invoke and practice with divine treasures to heal your physical, emotional, mental, and spiritual bodies, as well as to heal relationships and finance.

I wish you will have great healing results for your life as soon as possible. **Practice is vital.** Print these words on your heart and soul. You *will* do a good job for healing and transforming every aspect of your life.

To purify on the level of the body requires practice. Let me share with you a powerful one-sentence secret practice:

All my divine treasures heal, purify, and transform me.
Thank you, Divine.
All my divine treasures heal, purify, and transform me.
Thank you, Divine.
All my divine treasures heal, purify, and transform me.
Thank you, Divine.
All my divine treasures heal, purify, and transform me.
Thank you, Divine.

Chant three to five minutes per time; the longer, the better. Do it at least three times per day.

There are other practices you can use to purify your body. Some I have already mentioned in this chapter. You can give a Soul Order. A key wisdom is that the more purified you are, the fewer physical, emotional, and mental issues you will have. These issues cannot exist in a pure soul, heart, mind, and body.

This purification process does not have to take months and months. The more consistent time you give to practice, the greater the benefits and the more you can accelerate the healing process. The more time you give to practice with your divine treasures, the greater the efforts they will make to serve you well.

Purifying your soul, heart, mind, and body can transform every aspect of your life. I am extremely grateful that the Divine has given four priceless and most powerful treasures in this chapter to every reader: Divine Purification Soul Transplant, Divine Purification Heart Transplant, Divine Purification Mind Transplant, and Divine Purification Body Transplant.

These four divine treasures could transform your soul, heart, mind, and body very quickly. Practice more and more. The benefits are unlimited.

Hao!

Apply the Divine Soul Mind Body Healing and Transmission System to Heal All Life

*I*N THE UNIVERSE, everything can go both ways. Many heal-ing modalities only consider one way. If cancer forms, you have to remove it. If varicose veins appear; you have to remove them. What I am sharing is divine wisdom. It is the secret for healing all sicknesses. If a sickness can form, it can also disappear.

The Divine Soul Mind Body Healing and Transmission Sys-tem follows this wisdom. When we remove blockages of the soul, mind, and body, transformation occurs. Lothar's experience shows that if even pancreatic cancer forms, pancreatic cancer can also disappear.

To heal a sickness is to remove the soul, mind, and body blockages related to the sickness.

To transform a relationship is to remove the soul, mind, and body blockages in the relationship.

To transform a business and finances is to remove the soul, mind, and body blockages in the business and finances.

This book shares with you the *divine* way to heal you, humanity, Mother Earth, and all universes.

In this chapter, I will lead you to apply Divine Soul Mind Body Transplants to heal all life. Let us do the practices one by one to bless every aspect of life.

Physical Body

In chapter 2, I released for the first time the two most powerful ways to self-heal by applying Divine Soul Mind Body Transplants. Remember the one-sentence secret of this new divine sacred and secret wisdom:

**The Ling Gong, Message Center, and Snow Mountain Area
can heal, prevent sickness, rejuvenate, prolong life,
and transform every aspect of life, including
relationships and finances.**

Let us review and do these practices again:

Ling Gong Practice

Body Power. Put one palm or fist over your Ling Gong. Do Soul Tapping on your Ling Gong.

Soul Power. Say *hello*:

> *Dear soul, mind, and body of my Ling Gong,*
> *I love you, honor you, and appreciate you.*

You have the power to heal and rejuvenate me.
Dear all my Divine Soul Mind Body Transplants,
I love you, honor you, and appreciate you.
Please turn on to heal and rejuvenate me.
I am very grateful and honored.
Thank you.

Sound Power. Chant repeatedly, silently or aloud:

Divine Soul Mind Body Transplants heal and rejuvenate me. Thank you, Divine.
Divine Soul Mind Body Transplants heal and rejuvenate me. Thank you, Divine.
Divine Soul Mind Body Transplants heal and rejuvenate me. Thank you, Divine.
Divine Soul Mind Body Transplants heal and rejuvenate me. Thank you, Divine.

Mind Power. Visualize divine golden light and divine rainbow light vibrating in an area or areas where you need healing.

Practice for at least three to five minutes per time, the longer, the better. Practice as many times a day as you can, until you recover.

Message Center and Snow Mountain Practice

Body Power. Put one palm or fist over your Message Center. Put the other palm or fist over your lower back over your Snow Mountain Area, which is between your tailbone and the level of your navel. Do Soul Tapping on both areas continuously.

Soul Power. Say *hello:*

Dear soul, mind, and body of my Message Center,
Dear soul, mind, and body of my Snow Mountain
  Area,
I love you, honor you, and appreciate you.
You have the power to heal and rejuvenate me.
Dear all my Divine Soul Mind Body Transplants,
I love you, honor you, and appreciate you.
Please turn on to heal and rejuvenate me.
I am very grateful and honored.
Thank you.

Sound Power. Chant repeatedly, silently or aloud:

Divine Soul Mind Body Transplants heal and rejuve-
  nate me. Thank you, Divine.
Divine Soul Mind Body Transplants heal and rejuve-
  nate me. Thank you, Divine.
Divine Soul Mind Body Transplants heal and rejuve-
  nate me. Thank you, Divine.
Divine Soul Mind Body Transplants heal and rejuve-
  nate me. Thank you, Divine.

Mind Power. Visualize divine golden light and divine rainbow light vibrating in an area or areas where you need healing.

Practice for at least three to five minutes per time, the longer, the better. Practice as many times a day as you can, until you recover.

Now I will lead you to do a few practices for self-healing specific conditions. If you learn how to self-heal these few sample conditions, you can easily adapt these practices to apply Divine Soul Mind Body Transplants to self-heal other conditions.

Practices for Self-healing

LOWER BACK PAIN

Body Power. Put one palm or fist over your Message Center. Put the other palm or fist over your lower back. Do Soul Tapping on both areas continuously. (Tap gently on your lower back if it is painful.)

Soul Power. Say *hello:*

> *Dear soul, mind, and body of my Message Center,*
> *Dear soul, mind, and body of my lower back,*
> *I love you, honor you, and appreciate you.*
> *You have the power to heal my lower back.*
> *Dear my Divine Love Soul Mind Body Transplants,*[11]
> *I love you, honor you, and appreciate you.*
> *Please turn on to heal and rejuvenate my lower back.*
> *I am very grateful.*
> *Thank you.*

Mind Power. Visualize divine golden light vibrating in your lower back to heal your lower back.

Sound Power. Chant repeatedly, silently or aloud:

> *Divine Love Soul Mind Body Transplants heal and*
> *rejuvenate my lower back. Thank you, Divine.*
> *Divine Love Soul Mind Body Transplants heal and*
> *rejuvenate my lower back. Thank you, Divine.*

---

11. You received these Divine Soul Downloads when you read chapter 3.

Divine Love Soul Mind Body Transplants heal and
rejuvenate my lower back. Thank you, Divine.
Divine Love Soul Mind Body Transplants heal and
rejuvenate my lower back. Thank you, Divine.

Practice for at least three to five minutes per time, the longer, the better. Practice as many times a day as you can, until you recover.

COMMON COLD

Body Power. Put one palm or fist over your Message Center. Put the other palm or fist over your Snow Mountain Area. Do Soul Tapping on those areas continuously.

Soul Power. Say *hello:*

Dear soul, mind, and body of my Message Center,
Dear soul, mind, and body of my Snow Mountain
Area,
I love you, honor you, and appreciate you.
You have the power to heal my cold.
Dear my Divine Forgiveness Soul Mind Body
Transplants,[12]
I love you, honor you, and appreciate you.
Please turn on to heal my cold.
I am very grateful.
Thank you.

Mind Power. Visualize divine golden light vibrating in your lungs and entire respiratory system to heal your cold.

---

12. You also received these Divine Soul Downloads when you read chapter 3.

Sound Power. Chant repeatedly, silently or aloud:

> *Divine Forgiveness Soul Mind Body Transplants heal*
> *my cold. Thank you, Divine.*
> *Divine Forgiveness Soul Mind Body Transplants heal*
> *my cold. Thank you, Divine.*
> *Divine Forgiveness Soul Mind Body Transplants heal*
> *my cold. Thank you, Divine.*
> *Divine Forgiveness Soul Mind Body Transplants heal*
> *my cold. Thank you, Divine.*

Practice for at least three to five minutes per time, the longer, the better. Practice as many times a day as you can, until you recover.

BREAST CANCER

Body Power. Put one palm or fist over your Message Center. Put the other palm or fist over a cancerous area of your breasts. Do Soul Tapping on these areas continuously.

Soul Power. Say *hello*:

> *Dear soul, mind, and body of my Message Center,*
> *Dear soul, mind, and body of my breasts,*
> *I love you, honor you, and appreciate you.*
> *You have the power to heal my breast cancer.*
> *Dear my Divine Light Soul Mind Body Transplants,*
> *I love you, honor you, and appreciate you.*
> *Please turn on to heal my breast cancer.*
> *I am very grateful.*
> *Thank you.*

Mind Power. Visualize divine golden light vibrating in your breasts to heal your breast cancer.

Sound Power. Chant repeatedly, silently or aloud:

> *Divine Light Soul Mind Body Transplants heal my*
> *breasts. Thank you, Divine.*
> *Divine Light Soul Mind Body Transplants heal my*
> *breasts. Thank you, Divine.*
> *Divine Light Soul Mind Body Transplants heal my*
> *breasts. Thank you, Divine.*
> *Divine Light Soul Mind Body Transplants heal my*
> *breasts. Thank you, Divine.*

For chronic and life-threatening conditions such as breast cancer, chant for twenty to thirty minutes per time, for a total of at least two hours per day. The longer you chant, the better. It is also important to continue to practice after you have recovered, to prevent the sickness from recurring.

To apply the Divine Soul Mind Body Transplants you have received, you can use the practices I have given you in this book. You can invoke and practice with all of your divine treasures simultaneously, as we did in the first two practices in this chapter. I have just given you practices for applying Divine Soul Mind Body Transplants to self-heal three physical conditions: pain, a cold, and a life-threatening condition. When you see how to apply your Divine Soul Mind Body Transplants for these conditions, you can easily adapt these examples and apply these techniques to self-heal any unhealthy condition. In the last few practices, we asked our Divine Love Soul Mind Body Transplants to offer healing to our lower backs, Divine Forgiveness Soul

Mind Body Transplants to heal a cold, and Divine Light Soul Mind Body Transplants to heal breast cancer.

In fact, you can invoke and practice with any divine treasure to request a divine soul healing for any issue. Every divine treasure is a powerful unconditional universal servant. If you have a problem with your knee, for example, you can invoke and practice with any divine treasure you have received and ask it to offer healing to your knee. It will do so unconditionally. All you need to do is ask and chant. It is particularly powerful to apply customized Divine Soul Mind Body Transplants for specific systems, organs, parts of the body, or conditions. Please review chapter 3 to learn how you can receive customized Divine Soul Mind Body Transplants.

YUAN JING, YUAN CHI, YUAN SHEN

Dao is The Way. The Way is the universal law and principle. Dao produces and guides everyone and everything in every aspect of life. To review:

Dao produces one.
One produces two.
Two produces three.
Three produces everything.

These are the top principles of Daoist teaching. In fact, this is the highest philosophy and principle for everything in the universe.

Let me explain further.

Dao produces one.

Dao is one. Humanity is one. Countless planets are one. Countless stars are one. Countless galaxies are one. Countless universes are one. Everyone and everything in all universes are one. Divine oneness is Dao. Dao is divine oneness. Ancient Daoist teaching and divine teaching are the same in this respect.

One produces two.

Two is yin and yang. Heaven is yang. Mother Earth is yin. A man and a woman conceive a baby through intercourse. Heaven and Earth produce a soul through intercourse.

Two produces three.

Dao plus yin and yang are three. Man, woman, and baby are three. Heaven, Earth, and human being are three.

Three produces everything.

When a man and a woman conceive a baby, the next generation is produced. When Heaven and Earth produce a new soul, anything can be produced. On Mother Earth, generations are continually produced. Mother Earth is the yin world. In Heaven, souls are continually produced. Heaven is the yang world. Dao produces the yin and yang worlds. Dao and the yin and yang worlds together will produce everyone and everything in all universes.

I will use a human being as an example to explain the relationship between Dao and yin and yang. A man and a woman have intercourse. The sperm and egg merge. The secret is that at that moment, Dao responds in Heaven. Dao will prepare the body soul and the souls of all systems, organs, cells, cell units, DNA, RNA, smallest matter inside the cells, and spaces between cells. These souls all come to the mother's womb. The moment the egg and the sperm merge, all of the inner souls of this being are decided and confirmed. Dao selects all of the souls for this new being.

The very important wisdom I want to share is that at the moment the sperm and egg merge, Yuan Jing, Yuan Chi, and Yuan Shen are produced and reside with the embryo right away. "Yuan" means *original.* "Jing" means *tiny matter.* "Chi" means *energy* and *life force.* "Shen" means *soul.*

Because Yuan Jing, Yuan Chi, and Yuan Shen are produced when a person is conceived, they play a vital role in a person's entire life. Yuan Jing, Yuan Chi, and Yuan Shen must be continually developed to have great health in one's whole life. For rejuvenation and longevity, it is vital to highly develop Yuan Jing, Yuan Chi, and Yuan Shen. In Daoist teaching, there are secret practices for this.

Yuan Jing is the original essence of matter. It is the matter foundation for the whole body. Think about any building. It must have foundational material: wood, bricks, mortar, concrete, steel, and more. This is the vital role and function Yuan Jing has for the body.

For the fetus, Yuan Jing is nourished by nutrients in the mother's blood. After birth, food and practices nourish one's Yuan Jing. Yuan Jing must be developed continually for a being to grow and maintain good health. If your Yuan Jing is weak, your whole body will be weak. You will be tired and fatigued.

There are secret practices to develop Yuan Jing. Let me share with you a practical technique to develop Yuan Jing. We will use the Four Power Techniques of Soul Mind Body Medicine. Let us review them. These four practical techniques for self-healing are:

Body Power—using specific hand and body positions to develop energy, vitality, stamina, and immunity, and to heal, rejuvenate, and prolong life.

Sound Power—chanting mantras to boost energy and to

heal and rejuvenate. Mantras are special healing sounds from different spiritual practices throughout history.

Mind Power—creative visualization and using the potential power of the brain to boost energy and heal. Mind Power is *mind over matter,* which means the mind can heal, rejuvenate, and transform every aspect of life.

Soul Power—invoking souls to heal, rejuvenate, and transform every aspect of life. Soul Power is *soul over matter.*

Yuan Jing is stored in the kidneys. This is the way to develop Yuan Jing. Practice with me now:

Practice to Develop Yuan Jing

Body Power. Put your palms over your kidneys and do Soul Tapping of both kidneys continuously.

Soul Power. Say *hello:*

> *Dear soul, mind, and body of my Yuan Jing,*
> *I love you, honor you, and appreciate you.*
> *You are the essence of matter for my entire body.*
> *I deeply appreciate you.*
> *Boost your power and develop yourself.*
> *Thank you very much.*

> *Dear soul, mind, and body of Mother Earth and*
>   *Heaven,*
> *I love you, honor you, and appreciate you.*
> *You have the power to boost my Yuan Jing.*
> *Do a good job.*
> *Thank you very much.*

Sound Power. Chant repeatedly, silently or aloud:

> *Mother Earth and Heaven boost my Yuan Jing. Thank*
> * you very much.*
> *Mother Earth and Heaven boost my Yuan Jing. Thank*
> * you very much.*
> *Mother Earth and Heaven boost my Yuan Jing. Thank*
> * you very much.*
> *Mother Earth and Heaven boost my Yuan Jing. Thank*
> * you very much.*

Chant three to five minutes per time, three to five times per day. The longer and the more often you practice, the better the results.

The divine way to boost Yuan Jing is with Divine Soul Mind Body Transplants. At this moment, I will make a request of the Divine:

> *Dear Divine, I am extremely honored to ask you to*
> * give every reader three more major Divine Soul*
> * Downloads.*

The Divine is replying:

> *Dear my son, Zhi Gang, you want to serve. I will give.*

I am bowing down to the Divine one thousand times on the floor at this moment for the Divine's generosity to give these major treasures to every reader. The treasures are:

Divine Soul Mind Body Transplants of Divine Yuan Jing

They are the thirty-fifth, thirty-sixth, and thirty-seventh permanent divine gifts offered to you and every reader.

Imagine how many people's energy, vitality, stamina, and immunity can be boosted and enhanced by Divine Soul Mind Body Transplants of Divine Yuan Jing. I am deeply moved and touched by the Divine's love and blessing.

Prepare to receive these priceless divine treasures. Sit up straight. Put the tip of your tongue close to the roof of your mouth without touching. Open you heart and soul. In the next minute, the Divine will download these gifts to your soul:

Divine Order: Divine Golden Light Ball and Golden Liquid Spring of Divine Yuan Jing Soul Transplant Transmission!

Divine Order: Divine Golden Light Ball and Golden Liquid Spring of Divine Yuan Jing Mind Transplant Transmission!

Divine Order: Divine Golden Light Ball and Golden Liquid Spring of Divine Yuan Jing Body Transplant Transmission!

Divine Order: Join Divine Golden Light Ball and Golden Liquid Spring of Divine Yuan Jing Soul Transplant, Mind Transplant, and Body Transplant as one.

Yi Ya Ya Ya Ya Hei
Ya Ya Hei Hei Hei!

Hao! Hao! Hao!
Thank you. Thank you. Thank you.

Thank you, Divine. We continue to be blessed beyond any words.

The original soul of your Yuan Jing has just returned to the heart of the Divine. It has been replaced by a Divine Soul Transplant of Divine Yuan Jing. Similarly, the original mind and body of your Yuan Jing have been replaced by a Divine Mind Transplant of Divine Yuan Jing and a Divine Body Transplant of Divine Yuan Jing, respectively. The mind transplant is a divine golden light being that changed the consciousness of your Yuan Jing. The body transplant is a divine golden light being that now resides in your kidneys to change the energy and tiny matter of your Yuan Jing. You do not have your original Yuan Jing anymore. The soul, mind, and body of your Yuan Jing are completely changed. They are divine beings joined as one.

These Divine Soul Mind Body Transplants of Divine Yuan Jing carry divine frequency and vibration with divine love, forgiveness, compassion, and light. Divine Yuan Jing can quickly develop the matter foundation for your whole body. The benefits for your energy, stamina, vitality, and immunity are beyond words. This is the way to practice:

Divine Practice to Develop Yuan Jing

Soul Power. Say *hello:*

> *Dear my Divine Soul Mind Body Transplants of Divine Yuan Jing,*
> *I love you, honor you, and appreciate you.*

You carry divine frequency and vibration with divine
love, forgiveness, compassion, and light.
Please boost my energy, stamina, vitality, and immu-
nity.
I am extremely honored and appreciative.

Sound Power. Chant repeatedly, silently or aloud:

Divine Yuan Jing, Divine Yuan Jing, Divine Yuan
Jing, Divine Yuan Jing.
Divine Yuan Jing, Divine Yuan Jing, Divine Yuan
Jing, Divine Yuan Jing.
Divine Yuan Jing, Divine Yuan Jing, Divine Yuan
Jing, Divine Yuan Jing.
Divine Yuan Jing, Divine Yuan Jing, Divine Yuan
Jing, Divine Yuan Jing.

As you chant *Divine Yuan Jing*, the **Body Power** is to continue to do Soul Tapping on both kidneys. This is the divine way to boost Yuan Jing. Practice with me for five minutes now, before you read further.

Hao! Hao! Hao!
Thank you. Thank you. Thank you.

Emotional Body

Divine Soul Mind Body Transplants can transform every aspect of life, including emotions. In this section, I will show you how to transform common emotional imbalances by applying Divine Soul Mind Body Transplants.

ANGER

Anger is connected with the liver. This wisdom was released thousands of years ago in *The Yellow Emperor's Internal Classic*, the top authority book of traditional Chinese medicine. If you get angry easily, you could have blockages in your liver. If you have unhealthy conditions in your liver, you could get angry easily.

Practice for Self-healing Anger

Body Power. Put one palm or fist over your Message Center. Put the other palm or fist over your liver. Do Soul Tapping on these areas continuously.

Soul Power. Say *hello:*

> *Dear soul, mind, and body of my Message Center,*
> *Dear soul, mind, and body of my liver,*
> *I love you, honor you, and appreciate you.*
> *You have the power to heal my anger.*
> *Dear my Divine Forgiveness Soul Mind Body*
>   *Transplants,*
> *I love you, honor you, and appreciate you.*
> *Please turn on to heal my anger.*
> *I am very grateful.*
> *Thank you.*

Mind Power. Visualize divine golden light vibrating in your liver to heal your anger.

Sound Power. Chant repeatedly, silently or aloud:

Divine Forgiveness Soul Mind Body Transplants heal
  my anger. Thank you.
Divine Forgiveness Soul Mind Body Transplants heal
  my anger. Thank you.
Divine Forgiveness Soul Mind Body Transplants heal
  my anger. Thank you.
Divine Forgiveness Soul Mind Body Transplants heal
  my anger. Thank you.

Practice chanting for at least three to five minutes, the longer, the better. Practice as many times a day as you can, until your anger is removed.

DEPRESSION AND ANXIETY

Depression and anxiety are connected with the heart. If you have depression or anxiety, you could have blockages in your heart. If you have an unhealthy condition in your heart, you are more likely to be depressed or anxious.

Practice for Self-healing Depression and Anxiety

Body Power. Put your right palm or fist over your Message Center. Put your left palm or fist over your heart. Do Soul Tapping on these areas continuously.
  Soul Power. Say *hello*:

Dear soul, mind, and body of my Message Center,
Dear soul, mind, and body of my heart,
I love you, honor you, and appreciate you.

You have the power to heal my depression [or *anxiety*].
Dear my Divine Compassion Soul Mind Body Trans-
   plants,
I love you, honor you, and appreciate you.
Please turn on to heal my depression [or *anxiety*].
I am very grateful.
Thank you.

Mind Power. Visualize divine golden light vibrating in your heart to heal your depression (or anxiety).

Sound Power. Chant repeatedly, silently or aloud:

Divine Compassion Soul Mind Body Transplants heal
   my depression [or *anxiety*]. *Thank you.*
Divine Compassion Soul Mind Body Transplants heal
   my depression [or *anxiety*]. *Thank you.*
Divine Compassion Soul Mind Body Transplants heal
   my depression [or *anxiety*]. *Thank you.*
Divine Compassion Soul Mind Body Transplants heal
   my depression [or *anxiety*]. *Thank you.*

Practice chanting for at least three to five minutes, the longer, the better. Practice as many times a day as you can, until your depression (or anxiety) is removed.

WORRY

Worry is connected with the spleen. If you worry a lot, you could have blockages in your spleen. If you have unhealthy conditions in your spleen, you are more likely to be worried.

Practice for Self-healing Worry

Body Power. Put your right palm or fist over your Message Center. Put your left palm or fist over your spleen. Do Soul Tapping on these areas continuously.

Soul Power. Say *hello:*

> *Dear soul, mind, and body of my Message Center,*
> *Dear soul, mind, and body of my spleen,*
> *I love you, honor you, and appreciate you.*
> *You have the power to heal my worry.*
> *Dear all my Divine Soul Mind Body Transplants,*
> *I love you, honor you, and appreciate you.*
> *Please turn on to heal my worry.*
> *I am very grateful.*
> *Thank you.*

Mind Power. Visualize divine golden light vibrating in your spleen to heal your worry.

Sound Power. Chant repeatedly, silently or aloud:

> *Divine Soul Mind Body Transplants heal my worry.*
>   *Thank you.*
> *Divine Soul Mind Body Transplants heal my worry.*
>   *Thank you.*
> *Divine Soul Mind Body Transplants heal my worry.*
>   *Thank you.*
> *Divine Soul Mind Body Transplants heal my worry.*
>   *Thank you.*

Practice chanting for at least three to five minutes, the longer, the better. Practice as many times a day as you can, until your worry is removed.

SADNESS AND GRIEF

Sadness and grief are connected with the lungs. If you are sad or grieving, you could have blockages in your lungs. If you have unhealthy conditions in your lungs, you are more likely to be sad.

Practice for Self-healing Sadness and Grief

Body Power. Put one palm or fist over your Message Center. Put the other palm or fist over one of your lungs. Do Soul Tapping on these areas continuously.

Soul Power. Say *hello:*

> *Dear soul, mind, and body of my Message Center,*
> *Dear soul, mind, and body of my lungs,*
> *I love you, honor you, and appreciate you.*
> *You have the power to heal my sadness and grief.*
> *Dear my Mother's Love Soul Mind Body Transplants,*[13]
> *I love you, honor you, and appreciate you.*
> *Please turn on to heal my sadness and grief.*
> *I am very grateful.*
> *Thank you.*

---

13. You received these Divine Soul Downloads when you read chapter 3.

Mind Power. Visualize divine golden light vibrating in your lungs to heal your sadness and grief.

Sound Power. Chant repeatedly, silently or aloud:

> *Divine Mother's Love Soul Mind Body Transplants*
> *heal my sadness and grief. Thank you.*
> *Divine Mother's Love Soul Mind Body Transplants*
> *heal my sadness and grief. Thank you.*
> *Divine Mother's Love Soul Mind Body Transplants*
> *heal my sadness and grief. Thank you.*
> *Divine Mother's Love Soul Mind Body Transplants*
> *heal my sadness and grief. Thank you.*

Practice chanting for at least three to five minutes, the longer, the better. Practice as many times a day as you can, until your sadness and grief are removed.

FEAR

Fear is connected with the kidneys. If you are fearful, you could have blockages in your kidneys. If you have unhealthy conditions in your kidneys, you are more likely to be fearful.

Practice for Self-healing Fear

Body Power. Put one palm or fist over your Message Center. Put the other palm or fist over a kidney. Do Soul Tapping on these areas continuously.

Soul Power. Say *hello:*

> *Dear soul, mind, and body of my Message Center,*
> *Dear soul, mind, and body of my kidneys,*

I love you, honor you, and appreciate you.
You have the power to heal my fear.
Dear my Divine Removing Negative Beliefs Soul
    Mind Body Transplants,[14]
I love you, honor you, and appreciate you.
Please turn on to heal my fear.
I am very grateful.
Thank you.

Mind Power. Visualize divine golden light vibrating in your kidneys to heal your fear.

Sound Power. Chant repeatedly, silently or aloud:

Divine Removing Negative Beliefs Soul Mind Body
    Transplants heal my fear. Thank you.
Divine Removing Negative Beliefs Soul Mind Body
    Transplants heal my fear. Thank you.
Divine Removing Negative Beliefs Soul Mind Body
    Transplants heal my fear. Thank you.
Divine Removing Negative Beliefs Soul Mind Body
    Transplants heal my fear. Thank you.

Practice chanting for at least three to five minutes, the longer, the better. Practice as many times a day as you can, until your fear is removed.

GUILT

Guilt is a common emotion. Some people experience guilt in almost every aspect of their lives. If they do something, they feel

---

14. You received these Divine Soul Downloads when you read chapter 2.

guilty for doing it. If they do not do something, they feel guilty for not doing it. Guilt is an issue for millions of people.

Guilt can remove the joy of simple things. It can limit one's ability to function. Depression is often linked to guilt. Guilt can also lead to anxiety, worry, sadness, or fear.

There is no need to feel bad or ashamed that you have made a mistake. Mistakes are our best teachers. The lessons we learn from our mistakes can stay with us for the rest of our lives. A mistake is an excellent opportunity for learning and healing.

The important thing is to avoid making the same mistake over and over. If you are repeating your mistakes, this tells you that you are not really sorry for what you did originally. If you are really sorry, you will change your behavior. You will transform yourself. You will not repeat the same mistakes.

If you are serious about your spiritual journey, do not feel guilty about your mistakes. You cannot afford to paralyze yourself with guilt. You also cannot afford to repeat the same mistakes. Transform your guilt. Free yourself to move forward on your spiritual journey. You—all of us—will continue to make mistakes, but they will be new ones. Correct your mistakes, one after another.

Guilt is connected with the Message Center and the heart. The Message Center is the life-transformation center. Healing the Message Center will heal your guilt.

Practice with me now:

Practice for Self-healing Guilt

Body Power. Put your right palm or fist over your Message Center. Put your left palm or fist over your heart. Do Soul Tapping on these areas continuously.

Soul Power. Say *hello:*

> *Dear soul, mind, and body of my Message Center,*
> *Dear soul, mind, and body of my heart,*
> *I love you, honor you, and appreciate you.*
> *You have the power to heal my guilt.*
> *I am very grateful.*
> *Dear all my Divine Soul Mind Body Transplants,*
> *I love you, honor you, and appreciate you.*
> *Please turn on to heal my guilt.*
> *I am very grateful.*
> *Thank you.*

Mind Power. Visualize divine golden light vibrating in your Message Center and heart to heal your guilt.

Sound Power. Chant repeatedly, silently or aloud:

> *Divine Soul Mind Body Transplants heal my guilt.*
>   *Thank you.*
> *Divine Soul Mind Body Transplants heal my guilt.*
>   *Thank you.*
> *Divine Soul Mind Body Transplants heal my guilt.*
>   *Thank you.*
> *Divine Soul Mind Body Transplants heal my guilt.*
>   *Thank you.*

Practice chanting for at least three to five minutes, the longer, the better. Practice as many times a day as you can, until your guilt is removed. If you suffer from extreme feelings of guilt, treat it like a chronic condition. Chant for a total of at least two hours per day. Remember the story of Lothar in chapter 1. He practiced with his Divine Soul Mind Body Transplants for many hours per day. As a result, he self-healed his pancreatic cancer. This was unheard of. Something similar can happen for those who suffer from extreme guilt. Practice longer and experience the transformation more quickly.

Chanting is powerful and transforming by itself. The fourth book of my Soul Power Series, *Divine Soul Songs,* explains this in depth. When you chant any mantra, as we do in all of the practices in this book, you are giving your mind-sets, attitudes, beliefs, ego, and attachment a new message. When the message changes, actions, behaviors, attitudes, and thoughts will also change.

Mental Body

The mental body is the mind of a human being, an animal—of anything and everything. Mind is consciousness. Everyone and everything in the universe has a soul, mind (consciousness), and body. Blockages in the mind or consciousness are major blockages for every aspect of life. As I explained in chapter 2, some of the most important mind blockages are negative mind-sets, attitudes, and beliefs, as well as ego and attachment. At the same time, in chapter 2, the Divine has offered you and every reader gifts of Divine Soul Mind Body Transplants to remove negative mind-sets, attitudes, and beliefs, as well as ego and attachment. This is the love, compassion, and generosity of the Divine. Please apply these divine treasures and practice more in order to transform your mind and to heal and rejuvenate your mental body.

Spiritual Body

A human being consists of soul, mind, and body. Everyone and everything has a soul. *Soul is the boss.* To transform anyone and anything is to transform the soul first. Then, transformation of every aspect of life will follow.

A human's life is very short. The soul journey is eternal. A human's soul has reincarnated hundreds or even thousands of lifetimes. The purpose of the soul journey is to uplift the soul's standing in Heaven.

To uplift soul standing, the key is to purify the soul. I'm honored to offer the thirty-eighth, thirty-ninth, and fortieth divine treasures to every reader of this book:

Divine Soul Mind Body Transplants of Divine Pure Love

Prepare. Sit up straight. Put the tip of your tongue near the roof of your mouth without touching. Open your heart and soul to receive these three additional major treasures:

Divine Order: Divine Golden Light Ball and Golden Liquid Spring of Divine Pure Love Soul Transplant Transmission!

Divine Order: Divine Golden Light Ball and Golden Liquid Spring of Divine Pure Love Mind Transplant Transmission!

Divine Order: Divine Golden Light Ball and Golden Liquid Spring of Divine Pure Love Body Transplant Transmission!

238 DIVINE SOUL MIND BODY HEALING AND TRANSMISSION SYSTEM

Divine Order: Join Divine Pure Love Soul Mind Body Transplants as one.

Hei Ya Ya You!
Hei Ya Ya You!
Hei Ya Ya You You You!

Hao! Hao! Hao!
Thank you. Thank you. Thank you.

Congratulations! You are extremely blessed.

Now, let me lead you to apply these major divine treasures to purify your soul:

Practice to Purify Your Soul

Apply the Four Power Techniques:

Body Power. Put your left palm over your Message Center and your right hand in the traditional prayer position, with fingers pointing upward. This is the Soul Light Era prayer position.

Soul Power. Say *hello:*

> *Dear Divine Pure Love Soul Mind Body Transplants,*
> *I love you, honor you, and appreciate you.*
> *Please turn on to purify my soul.*
> *I am very grateful.*
> *Thank you.*

Sound Power. Chant repeatedly, silently or aloud:

> *Divine Pure Love Soul Mind Body Transplants purify*
> *my soul. Thank you.*

Divine Pure Love Soul Mind Body Transplants purify
   my soul. Thank you.
Divine Pure Love Soul Mind Body Transplants purify
   my soul. Thank you.
Divine Pure Love Soul Mind Body Transplants purify
   my soul. Thank you.

This practice is vital for your spiritual journey. I sincerely suggest that you do this practice as many times per day as you can, and continue to do this practice daily for your entire life. The benefits are unlimited, because purification is unlimited. The higher the level of purity your soul reaches, the higher the soul standing your soul could reach.

Another important issue for the spiritual body is to clear your own personal bad karma. Bad karma is soul blockages. Soul blockages are the root blockages for every aspect of life, including sickness in the physical body, emotional body, mental body, and spiritual body. The Divine made a law, a spiritual law, which is karma.

Karma is the record of services. Karma is divided into two kinds: good karma and bad karma. Good karma is given for your good service in previous lifetimes and in this lifetime. Good service includes the services of love, forgiveness, peace, healing, blessing, harmony, and enlightenment to humanity, animals, nature, Mother Earth, and all universes. Good service is recorded in the Akashic Records as virtue in your Akashic Record book.

Mother Earth and the physical world are yin. Heaven and the Soul World are yang. Physical money on Mother Earth is yin money. Money in Heaven is yang money. Heaven's money is *virtue*. If you serve well, you gain virtue. This yang money is given to your virtue bank in Heaven. When you need physical money, yang money in Heaven can transform to yin money on Mother Earth. If you do not have enough virtue deposited into your virtue bank, you will not have enough funds in Heaven's bank to withdraw and transform to yin money or physical money. Service and virtue are vital for every aspect of life, including finances.

To serve humanity, Mother Earth, and all universes unconditionally is to accumulate virtue. To chant constantly is to accumulate virtue constantly. I share the secret with humanity to chant constantly, or at least as much as you can.

If you have time, chant. After waking up, while showering, during your commute, at break times, before meals, after meals, before sleep—at every moment you have, chant. (You can always chant silently or aloud.)

To chant is to heal, especially chanting Divine Soul Songs. Divine Soul Songs carry divine frequency and vibration, with divine love, forgiveness, compassion, and light. Divine Soul Songs can heal all sicknesses, including chronic and life-threatening conditions. It does take time to heal, especially from chronic and life-threatening conditions. Be patient. Chant constantly and persistently.

Remember the story I shared in chapter 1 about my student Lothar, who was diagnosed with a seventeen-centimeter pancreatic cancer tumor in July 2008. He chanted six to ten hours per day, and received divine karma cleansing and Divine Soul Mind Body Transplants. By April 2009, his pancreatic cancer completely disappeared.

Remember also the story about Walter. In July 2003, when the Divine chose me as a divine servant, vehicle, and channel, the Divine immediately gave me the honor of transplanting a divine soul of the liver to Walter, who had a three-centimeter cancerous tumor on his liver. Walter also received divine karma cleansing. He chanted more than two hours per day. Within two and a half months, his liver cancer disappeared. His liver is still in perfect condition to this day, six years later.

To chant is to heal and rejuvenate. Divine frequency and vibration, which carry divine love, forgiveness, compassion, and light, can make your cells younger. Rejuvenation is happening while you chant.

To chant is to transform every aspect of life. Divine frequency and vibration, which carry divine love, forgiveness, compassion, and light, can remove blockages from every aspect of your life. Chanting accelerates your life transformation process.

To chant is to enlighten your soul, heart, mind, and body. Divine frequency and vibration, which carry divine love, forgiveness, compassion, and light, can purify your soul, heart, mind, and body. Your soul blockages can be removed because you are chanting. To chant is to serve.

In chapter 2 on karma in *The Power of Soul,* the third book of my Soul Power Series, I shared one of the simplest and most effective techniques to clear your own bad karma: sing the Divine Soul Song *Love, Peace and Harmony:*

Lu la lu la li
Lu la lu la la li
Lu la lu la li lu la
Lu la li lu la
Lu la li lu la

Wo ai wo xin he ling
Wo ai quan ren lei
Wan ling rong he mu shi sheng

Xiang ai ping an he xie
Xiang ai ping an he xie

I love my heart and soul
I love all humanity
Join hearts and souls together
Love, peace and harmony
Love, peace and harmony

The second line, *I love all humanity,* is the key for self-clearing karma. When you chant *I love all humanity,* you are giving service to humanity. You are shining divine light. Your chanting is like a lightbulb. If you have just one lightbulb turned on in a room, it is quite bright around the lightbulb, but the rest of the room may not be very bright.

Imagine that thirty people are chanting together in a room. They are like thirty one-hundred-watt lightbulbs shining in one room. That room is much brighter now than it was before.

Now imagine that millions of people are chanting together on Mother Earth. This means millions of lightbulbs are shining together. Mother Earth's frequency and vibration will be transformed instantly. This is the power and significance of chanting.

When you sing the Divine Soul Song *Love, Peace and Harmony,* be sure to do it from the bottom of your heart and soul. Then, the moment you sing, you are literally giving love to humanity, Mother Earth, and all universes. This is one of the greatest services. This great service will give you virtue automatically. Your bad karma will be reduced on the spot.

There are no limits to singing this Divine Soul Song. The more you sing, the faster you will clear your bad karma.

There are many other services you can give humanity. As long as you are doing something that benefits people's lives, including their health, relationships, and finances, you *are* serving. There are unlimited services.

The best service to offer is *unconditional universal service.* This means that you serve without expectation. Unconditional universal service is recorded in the Akashic Records, and you will be given more virtue instantly. Virtue is spiritual currency. The spiritual journey depends on virtue. Virtue is given by Heaven only for your good services. Unconditional universal service gains the greatest virtue. Chanting *Love, Peace and Harmony* can be great unconditional universal service.

Dr. Masaru Emoto has done much research on water crystals. When water is given messages of love by words or by thought, beautiful crystals form. When water is told *I hate you,* the water crystals are far from beautiful.

A few spiritual fathers chanted together to serve some polluted water; the polluted water was transformed. In 2002, the Divine told me that millions of people chanting together is the solution for purifying pollution on Mother Earth, including air, water, and land pollution. The results could be beyond comprehension. This is divine guidance and a divine prediction.

Millions of people chanting together can transform people's health. Millions of people radiating divine love and light together could offer remarkable healing to humanity.

Millions of people chanting together could prevent sickness for humanity.

Millions of people chanting together could rejuvenate and prolong the life of humanity.

Millions of people chanting together can transform the relationships of humanity.

Millions of people chanting together can transform the finances of humanity.

Millions of people chanting together can enlighten the soul, heart, mind, and body of humanity.

Millions of people chanting together can bring love, peace, and harmony to humanity, Mother Earth, and all universes.

I wish you will help that day come sooner.

Chanting, chanting, chanting.
Divine chanting is healing.
Chanting, chanting, chanting.
Divine chanting is rejuvenating.
Singing, singing, singing.
Divine singing is transforming.
Singing, singing, singing.
Divine singing is enlightening.

Humanity is waiting for divine chanting.
All souls are waiting for divine singing.
Divine chanting removes all blockages.
Divine singing brings inner joy.

Divine is chanting and singing.
Humanity and all souls are nourishing.
Humanity and all souls are chanting and singing.
World Love, Peace and Harmony are coming.

World Love, Peace and Harmony are coming.

World Love, Peace and Harmony are coming.

Pets

Many pets have reincarnated for many lifetimes. In this lifetime, your pets can also receive the Divine Soul Mind Body Healing and Transmission System for their physical and other issues. A pet who receives the Divine Soul Mind Body Healing and Transmission System for one issue is extremely blessed. Some pets have even had their karma cleansed and their curses and negative memories removed. Just think about how blessed those pets are.

Once your pet receives the Divine Soul Mind Body Healing and Transmission System, you can practice for your pet. Invoke your pet's Divine Soul Mind Body Transplants and chant, just as I have led you to do in most of the practices in this book.

At the soul level, you can even teach your pet how to practice. Tell your pet's soul, "When I can join you, we will practice together. Until then, please practice by yourself. Do a good job." You can tell the soul of your pet to continue to practice throughout the day or night.

Here is one way to practice if your pet has received Divine Soul Mind Body Transplants:

Practice with Your Pet's Divine Treasures

Soul Power. Say *hello:*

> *Dear soul, mind, and body of my pet's Divine Soul*
>   *Mind Body Transplants,*
> *I love you, honor you, and appreciate you.*
> *Please turn on.*
> *Please heal, bless, rejuvenate, and transform my pet's*
>
> _____.
>
> *Thank you.*

Sound Power. Chant repeatedly, silently or aloud:

> *Divine Soul Mind Body Transplants heal, bless, reju-*
> *venate, and transform my pet. Thank you, Divine.*
> *Divine Soul Mind Body Transplants heal, bless, reju-*
> *venate, and transform my pet. Thank you, Divine.*
> *Divine Soul Mind Body Transplants heal, bless, reju-*
> *venate, and transform my pet. Thank you, Divine.*
> *Divine Soul Mind Body Transplants heal, bless, reju-*
> *venate, and transform my pet. Thank you, Divine.*

Practice for at least for three to five minutes per time, the longer, the better. Practice as many times a day as you can.

When you chant with your pet, tell your pet's soul, *practice with me.* Your pet's soul will chant with you.

If your pet has a chronic or life-threatening condition, practice as much as you can throughout the day. If you are away from your pet during the day, that is not a problem. Tell the soul of your pet to continue chanting this mantra until you are able to join your pet.

If your pet has not received Divine Soul Mind Body Transplants, you can practice for your pet using your own divine treasures. In fact, you can offer healing to others using your own divine treasures in a similar way. Here is how to do it:

Practice for Your Pet with Your Own Divine Treasures

Soul Power. Say *hello:*

> *Dear soul, mind, and body of all my divine treasures,*
> *I love you, honor you, and appreciate you.*

Please turn on.
Please heal my pet's _____.
Thank you.

Sound Power. Chant repeatedly:

Divine treasures heal my pet. Thank you, Divine.
Divine treasures heal my pet. Thank you, Divine.
Divine treasures heal my pet. Thank you, Divine.
Divine treasures heal my pet. Thank you, Divine.

The Divine Soul Mind Body Healing and Transmission System brings your pet, as well as you, all humanity, and Mother Earth a new divine opportunity and divine empowerment for healing and transformation. It is a very special way for you to serve your pet and for your pet itself to offer service.

Relationships

Everyone has many relationships, and many kinds of relationships. The Divine Soul Downloads you have received in this book can bring healing and blessings to every relationship. If the relationship is not harmonious, divine treasures can bring healing. If the relationship is strong, harmonious, and loving, divine treasures can nurture it. Here is how to practice:

Practice to Heal or Nurture Relationships

Soul Power. Say *hello:*

Dear soul, mind, and body of my Divine Forgiveness
Soul Mind Body Transplants,[15]

---

15. You received these Divine Soul Downloads when you read chapter 3.

I love you, honor you, and appreciate you.
Please turn on to heal my relationship with _____.
I am very grateful.
Thank you.

Sound Power. Chant repeatedly:

Divine Forgiveness Soul Mind Body Transplants heal
   my relationship with _____. Thank you, Divine.
Divine Forgiveness Soul Mind Body Transplants heal
   my relationship with _____. Thank you, Divine.
Divine Forgiveness Soul Mind Body Transplants heal
   my relationship with _____. Thank you, Divine.
Divine Forgiveness Soul Mind Body Transplants heal
   my relationship with _____. Thank you, Divine.

or
Soul Power. Say *hello:*

Dear soul, mind, and body of all my Divine Soul
   Mind Body Transplants,
I love you, honor you, and appreciate you.
Please turn on to nurture my relationship with _____.
I am very grateful.
Thank you.

Sound Power. Chant repeatedly:

Divine Soul Mind Body Transplants nurture my rela-
   tionship with _____. Thank you, Divine.

Divine Soul Mind Body Transplants nurture my relationship with _____. Thank you, Divine.
Divine Soul Mind Body Transplants nurture my relationship with _____. Thank you, Divine.
Divine Soul Mind Body Transplants nurture my relationship with _____. Thank you, Divine.

Practice for at least three to five minutes per time, the longer, the better. Practice as many times a day as you can to heal and bless your relationships.

Finances

In the human realm, money is the currency for exchange. In the Soul World, virtue is the currency for exchange. Physical money is yin money. Virtue is yang money. They exchange. When a person has financial difficulties, it is due to soul, mind and body blockages. The root blockage is the soul blockage, which is bad karma. Mind blockages are blockages in the consciousness of a business or finances. Body blockages are blockages in energy and tiny matter. These blockages could affect the personnel, infrastructure, planning, marketing, leadership, information technology, and any other aspect of a business.

For success in business and finances, proper physical components are very important. Most people have not realized that the spiritual component is no less important. Many businesses are not successful, despite having good personnel, plans, and strategies. Almost always, one reason for this is bad karma and the mind and body blockages of the business.

To clear the soul, mind, and body blockages of the business or finances is the first step.

To receive Divine Soul Mind Body Transplants of the business or finances is the second step.

To invoke and chant with Divine Soul Downloads, together with having the proper physical components, is the third step.

Organizations

According to the teachings of this book, to transform an organization involves the same three steps of the Divine Soul Mind Body Healing and Transmission System: (1) Remove soul, mind, and body blockages. (2) Receive Divine Soul Mind Body Transplants for the organization. (3) Invoke and chant to transform the organization.

Now, let me offer the forty-first divine treasure in this book to help you transform an organization, and more:

Divine Soul Transplant of Divine Golden Light Ball and Golden Liquid Spring of Divine Harmony

Prepare! Sit up straight. Put the tip of your tongue near, but not touching, the roof of your mouth. Open your heart and soul to receive this divine treasure. In the next twenty seconds, the Divine will download it to your soul.

Divine Order: Divine Golden Light Ball and Golden Liquid Spring of Divine Harmony Soul Transplant Transmission!

Hao! Hao! Hao!
Thank you. Thank you. Thank you.

We are extremely blessed. Thank you, Divine. We cannot thank you enough.

Next, prepare to receive the forty-second divine treasure for every reader of this book:

Divine Mind Transplant of Divine Golden Light Ball and Golden Liquid Spring of Divine Harmony

Put the tip of your tongue near the roof of your mouth, without touching. Sit up straight. Open your heart and soul.

Divine Order: Divine Golden Light Ball and Golden Liquid Spring of Divine Harmony Mind Transplant Transmission!

Hao! Hao! Hao!
Thank you. Thank you. Thank you.

Thank you, Divine. We are extremely honored.

I will now offer the forty-third permanent divine gift in this book:

Divine Body Transplant of Divine Golden Light Ball and Golden Liquid Spring of Divine Harmony

Prepare! Sit up straight. Put the tip of your tongue near, but not touching, the roof of your mouth. Open your heart and soul to receive this divine treasure. In the next twenty seconds, the Divine will download it to your soul.

252 DIVINE SOUL MIND BODY HEALING AND TRANSMISSION SYSTEM

Divine Order: Divine Golden Light Ball and Golden Liquid Spring of Divine Harmony Body Transplant Transmission!

Hao! Hao! Hao!
Thank you. Thank you. Thank you.

Thank you, Divine. We are blessed beyond any words.
Now, I will send a

Divine Order: Join Divine Golden Light Ball and Golden Liquid Spring of Divine Harmony Soul Transplant, Mind Transplant, and Body Transplant as one.

Ya Hei Ya Hei Yi Ya Ya You!

Thank you, Divine.
Practice with me now:

Practice to Heal and Transform Organizations

Body Power. Put your hands in the Soul Light Era prayer position (left palm over Message Center, right hand in the traditional prayer position).
   Soul Power. Say *hello*:

> *Dear soul, mind, and body of my Divine Harmony*
>   *Soul Mind Body Transplants,*
> *I love you, honor you, and appreciate you.*
> *Please turn on to heal and transform my organization*

[name your organization and make specific requests].
I am very grateful.
Thank you.

Mind Power. Visualize divine golden light vibrating in your organization and every aspect of it, including its people, physical structures and objects, and relationships.

Sound Power. Chant repeatedly, silently or aloud:

> *Divine Harmony Soul Mind Body Transplants heal*
> *and transform my organization. Thank you.*
> *Divine Harmony Soul Mind Body Transplants heal*
> *and transform my organization. Thank you.*
> *Divine Harmony Soul Mind Body Transplants heal*
> *and transform my organization. Thank you.*
> *Divine Harmony Soul Mind Body Transplants heal*
> *and transform my organization. Thank you.*

Practice chanting for at least three to five minutes, the longer, the better.

Humanity

Millions of people are suffering. Humanity needs healing on all levels. In June 2009, the UN Food and Agriculture Organization estimated that one billion people live in hunger. The Divine Soul Downloads and techniques in this book can bring great healing, blessing, rejuvenation, and transformation to humanity. I wish you will offer this service to humanity unconditionally. You can bring great light and blessing to humanity. It is a huge service that is especially needed in this time of Mother Earth's transition. In order to heal and transform humanity, you can use your Divine Soul Mind Body Transplants of Divine Love, Divine Forgiveness, Divine Compassion, and Divine Light that you received when you read chapter 3. Here is how to do it:

Practice to Heal and Transform Humanity

Body Power. Use the Soul Light Era prayer position.
    Soul Power. Say *hello*:

> *Dear soul, mind, and body of my Divine Love, Divine Forgiveness, Divine Compassion, and Divine Light Soul Mind Body Transplants,*
> *I love you, honor you, and appreciate you.*
> *Please turn on to heal humanity's suffering in the physical, emotional, mental, and spiritual bodies.*
> *Please transform the consciousness of humanity.*
> *Please offer the blessings that are appropriate at this time.*
> *I am very grateful.*
> *Thank you.*

    Mind Power. Visualize divine golden light vibrating in all humanity.
    Sound Power. Chant repeatedly, silently or aloud:

> *Divine Love, Divine Forgiveness, Divine Compassion, and Divine Light Soul Mind Body Transplants heal and transform humanity.*
> *Thank you, Divine.*

Divine Love, Divine Forgiveness, Divine Compassion,
  and Divine Light Soul Mind Body Transplants heal
  and transform humanity.
Thank you, Divine.
Divine Love, Divine Forgiveness, Divine Compassion,
  and Divine Light Soul Mind Body Transplants heal
  and transform humanity.
Thank you, Divine.
Divine Love, Divine Forgiveness, Divine Compassion,
  and Divine Light Soul Mind Body Transplants heal
  and transform humanity.
Thank you, Divine.

Chant for at least three to five minutes, the longer, the better.

Cities, Countries, Mother Earth, and All Universes

Cities, countries, Mother Earth, and universes are also out of balance and suffering.

At this time, every country worldwide faces major economic challenges. A country that lacks financial resources on Mother Earth lacks virtue in its virtue bank in Heaven. Every country worldwide needs to accumulate more virtue.

Cities, countries, Mother Earth, and universes are also suffering from war, pollution, and many other issues. This is part of humanity and Mother Earth's purification process. War and pollution also create huge new bad karma for humanity, cities, and countries.

As I have taught in the first four books of my Soul Power Series, Mother Earth is in the process of purification. Natural disasters, climate changes, hurricanes, tsunamis, political, religious, and ethnic wars, economic collapse, disease, proliferation of nuclear arms, and more, are part of this purification. Mother Earth is having her karma cleansed. This is something she must do herself at this time.

You may not have realized that all universes need healing. There is a renowned ancient philosophical and spiritual statement:

**A human being is the small universe;
the universe is the big universe.**

What a human being has, the universe has. What a human being needs, the universe needs.

Now, I am honored to ask the Divine to offer the final three divine treasures in this book as a gift to you and every reader. Prepare to receive the forty-fourth, forty-fifth, and forty-sixth Divine Soul Downloads offered in this book:

**Divine Soul Mind Body Transplants of the
Divine Soul Song *Love, Peace and Harmony***

Sit up straight. Put the tip of your tongue near, but not touching, the roof of your mouth. Open your heart and soul to receive these divine treasures. In the next minute, the Divine will download them to your soul.

**Divine Order: Divine Golden Light Ball and
Golden Liquid Spring of the Divine Soul Song *Love,
Peace and Harmony* Soul Transplant
Transmission!**

**Divine Order: Divine Golden Light Ball and
Golden Liquid Spring of the Divine Soul Song** *Love,
Peace and Harmony* **Mind Transplant
Transmission!**

**Divine Order: Divine Golden Light Ball and
Golden Liquid Spring of the Divine Soul Song** *Love,
Peace and Harmony* **Body Transplant
Transmission!**

Hao! Hao! Hao!
Thank you. Thank you. Thank you.

Congratulations! You have just received three more of the
Divine's major treasures. You are extremely blessed. We are extremely honored and grateful. We cannot thank and honor the
Divine enough for his generosity. The forty-six Divine Downloads you have received give you much divine virtue to transform
your life. There are no words to express our greatest gratitude.

Finally, I will give another

**Divine Order: Join Divine Golden Light Ball and
Golden Liquid Spring of the Divine Soul Song** *Love,
Peace and Harmony* **Soul Transplant, Mind Transplant,
and Body Transplant as one.**

He La La Yi Ya You Yi Ya You!

Let us practice now:

Practice to Transform All Souls in All Universes

Soul Power. Say *hello:*

> *Dear soul, mind, and body of my Divine Soul Song*
>   Love, Peace and Harmony *Soul Mind Body Trans-*
>   *plants,*
> *I love you, honor you, and appreciate you.*
> *Please turn on to serve the divine mission for all souls*
>   *in all universes.*
> *Please offer blessings of love, peace, and harmony to*
>   *heal, transform, and enlighten cities, countries,*
>   *Mother Earth, and all universes.*
> *I am very grateful.*
> *Thank you.*

> *Dear every soul in all universes,*
> *I love you, honor you, and appreciate you.*
> *I invite you to join me in this practice.*
> *Let us sing the Divine Soul Song* Love, Peace and
>   Harmony *together.*
> *I am very grateful.*
> *Thank you.*

Mind Power. Visualize divine golden light vibrating in everyone and everything in all universes.

Sound Power. Sing or chant the words to *Love, Peace and Harmony:*

> *Lu la lu la li*
> *Lu la lu la la li*

Lu la lu la li lu la
Lu la li lu la
Lu la li lu la

I love my heart and soul
I love all humanity
Join hearts and souls together
Love, peace and harmony
Love, peace and harmony

Chant for at least three to five minutes, the longer, the better.
Hao! Hao! Hao!
Thank you. Thank you. Thank you.
To do this practice is to offer unconditional universal service.
The benefits are without limit.

Conclusion

$\mathcal{J}$AM DELIGHTED TO conclude this book.

This book, *Divine Soul Mind Body Healing and Transmission System: The Divine Way to Heal You, Humanity, Mother Earth, and All Universes,* has delivered the key secrets, wisdom, knowledge, and practices to serve every aspect of your life.

The whole book can be summarized as follows:

- Everyone and everything consists of soul, mind, and body.
- The Divine Soul Mind Body Healing and Transmission System can transform everyone and everything in three steps:
  - Remove soul, mind, and body blockages.
  - Receive Divine Soul Mind Body Transplants.
  - Apply Divine Soul Mind Body Transplants by invoking and chanting to transform every aspect of your life.

This book can be summarized further in one sentence:

Divine Soul Mind Body Transplants can heal you, humanity, Mother Earth, and all universes.

I am extremely honored that the Divine has preprogrammed so many Divine Soul Mind Body Transplants in this book. These transplants are priceless treasures that can heal, rejuvenate, transform, and enlighten all life. These treasures are permanent treasures.

Read this book more times.

Practice more and more.

Receive more and more benefits.

Serve more and more.

Heal you and your loved ones.

Rejuvenate you and your loved ones.

Transform and enlighten you, your loved ones, humanity, Mother Earth, and all universes.

> *I love my heart and soul*
> *I love all humanity*
> *Join hearts and souls together*
> *Love, peace and harmony*
> *Love, peace and harmony*
>
> *God gives his heart to me*
> *God gives his love to me*
> *My heart melds with his heart*
> *My love melds with his love*

Love you. Love you. Love you.

Thank you. Thank you. Thank you.

Acknowledgments

$\mathcal{I}$ DEEPLY APPRECIATE THE Divine for his generosity, love, teaching, nourishment, blessing, transformation, and enlightenment for every reader and me.

I deeply appreciate Master Zhi Chen Guo and all of my spiritual fathers and mothers on Mother Earth and in the Soul World, and my masters in tai chi, qi gong, kung fu, the *I Ching*, and feng shui.

I deeply appreciate my father, Sha Bai Lu, and my mother, Zhang Yi Chuan, for their love, compassion, education, and nurturance.

I deeply appreciate my Worldwide Representatives: Marilyn Smith, Francisco Quintero, Joyce Brown, Lothar Zahler, Patty Baker, Allan Chuck, Shu Chin Hsu, David Lusch, Patricia Smith, Michael Stevens, Peggy Werner, Petra Herz, and Lynne Nusyna, for their great contributions to the divine mission. The divine mission is to serve humanity and all souls, in order to create love, peace, and harmony for humanity, Mother Earth, and all universes.

I deeply appreciate Allan Chuck as the primary and final editor of this book. He is the best editor to keep my voice to bring my message to the world. I also deeply appreciate Elaine Ward for assisting Allan to edit this book.

I deeply appreciate my more than four hundred Master Teachers and Healers of Soul Healing and Enlightenment worldwide and my more than one thousand Soul Healing Teachers and Healers worldwide, as well as thousands of students worldwide for their great service to the divine mission.

I deeply appreciate Judith Curr as my co-publisher for her great support and blessing of my Soul Power Series. I deeply appreciate Johanna Castillo as my main editor at Atria Books for her great support and contributions to my books. Many others at Simon & Schuster and Simon & Schuster Canada have given my work and me great support. They include Christine Saunders, Amy Tannenbaum, Deb Darrock, Tom Spain, Michael Noble, Kitt Reckord, Christine Duplessis, and Melissa Ong, to mention only a few.

I deeply appreciate Sarah Ginsberg for her support of the audio version of this book and the previous four books of my Soul Power Series.

I deeply appreciate Mr. Chun Yen Chiang for co-creating the Soul Symphony of Yin Yang and the Soul Symphony of Five Elements with me.

I deeply appreciate my wife and our three children for their great support of my work.

I deeply thank everyone who has supported my service worldwide. Thank you all.

I am honored to be the servant of you, humanity, Mother Earth, and all universes.

I wish this book will serve you well.

Lu la lu la li
Lu la lu la la li
Lu la lu la li lu la
Lu la li lu la
Lu la li lu la

I love my heart and soul
I love all humanity
Join hearts and souls together
Love, peace and harmony
Love, peace and harmony

A Special Gift

As a special gift for you, you can visit www.DrSha.com to listen to and dowload an excerpt from the second movement of the Soul Symphony of Yin Yang.

This first divine soul symphony was completed in early 2009 by the Divine Music Composer Mr. Chun Yen Chiang and me. As I write this, it was just previewed to great admiration and a warm reception at the First International Soul Song & Soul Music Concert for Healing and Rejuvenation in Neuss, Germany on June 13, 2009.

As with this book, Mr. Chiang and I did not co-create this music from our minds. We received Divine Soul Downloads for the music. We flowed out the melodies and the entire work. Mr. Chiang wrote out the complete score.

Like the Divine Soul Songs I have received, this soul symphony is Heaven's music, with divine frequency and vibration. Each movement carries its special qualities of divine love, forgiveness, compassion, and light. Each movement can offer you healing, rejuvenation, and life transformation.

As I have explained in many of my books, Yin Yang is one of the highest philosophies to represent and explain everything. The Soul Symphony of Yin Yang encompasses the full range of yin and yang, including all elements, universes, and possibilities within. A CD of the entire work, performed by the China Philharmonic Orchestra, is now available.

Divine Soul Symphonies are your servants. I wish this soul symphony will serve you well.

Thank you. Thank you. Thank you.

Index

Dr. Sha's Teachings and Services

Other Books and Audiobooks

*Power Healing: The Four Keys to Energizing Your Body, Mind &
Spirit.* HarperSanFrancisco, 2002.

*Soul Mind Body Medicine: A Complete Soul Healing System for
Optimum Health and Vitality.* New World Library, 2006.

Living Divine Relationships. Heaven's Library, 2006.

Body Space Medicine by Dr. Zhi Chen Guo (foreword by Dr.
Sha). Heaven's Library, 2007.

Soul Wisdom: Practical Soul Treasures to Transform Your Life (revised trade paperback edition). Heaven's Library/Atria, 2008.
Also available as an audiobook.

*Soul Communication: Opening Your Spiritual Channels for Success
and Fulfillment* (revised trade paperback edition). Heaven's
Library/Atria, 2008. Also available as an audiobook.

*The Power of Soul: The Way to Heal, Rejuvenate, Transform, and
Enlighten All Life.* Heaven's Library/Atria, 2009. Also available as an audiobook.

Divine Soul Songs: Sacred Practical Treasures to Heal, Rejuvenate, and Transform You, Humanity, Mother Earth, and All Universes. Heaven's Library/Atria, 2009. Also available as an audiobook.

La Sabiduría del Alma (Spanish-language version of *Soul Wisdom*). Heaven's Library/Atria Español, 2009.

Multimedia eBook

Soul Mind Body Medicine: A Complete Soul Healing System for Optimum Health and Vitality. Heaven's Library/Alive! eBooks Network, 2008; www.HeavensLibrary.com. Includes one hour of new audio content and one hour of new video content with Dr. Sha.

Healing, Blessing, and Life Transformation

Divine Soul Song Singing Teleconference for the World Soul Healing, Peace and Enlightenment Movement, Monday through Friday, 5:30–6:00 PM Pacific Time. Register once at www.DrSha.com for this ongoing Divine Soul Song singing service.

Free Soul Healing Blessings for Humanity Webcast and Teleconference, Saturday, 11 AM–12 noon Pacific Time.

Divine Soul Massage Teleconference Session with Master Sha, Sunday, 4:00–5:00 PM Pacific Time.

Divine Remote Group Healing, Rejuvenation, and Transformation Teleconference Session with Master Sha, Sunday, 5:00–7:00 PM Pacific Time.

Divine Soul Mind Body Healing and Transmission System, Divine Soul Mind Body Transplants, other Divine Soul

Downloads, Divine Soul Orders, and other Divine Blessings
(www.DrSha.com)
Love Peace Harmony Center—Boulder, Colorado
Soul Healing Center—San Francisco, California
Soul Healing Center—Frankfurt, Germany
Soul Healing Center—Toronto, Canada

CDs

The Voice of the Universe: Power Healing Music. Qi Records, 2002.
Four powerful universal mantras for the Soul Light Era recorded by Dr. Sha:

- *God's Light*
- *Universal Light*
- *Shining Soul Light*
- *Follow Nature's Way*

The Music of Soul Dance. Institute of Soul Healing and Enlightenment, 2007. A ten-CD boxed set of Heaven's music to in-
spire and help guide your Soul Dance.
Blessings from Heaven. Institute of Soul Healing and Enlighten-
ment, 2007. Divine Soul Music by Divine Composer Chun
Yen Chiang and Dr. Sha.
Love, Peace and Harmony. Institute of Soul Healing and Enlight-
enment, 2007. The first Soul Song given by the Divine to Dr.
Sha and humanity.
God Gives His Heart to Me. Institute of Soul Healing and En-
lightenment, 2008. The second Soul Song given by the Di-
vine to Dr. Sha and humanity.
Soul Songs for Healing and Rejuvenation. www.MasterShaSoul
Song.com, 2008–2009. Divine Soul Songs for healing and

rejuvenating various organs, systems, and parts of the body; for balancing emotions; and for weight loss.

Divine Soul Song of Compassion. Institute of Soul Healing and Enlightenment, 2009. The third Soul Song given by the Divine to Dr. Sha and humanity.

Divine Soul Song of Yin Yang. Institute of Soul Healing and Enlightenment, 2009.

Soul Symphony of Yin Yang. Institute of Soul Healing and Enlightenment, 2009. The first Divine Soul Symphony co-created by Chun Yen Chiang and Dr. Sha.

Divine Soul Songs for Healing and Rejuvenation of Five Elements. Institute of Soul Healing and Enlightenment, 2009.

Soul Symphony of Five Elements. Institute of Soul Healing and Enlightenment, 2009.

DVDs

Power Healing to Self-Heal Ten Common Conditions. Institute of Soul Healing and Enlightenment, 2004. On this DVD, Dr. Sha teaches the Four Power Techniques to self-heal:

- Anxiety
- Back pain
- Carpal tunnel syndrome
- Common cold
- Constipation
- Energy boosting
- Headache
- Knee pain
- Menopause
- Weight loss

Dr. Sha also offers blessings for each condition.

Power Healing with Master Zhi Gang Sha: Learn Four Power Techniques to Heal Yourself. Institute of Soul Healing and Enlightenment, 2006. This four-DVD set offers a comprehensive teaching of the wisdom, knowledge, and practices of Power Healing and Soul Mind Body Medicine. All aspects of Body Power, Sound Power, Mind Power, and Soul Power are covered in depth. Dr. Sha reveals and explains many secret teachings and leads you in practices.

Soul Masters: Dr. Guo & Dr. Sha. 926363 Ontario Limited, 2008. Feature-length documentary film shown at the 2008 Sun Valley Spiritual Film Festival.

Soul Enlightenment: Fulfill Your Soul's Journey. Institute of Soul Healing and Enlightenment, 2008.

Conversation with Master Sha & Master Guo. Institute of Soul Healing and Enlightenment, 2008.

First International Soul Song, Soul Music and Soul Dance Concert for Healing and Rejuvenation. Institute of Soul Healing and Enlightenment, 2009.

www.DrSha.com
www.HeavensLibrary.com
1.888.3396815
DrSha@DrSha.com

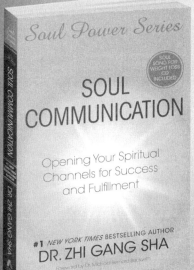